Bush, the Detainees,
& the Constitution

ALSO BY HOWARD BALL

The Bakke *Case*
Cancer Factories
Compromised Compliance
Controlling Regulatory Sprawl
Courts and Politics
A Defiant Life: Thurgood Marshall
Hugo L. Black
Judicial Craftsmanship or Fiat?
Justice in Mississippi
Murder in Mississippi
Of Power and Right
Prosecuting War Crimes and Genocide
The Supreme Court in the Intimate Lives of Americans
U.S. Homeland Security
The U.S. Supreme Court
USA Patriot Act of 2001
The Vision and the Dream of Hugo L. Black
War Crimes and Justice
The Warren Court's Perception of Democracy
"We Have a Duty"

Bush, the Detainees, & the Constitution

THE BATTLE OVER PRESIDENTIAL POWER
IN THE WAR ON TERROR

Howard Ball

 University Press of Kansas

Published by the University Press of Kansas (Lawrence, Kansas 66045),
which was organized by the Kansas Board of Regents and is operated
and funded by Emporia State University, Fort Hays State University,
Kansas State University, Pittsburg State University, the University of
Kansas, and Wichita State University

Library of Congress Cataloging-in-Publication Data
Ball, Howard, 1937–
Bush, the detainees, and the Constitution : the battle over presidential
power in the War on Terror / Howard Ball.
p. cm.
Includes bibliographical references and index.
ISBN 978-0-7006-1529-2 (cloth : alk. paper)
1. War and emergency powers—United States. 2. Executive power—
United States. 3. Presidents—United States. 4. Constitutional law—
United States. 5. Political prisoners—United States. 6. Civil rights—
United States. 7. Terrorism—United States—Prevention. 8. War on
Terrorism, 2001—Political aspects. I. Title.
KF5060.B35   2007
342.73'062—dc22   2007021676

British Library Cataloguing-in-Publication Data is available.

Printed in the United States of America

10 9 8 7 6 5 4 3 2 1

The paper used in this publication is acid-free and contains 50 percent
postconsumer waste. It meets the minimum requirements of the
American National Standard for Permanence of Paper for Printed
Library Materials Z39.48-1992.

For my "brothers," Charles and Tom

In blessed memory of Suzette Talarico, a bright, vibrant woman who fought tirelessly against injustice, intolerance, and cancer

and for Carol

Contents

Introduction: Is the American Republic Invulnerable? *1*

1. Presidential Power versus the Constitution's Limits on Power, *6*

2. Capturing the Enemy, *37*

3. Treatment of the Enemy, *56*

4. Bush versus the U.S. Supreme Court, Round One, 2003–2004, *87*

5. Bush versus the U.S. Supreme Court, Round Two, 2004–2006, *125*

6. Bush Trumps the U.S. Supreme Court: The 2006 Military Commissions Act, *175*

Epilogue: The 2006 Midterm Elections and a Return to the U.S. Supreme Court, *187*

Appendix 1. Authorization for Use of Military Force (AUMF) Resolution, September 18, 2001, *199*

Appendix 2. Presidential Military Order 1, November 13, 2001, *201*

Appendix 3. The Third Geneva Convention of 1949: Relative to the Treatment of Prisoners of War. Geneva, August 12, 1949 (Preamble, Parts I and II), *205*

Appendix 4. Convention against Torture and Other Cruel, Inhuman, or Degrading Treatment or Punishment, Entered into Force June 26, 1987 (Preamble, Part I), *215*

Appendix 5. Detainee Treatment Act of 2005 (Title X— Matters Relating to Detainees), *221*

Appendix 6. Military Commissions Act of 2006 (Excerpts), *229*

Notes, *233*

Index, *267*

Bush, the Detainees,
& the Constitution

Introduction:
Is the American Republic Invulnerable?

It takes a lot of degeneration before a country falls into dictatorship, but we should avoid these ends by avoiding these beginnings.
SANDRA DAY O'CONNOR, 2006[1]

How America has treated "enemy combatants"[2] since September 2001 is a story that brings into play the character of representative government, the meaning and scope of due process of law, the jurisdiction of the federal courts, and the viability of the concepts of checks and balances and the separation of powers. In President George W. Bush's war on terror, the war powers of the president (who is commander in chief of the armed forces) butted up against these constitutional restraints. For over five years, these constraints were impotent in the face of an aggressive chief executive.

Since September 2001 the president and his chief lieutenants (Vice President Dick Cheney, Secretary of Defense Donald Rumsfeld, and U.S. Attorneys General John Ashcroft and Alberto R. Gonzales) have radically departed from earlier official governmental conduct regarding the treatment of enemy detainees. The legal arguments presented to the president by the Justice Department from 2001 to the present, as well as the arguments presented by the U.S. government to the justices of the U.S. Supreme Court in 2004 and 2006, place in sharp focus the critically important—and very controversial—issue of presidential powers versus the principles of separation of powers and checks and balances.

The 2004 and 2006 Supreme Court enemy combatants opinions were watershed decisions that touch upon grave and important issues of constitutional and political importance for Americans and for the rest of the world. The justices addressed a number of weighty issues, chief among them the following questions:

What is the scope of the right of habeas corpus in the war on terror? Habeas corpus is an ancient protection, a venerable part of the English common law brought to America in the seventeenth century. If an individual who has been imprisoned by a government alleges that the action is arbitrary and unlawful, he or she can ask a judge to issue a writ of habeas corpus. If the request is successful, a judge issues a court order addressed to a prison official ordering that the detainee be brought to the court so it can be determined whether or not that person has been imprisoned lawfully and whether or not he or she should be released from custody.

Habeas corpus was considered such a fundamental right by the framers of the U.S. Constitution that at the 1787 convention they incorporated the right into Article I, Section 9, the section that limits the powers of Congress: "The Privilege of the Writ of Habeas Corpus shall not be suspended, unless when in Cases of Rebellion or Invasion the public Safety may require it." Since the war on terror began in 2001, there have been constant efforts by the Bush administration and Congress to prohibit the use of habeas corpus by captured enemy combatants held in prisons in Guantánamo Bay, Cuba.[3] And in October 2006, with the passage of the Military Commissions Act (MCA), all enemy combatants were barred from seeking habeas corpus relief in federal courts; further, the MCA prohibited judicial review of actions taken against detainees (see chapter 6).

Did Congress, when it passed the Authorization for Use of Military Force (AUMF) Resolution in 2001 and the Iraq Resolution in 2002, give the president a nearly unlimited authority to do as he wanted regarding al Qaeda detainees, weapons of mass destruction, the establishment of military commissions, and other matters ostensibly linked to the war on terror? Can Congress "unconsciously suspend the writ of habeas corpus," as the federal government claimed in March 2006?[4]

Can the federal courts' authority to hear habeas actions from foreign detainees and American citizens who are labeled by the government as enemy combatants be taken away in time of war? President Bush signed the Detainee Treatment Act (DTA) of 2005, claiming that the DTA did take that authority from the courts (see appendix 5), and after the Supreme Court struck down those provisions of the DTA in *Hamdan v. Rumsfeld* (2006), the administration attempted with the MCA to place similar prohibitions on federal judicial behavior. Is President Bush or any other president, as commander in chief, the sole official statutorily or constitutionally empowered to make decisions and issue orders that deny due process to citizens and others declared by him to be enemy combatants who are then held indefinitely by the military?

If not so authorized, can a president act in contravention to the constraints placed on him by the U.S. Constitution and the customs and conventions of international law in order to maintain the nation's sovereignty?[5]

Can the U.S. military, on the basis of general guidelines from civilian leaders, torture detainees in the effort to acquire actionable intelligence?

Central to the question of how a democracy battles its enemy in this age of asymmetrical warfare is the question of whether or not a president can be constrained constitutionally, by Congress, or by the U.S. Supreme Court, as well as by his own counsel when balancing national security with the demands of due process of law found in the U.S. Constitution and in international treaties.

Given the Bush administration's radical departure from past American governmental treatment of enemy prisoners, the legal arguments presented in 2004 and 2006 place the critically important issues of the president's war powers and the restraints on these powers (via the separation of powers and checks and balances principles) in clear perspective.

What has emerged since September 11, 2001, is a very troublesome story about the relationship between absolute presidential power in a war on terror and the principles of representative government. Until the presidency of George W. Bush, it has not been necessary to tell that story because that conflict, historically, flared up only rarely and usually ended disastrously for the president—as the sad end of the presidency of Richard M. Nixon illustrates.

It is also a tragic story because its telling is highlighted by the consistency of the false premises used by President Bush and his associates, in particular, Vice President Cheney, Secretary of Defense Rumsfeld, and the ideologues—including a number of influential lawyers—on the staffs of these three resolute men.

Unable to acquire actionable evidence before or after September 11, the president and his men resorted to actionable suspicion to make decisions to take the United States into war, to commit too few troops to that war, to deny captured enemy prisoners fundamental due process rights required by domestic and international law, to permit the torture of these prisoners, and to argue in the federal courts that the president has unilateral authority to act as he has in the fight against international terrorism. Put simply, President Bush and his subordinate officials, as war leaders, for five years have ridden roughshod over the foundation stones embedded in the U.S. Constitution.

In *The Federalist Papers,* a series of over eighty essays written in 1787–1788 by Alexander Hamilton, John Jay, and James Madison in defense of the proposed 1787 Constitution,[6] Madison wrote of the critical importance of the separation of powers among the legislative, the executive, and the judicial branches and of the checks and balances that were contained in the Constitution. When three separate institutions of government[7] share power, there is representative government. He defined tyranny as the coalescing of the powers of the three branches of government into the hands of one of them:

> No political truth is certainly of greater intrinsic value, or is stamped with the authority of more enlightened patrons of liberty than that . . . the accumulation of all powers, legislative, executive, and judiciary, in the same hands, whether of one, a few, or many, and whether hereditary, self-appointed, or elective, may justly be pronounced the very definition of tyranny.[8]

Over the course of almost 220 years of representative government, "the American people have [had] a touching faith in the invulnerability of their republic."[9] However, sadly, the world has seen a different and unchecked authority emanating from the White House since September 11, 2001. The post-2001 military and national security strategy developed and boldly implemented by President Bush and his lieutenants is a startling tale of one of the three branches of government—the presidency—trying to assume all powers: executive, legislative, and judicial, as well as that of commander in chief of the nation's armed forces. Whether justified in the name of national security or in the cause of maintaining order, this uniting of all power in the hands of the president is tyranny.

This book is an effort to understand what has been happening since September 11, 2001, and to ask whether Congress or the judiciary can act in a timely manner to avoid the unfolding tragedy. It will raise, examine, and answer the legal, political, military, ethical, and constitutional questions surrounding the actions President Bush has taken in the area of national security after September 11. It will examine the rationale presented by the Bush administration to explain its radical departure from earlier governmental policy regarding the treatment of captured combatants. It will critically evaluate these actions in light of past U.S. history and legal and ethical precedents. Finally, it will examine the entry of the federal courts into this discussion, especially the actions of the U.S. Supreme Court. The issue of detainee treatment, as noted above, is complex and controversial. The history of the Bush administration's policies regarding the treatment of detainees will be used as the lens through which one can see the steps the administration has taken to appropriate more and more power.

Studying the treatment of these prisoners through an examination of the handful of cases that came to the Court in 2004–2006, one finds example after example of executive branch actions—most of them secret until they were revealed in 2004—that assertively denied persons the basic protections of the Constitution and of international law. Were it not for the U.S. Supreme Court and the 2006 midterm congressional elections, this story's ending would have been very different—much more dreadful than the one told in this book.

1. Presidential Power versus the Constitution's Limits on Power

Constitutional guarantees are in place . . . because we value the Constitution.

PRESIDENT GEORGE W. BUSH, APRIL 2004[1]

The Constitution [is] just a goddamned piece of paper.

PRESIDENT GEORGE W. BUSH, DECEMBER 2005[2]

After 9/11, the U.S. president, George W. Bush, declared war against terrorism. On September 20, 2001, before a joint session of Congress televised to the nation, Bush presented his administration's position: "Our war on terror begins with al Qaeda, but it does not end there. It will not end until *every* terrorist group of global reach has been found, stopped, and defeated" (my emphasis).[3]

This war against terrorism was not perceived by the president as a figurative war like earlier presidentially declared wars on drugs or on poverty or on cancer, metaphorical battles Americans have fought without much success for decades. Whereas other nations struck by terrorist actions (Spain, Great Britain, Israel, Indonesia) labeled them vicious crimes whose perpetrators would be subject to prosecution under their respective criminal codes, the United States saw the 9/11 terrorist attacks "not only as crimes but [as] acts of war."[4]

PRESIDENT BUSH'S DECLARATION OF AN OPEN-ENDED WAR ON TERROR

The president's declaration of a "war on terror" was a uniquely American response to the actions of terrorists. Most Europeans, "with their long experience of terrorism by the Red Army Brigade, the Irish Republican Army, Basque separatists, and other groups," wrote Mark Landler, "tend to view [9/11 and other acts of terror] as a matter for law-enforcement, security and intelligence agencies, rather than a clash of civilizations." Landler observed after the London terror bombings in July 2005 that even that terrible act "will not make Europeans more receptive to American-style measures, like the detention and co-erced interrogations of suspected terrorists at Guantánamo Bay."[5] (It should be noted, however, that after the July 2005 London terrorist bombings, the British government rapidly adopted much more stringent detention measures.)

The European view, however, was not shared by President Bush, National Security Adviser Condoleezza Rice, Vice President Dick Cheney, and Secretary of Defense Donald Rumsfeld. For them, September 11, 2001, was not only the formal beginning of a war against terror; it was also the beginning of plans for invading Afghanistan in order to defeat the Taliban government that had given aid and shelter to al Qaeda terrorists and the continuation of the development of a top-secret plan to invade Iraq. (The 2003 invasion was a goal President Bush and his chief lieutenants had planned for as early as January 2001.)[6] Eighteen months later, the United States attacked Iraq.

Because these terrorist acts were deemed opening salvoes in a literal, open-ended war, lawyers for the president maintained that the military could hold al Qaeda and Taliban detainees, as well as American citizens—*all* classified as enemy combatants—indefinitely and outside the protections of international humanitarian law. Even though the term does not exist in international law, in the White House, the Pentagon, and the Department of Justice (DOJ), the only operative term for all detainees is "enemy combatants." As U.S. Attorney General Alberto R. Gonzales said to the American Bar Association (ABA): "Captured *enemy combatants,* whether *soldiers* or *saboteurs,* may be detained for the duration of hostilities. They need not be 'guilty' of anything; they are detained [indefinitely] simply by virtue of their status as *enemy combatants* in war" (my emphasis).[7]

Gonzales's language actually mimicked the language of the Third Geneva Convention of 1949 regarding prisoners of war, which states that there are two types of combatants in war: *lawful* and *unlawful.* Lawful combatants—"soldiers"—must be classified as prisoners of war and receive treatment in accord with the international laws of war, most especially the Third Geneva Convention. Unlawful combatants—"saboteurs" and "spies"—are not entitled to the protections afforded POWs and can be treated in accordance with the detaining power's military or criminal codes. However, contrary to the Third Geneva Convention's language, U.S. policy has not provided detainees with *any* rights, including the right to seek habeas corpus relief in a federal court. (It should be noted that Pentagon lawyers did prepare procedural rules for the treatment of enemy combatants brought before the military commissions President Bush created in his November 2001 military order, "Detention, Treatment, and Trial of Certain Non-Citizens in the War against Terrorism." This became a moot issue after the U.S. Supreme Court handed down the *Hamdan v. Rumsfeld* [126 S.Ct. 2749] decision in June 2006.)[8] However, the habeas issue emerged again after President Bush signed the MCA of 2006 in mid-October.

Since October 2001, when American military forces were first used against the Taliban in Afghanistan, the Bush administration has been responsible for "the wholesale incarceration of [captured] foreigners—perhaps for life—who have no real chance to confront their accusers or answer the charges against them."[9] This imprisonment without formal charges and trial (along with the often brutal interrogation of detainees in Afghanistan, Iraq, and Cuba by the U.S. military and in secret locations around the globe by the CIA's operatives) remains beyond the pale of the Geneva Conventions and other international as well as domestic laws. The decision by President Bush to treat all captured personnel as enemy combatants came very early in the war on terror.

On February 7, 2002, the president sent a memorandum to his key players in this war (Cheney, Secretary of State Colin Powell, Rumsfeld, Gonzales, Chief of Staff to the President Andrew Card, Director of Central Intelligence George Tenet, Assistant to the President for National Security Affairs Condoleezza Rice, and Chairman of the Joint Chiefs of Staff Richard Myers). In it he wrote:

> I . . . determine that none of the provisions of [1949] Geneva [Conventions] apply to our conflict with al Qaeda in Afghanistan or elsewhere throughout the world. . . . I also accept the legal conclusion of the Department of Justice and determine that [the] Geneva [language concerning definition of and treatment of prisoners of war] does not apply to either al Qaeda or Taliban detainees. . . . Based on the facts supplied by the Department of Defense and the recommendation of the Department of Justice, I determine that the Taliban detainees are unlawful combatants and, therefore, do not qualify as prisoners of war under Article 4 of Geneva. I note that, because Geneva does not apply to our conflict with al Qaeda, al Qaeda detainees also do not qualify as prisoners of war.[10]

This has been the categorical position of the Bush administration, from the beginning of the battles in October 2001[11] in Afghanistan through the 2006 *Hamdan v. Rumsfeld* opinion of the U.S. Supreme Court. (Chapters 2 and 3 will fully examine Bush's memo and his administration's capture and treatment of captured al Qaeda and Taliban soldiers.)

The remainder of this chapter places the Bush administration's treatment of enemy combatants in a broader political and public policy context. From the instant the terrorist attacks occurred on September 11, 2001, the president, the vice president, the U.S. attorney general, and the secretary of defense—the chief architects of President Bush's wartime policies abroad and domestically—successfully developed and implemented controversial public policies that immediately enhanced the powers of the president at the expense of Congress and the federal courts. These audacious actions of what Cheney termed the "unitary" executive were left unchecked and violated the fundamental constitutional concepts of separation of powers and checks and balances.

Since George Bush was sworn in as president, Vice President Cheney has been Bush's mentor and the majordomo of the administration. At one point, given Cheney's penchant for giving advice and counsel to Bush in front of others at cabinet meetings, National Security Council meetings, and the like, Bush "asked Cheney to pull back a little at big meetings, to give the President more room to move, to take charge. Bush asked Cheney not to offer him advice in crowded rooms. Do that privately. Cheney did."[12]

Many organizations and writers have called the president a despot for running roughshod over the Constitution after September 11, 2001. Jonathan Alter, a respected reporter for *Newsweek* magazine, was one such critic. In December 2005 he wrote, "We're seeing clearly now that Bush thought 9/11 gave him license to act like a dictator, or in his own mind, no doubt, like Abraham Lincoln during the Civil War."[13] Paradoxically, the situation was more complex than Alter suggested. President Bush was given license to act unilaterally—without any oversight—against terrorists, at home and abroad, by the Republican-controlled U.S. Congress. Furthermore, Lincoln's actions in the early days of the Civil War occurred when Congress was not in session. However, when Lincoln asked Congress, post hoc, to authorize his actions—which Congress did—he acknowledged that he had used Article I and Article II powers.

THE MANIFESTATIONS OF THE CENTRALIZATION OF PRESIDENTIAL POWER IN THE WAR ON TERROR SINCE 2001

When, immediately after 9/11, President Bush defined the war on terror as a "continuing threat," he "set in place a network of laws and policies of expansive scope and uncertain duration," unchecked by an acquiescent Congress that went along with the legislative proposals proffered by the White House. These presidential proposals focused heavily on reining in America's domestic enemies as well as al Qaeda terrorists; "the broadest sweep of these [war on terror] policies applies domestically; *there is magnified concern for any appreciable lack of limits*" (my emphasis).[14]

Many claim that President Bush's actions in the war on terrorism jeopardize personal liberty and the continuing viability of the concepts of separation of powers and checks and balances—concepts that are fundamental to our system of governing. Bush's successful push for antiterrorist legislation, as well as his top-secret orders to agencies such as the National Security Agency (NSA), illuminates his and Cheney's belief that there are no limits to presidential powers in America's war on terror. Some of the major bills and governmental actions to fight that war follow.[15]

Authorization for Use of Military Force (September 18, 2001)
and Iraq Joint Resolutions (October 16, 2002)

From the day the terrorists struck the World Trade Center Twin Towers in New York City and the Pentagon in Virginia, Bush has insisted that the United States was in a bloody no-end-in-sight war against terrorism, and the administration has relied on the president's authority as commander in chief, as well as the undefined *inherent powers* attached to the presidency, to centralize decision making in the executive branch—ignoring the reality that on war and national security matters, the Constitution clearly establishes shared power between Congress and the president. Article II states: "The *executive power* shall be vested in a President of the United States of America. . . . The President shall be commander in chief of the Army and Navy of the United States, and of the militia of the several states, when called into the actual service of the United States." However, Article I, the national legislative article, states:

> The Congress shall have power . . . To declare war, grant letters of *marque* and reprisal, and make rules concerning captures on land and water; To raise and support armies, but no appropriation of money to that use shall be for a longer term than two years; To provide and maintain a navy; To make rules for the government and regulation of the land and naval forces; To provide for calling forth the militia to execute the laws of the union, suppress insurrections and repel invasions; To provide for organizing, arming, and disciplining, the militia, and for

governing such part of them as may be employed in the service of the United States, reserving to the states respectively, the appointment of the officers, and the authority of training the militia according to the discipline prescribed by Congress.

On September 18, 2001, without any substantive input into the drafting of the legislation, Congress passed a joint resolution drafted by the White House: The Authorization for Use of Military Force (AUMF) Joint Resolution (Public Law 107-40). As passed and as implemented by the Bush White House, the resolution granted Bush the broadest authority to do battle against any nation, organization, or person he determined to have been involved in 9/11 or to be part of planning future terrorist actions against the United States. Section 2(a) is the operative segment of the AUMF:

IN GENERAL—That the President is authorized to use *all necessary and appropriate force* against those nations, organizations, or persons he determines planned, authorized, committed or aided the terrorist attacks that occurred on September 11, 2001, or harbored such organizations or persons, *in order to prevent any future acts of international terrorism* against the United States by such nations, organizations, or persons. [My emphasis]

The Bush White House was so convinced of the extent of presidential power that White House senior staff and Department of Justice lawyers pressed for even more in the above section of the AUMF. Minutes before the final vote in the U.S. Senate, they were lobbying to insert "in the United States" after the phrase "use all necessary and appropriate force," which would have "essentially grant[ed] war powers to anything a president deigned to do within the United States. Senators shot that [proposal] down. 'That,' said one senator, 'would be without precedent.'"[16] Through 2006, when a federal district court judge and a slim U.S. Supreme Court majority handed down decisions that attempted to curtail both his wiretapping actions and his military commissions, Bush was able to do just about anything he wanted to in the United States and abroad in his war against terrorism.

The AUMF Resolution passed by Congress in 2001 is two-pronged. First, it authorizes the president to use "all necessary and appropriate force against those nations, organizations, or persons he determines" planned the 9/11 attacks. Second, it also authorizes the president to use that force "in order to prevent any future acts of international terrorism against the United States." Since it was signed, the president and his surrogates in the executive branch

have used it, along with the inherent presidential powers in Article II, to justify all of their actions in the fight against international terrorism, from the
treatment of detainees to the use of presidentially created military commissions to try some of them as war criminals.

Little more than one year later, with the Iraq Joint Resolution (Public Law
107-243) on October 16, 2002, the quiescent Congress again granted the president broad authority, this time to go to war against Saddam Hussein because,
the president insisted—falsely—Iraq had been involved in the 9/11 terrorist
attacks and was manufacturing weapons of mass destruction for future use
against the United States. On October 11, 2002, BBC News, in response to a
draft version, observed that the president was fully authorized to use force "as
he sees fit."[17]

Section 3(a) of the 2002 Iraq Resolution is the operative section: "The
President is authorized to use the Armed Forces of the United States as he determines to be necessary and appropriate in order to . . . Defend the national
security of the United States against the continuing threat posed by Iraq." Section 3(b) mandates that the president "make available to the Speaker of the
House of Representatives and the President pro tempore of the Senate *his determination* that . . . acting pursuant to this joint resolution is consistent with
the United States and other countries continuing to take the necessary actions
against international terrorist organizations, including those nations, organizations, or persons who planned, authorized, committed, or aided the terrorist attacks that occurred on September 11, 2001" (my emphasis).[18]

Congress, in 2001 and in 2002, caved in to the president's demands. There
was no substantive debate, there were no committee hearings. There was just
blind trust that the president was telling the truth. The consequence of these
congressional resolutions became crystal clear in the years immediately after
2001: "The checking and balancing functions of other institutions have been
marginalized" as a result of these "exceedingly permissive resolutions from
Congress."[19] For almost three years, until the federal judiciary, especially the
U.S. Supreme Court, intervened in June 2004, President Bush did not have
any institutional checks on his actions against terror at home and abroad. The
passage of the 2001 AUMF Resolution and the 2002 Iraq Resolution enabled
Bush and Cheney to exercise "their vast, creative prerogatives in the 'war on
terror.' Namely, to do what they want, when they want to, for whatever reason
they decide."[20]

The USA Patriot Act (October 26, 2001)

In a similar fashion, the Bush administration, led by U.S. Attorney General John Ashcroft and Deputy Attorney General Viet Dinh, in the five weeks after September 11 drafted and then (with the help of many other White House lobbyists) pushed through Congress a 342-page-long antiterrorist bill *substituted* in lieu of the drafts prepared by legislators, the 2001 USA Patriot Act (Public Law 107-56). There were no hearings on the controversial substitute legislation in the House of Representatives and there was only about one day's debate in the Senate before it was passed by the legislators. Indeed, the final draft of the administration's substitute legislation was given to members of the House of Representatives the morning of the vote on the bill—clearly, there was no "realistic opportunity to study the bill's tremendous implications."[21]

The Patriot Act gave extensive and secret power to the executive branch, especially the administration's intelligence-gathering agencies—the Federal Bureau of Investigation (FBI), the NSA, the Central Intelligence Agency (CIA), the Defense Intelligence Agency (DIA)—to fight terrorists in America and worldwide. These agencies have mostly unchecked powers to gather intelligence information and then to apprehend and bring to some sort of justice suspected terrorists and their supporters in the United States as well as abroad.

The act clearly amends the 1978 Foreign Intelligence Surveillance Act (FISA, Public Law 95-511) because the Patriot Act allows searches of and seizures from citizens and persons suspected of criminal activities without a search warrant or any showing of probable cause. The 1978 legislation was passed because Senate and House intelligence committee investigations uncovered domestic intelligence abuses by the FBI, the CIA, the NSA, and other agencies during the administrations of President Lyndon Baines Johnson (D; 1963–1969) and Richard M. Nixon (R; 1969–1974). In those hot- and cold-war years, the lines of division between domestic and foreign intelligence-gathering surveillance were blurred. The CIA, the NSA, and army intelligence were used domestically, in violation of the protocols established regarding the authority and scope of responsibilities of those agencies. The 1978 legislation established a set of legal protocols for "foreign intelligence" surveillance separate from ordinary law enforcement surveillance, that is, actions of the FBI.[22]

FISA was aimed at "regulating the collection of foreign intelligence information in furtherance of U.S. counterintelligence," whether or not any laws were or will be broken.[23] FISA created a supersecret federal court, the Foreign Intelligence Surveillance Court. Federal authorities had to go to the court for permission to use wiretaps on foreign agencies, nations, or individuals. The agency had to show one of the seven federal judges (after the Patriot Act, eleven) that the sole purpose of the requested surveillance was *foreign* intelligence. The Bush administration's drafters of the Patriot Act, Ashcroft and Dinh, vigorously sought to lift the FISA restraints on the use of wiretap information. They were successful in blurring the distinction between law enforcement purposes (FBI activities) and foreign intelligence and counterintelligence purposes (the CIA and the military intelligence agencies).

The act contains ten sections, or titles. It allows a governmental agency to monitor, without a warrant, every e-mail message that an individual sends or receives. Secret, warrantless searches—not limited solely to terrorism suspects—can be conducted by governmental agencies who show that there "might be an adverse result" if the person were to find out about the search. Privacy standards that were established by legislation and by U.S. Supreme Court opinions in the preceding sixty years were instantly eroded in the 2001 Act.[24] Title II, "Enhanced Surveillance Procedures," gives yet another controversial power to the executive branch. It authorizes federal agencies to intercept wire, oral, and electronic communications relating to terrorism or relating to computer fraud and abuse. Unlike FISA, which contained prohibitions and regulations, the section allows law enforcement and counterintelligence agencies to share information and to conduct sneak-and-peek searches.[25]

Furthermore, and equally disturbing to many in the legal community, the Patriot Act "grants vast powers to law enforcement that have nothing to do with counter-terrorism."[26]

The Roundup of Members of the Immigrant Community in the United States after September 11, 2001

Within days of September 11, 2001, FBI and Immigration and Naturalization Service (INS) agents began a secret roundup and "unprecedented" detention of thousands of people across the United States, "most of whom are Muslim or bear Arabic names. 'It's the first time in [American] history,' argued Kate Martin, who works for the Center for National Security Studies, 'that the government has arrested people in secret. We have 200 years of law and tradition saying that arrests are public. . . . We do not have secret arrests.'"[27]

After the passage of the USA Patriot Act in late October 2001, there was, as critics observed, a "domestic reign of terror visited on the U.S. immigrant community [because the act] authorized the INS to detain immigrants without charge for up to seven days. But as a belated report by the Justice Department's Inspector General revealed, many captives were in fact held illegally without charge for as long as eight months, denied access to attorneys, and then, after secret hearings, deported."[28]

Furthermore, according to the Department of Justice's own report by the Office of the Inspector General (OIG), released in June 2003, of the thousands of immigrants rounded up, only one person was ultimately convicted of "supporting" terrorism.[29] The report criticized the Department of Justice and the INS for using "the Patriot Act and federal immigration statutes to detain, in the federal detention center in New York City (the Metropolitan Detention Center), more than 1,100 aliens for months without their families' knowing where they were and what crimes they may have committed. . . . It was not until the second half of 2002 that the detainees were investigated and [almost all of them] released."[30] The INS consistently violated the federal rule that detainees had to be served notice, within seventy-two hours of being detained, of the charges for which they were being held. The FBI, which by law is responsible for clearance investigations of all detainees held by the INS, failed to act in the prescribed manner.

In consequence, for example, detainees in the Manhattan INS detention center remained in restrictive custody for months. According to the Department of Justice's OIG report, the FBI clearance process took an average of eighty days. Although the federal law allowed for release on bail bond, the Department of Justice instituted a "no bond" policy after September 11, 2001, in order to keep the thousands of detainees confined in the center until clearance investigations had been completed by the FBI. Clearly, such behavior by FBI and the INS personnel violated the language of the Patriot Act, as well as INS regulations and other federal regulations. It violated these thousands of persons' civil rights under the Constitution.

However, in early January 2004, the U.S. Supreme Court declined to review the government's refusal to release names and other information—including the whereabouts—about the thousands of foreigners being held. They declined to grant certiorari in *Center for National Security Studies v. U.S. Department of Justice* (03-472), in a petition that "pitted two fundamental values against each other—the right of the public to know details of how its government operates versus the government's need to keep some information secret to protect national security."[31] The Court's denial of certiorari meant that the 2–1 ruling of the U.S. Court of Appeals for the District of Columbia Circuit stood.

Federal judges and the justices of the U.S. Supreme Court, like their legislative brethren, accepted presidential arguments. The federal appellate judges wrote, "The need for deference [to the executive] in this case is just as strong as in earlier cases. America faces an enemy just as real as its former cold war foes." The lone dissenter, Judge David A. Tatel, wrote, "By accepting the government's vague, poorly explained allegations, and by filling in the gaps in the government's case with its own assumptions about facts absent from the record, this court has converted deference into acquiescence."[32] It was only in 2004, when petitions for certiorari review came to the U.S. Supreme Court, that the justices began to substantively examine the behavior of President Bush in light of the constraints on presidential power found in the Constitution.

The Negation of the Protections of the U.S. Constitution's Due Process Amendments in the Name of National Security

The U.S. Constitution protects everyone—citizens, legal aliens, illegal aliens—from a variety of governmental actions that threaten a person's liberty without due process of law and fundamental fairness. Throughout the document, reference is made to either "persons"/"people" or "citizens" in the nation's fundamental law. Only citizens can vote; however, the due process protections in Amendments Four through Ten of the Bill of Rights apply to all "persons" who reside within the sovereign territory of the United States. The Fourth Amendment states:

> The right of the *people* to be secure in their persons, houses, papers, and effects, against unreasonable searches and seizures, shall not be violated, and no Warrants shall issue, but upon probable cause, supported by Oath or affirmation, and particularly describing the place to be searched, and the *persons* or things to be seized. [My emphasis]

Since September 11, 2001, President Bush's surrogates in the Department of Justice and other federal law enforcement agencies have undermined the Fourth Amendment's protections in a number of ways.

First, the president "has exerted his authority to exclude the judiciary from the warrant application process by issuing his own arrest warrants."[33] Under President Bush's November 2001 military order (discussed in chapter 2), once

Bush determines that a noncitizen "enemy combatant" may be involved in alleged war crimes, federal law enforcement agents "shall" detain that person "at an appropriate location designated by the secretary of defense outside or within the United States."[34] That person, according to the order, cannot go into federal district court to seek a writ of habeas corpus to challenge the legality of the arrest. The Fourth Amendment is categorically ignored.

Second, President Bush and the FBI have attempted to dilute the Fourth Amendment's probable cause language. In the months following September 11, 2001, the FBI, the INS, and other law enforcement agencies rounded up, arrested, and detained many thousands of persons without any charges and without having to show an impartial magistrate the probable cause required for such government action. Although he has since modified his position, federal appeals court judge Richard Posner, a conservative jurist, labeled this governmental action "imprisonment on suspicion while the police look for evidence to confirm their suspicion."[35] "Of all the checks and balances in the Fourth Amendment," wrote Dave Kopel in 2001, "the most important is that the person who is searched knows that he has been searched."[36] Under the Patriot Act, a person can be searched again and again by a federal law enforcement agency without his or her knowledge.

The Fifth Amendment states, in part:

> No *person* shall be held to answer for a capital, or otherwise infamous crime, unless on a presentment or indictment of a Grand Jury, . . . nor be deprived of life, liberty, or property, without due process of law." [My emphasis]

Yet the military order allowed President Bush to have people arrested outside of the judicial process and held incommunicado at military bases without *any* due process. Such a person is barred from filing a writ of habeas corpus in a federal court. Furthermore, the order states: "I [President Bush] reserve the authority to direct the secretary of defense, at any time hereafter, to transfer to a governmental authority [a foreign nation] control of any individual subject to this order."[37] (Chapter 3 discusses the policy of "extraordinary rendition" of detainees to other nations by the CIA.)

The Sixth Amendment, another constitutional guarantee to all *persons* held within the nation's jurisdiction, states:

> In all criminal prosecutions, the *accused* shall enjoy the right to a speedy and public trial, by an impartial jury of the State and district wherein the crime shall have been committed, which district shall have been previously ascertained by

law, and to be *informed of the nature and cause of the accusation;* to be confronted with the witnesses against him; to have compulsory process for obtaining witnesses in his favor, and to have the Assistance of Counsel for his defence. [My emphasis]

Under President Bush's military order, he alone decides who can be tried before a jury in a criminal trial in federal court and who is to be tried before a military commission he established in the order.[38] The order totally ignored the language of the Sixth Amendment. As one conservative critic wrote, "The Constitution's [Sixth Amendment] is not a 'peace provision' that can be suspended during wartime. Reasonable people can argue about how to prosecute war criminals who are captured overseas in a theater of war, but the President cannot make himself the policeman, the prosecutor, and judge over people on United States soil. In America, the president's power is 'checked' by the judiciary and by citizen juries."[39]

Warrantless Wiretaps Secretly Conducted by the NSA

FISA allows America's intelligence-gathering agencies to use the latest technologies in the effort to acquire foreign intelligence useful to the protection of the nation. It permits federal law enforcement and intelligence-gathering agencies (almost twenty in number) to receive permission—a search warrant—from the Foreign Intelligence Surveillance Court to use wiretaps in the national interest. However, immediately after September 11, 2001, the president secretly ordered the NSA to conduct warrantless wiretaps and Internet intercepts on all appropriate foreign telephone calls to the United States and also instructed the NSA to collect data on hundreds of millions of domestic telephone numbers.

The NSA was created in 1952 during the administration of President Harry S. Truman (D; 1945–1953) "to consolidate the government's code-breaking and code-making capabilities, and initially there were few limits on the NSA's ability to conduct electronic surveillance inside the United States."[40] However, by the early 1970s, the domestic abuses of the FBI, CIA, and the NSA became known. Congressional committees chaired by Senator Frank Church (D–ID) and Congressman Otis Pike (D–NY) uncovered the fact that these agencies were conducting unauthorized spying on people involved in the civil rights and the anti–Vietnam War movements. In response, Congress passed FISA, requiring such surveillance organizations to obtain search warrants. The NSA abided by the rules and restrictions placed on its activities by Congress in the

1970s and 1980s, but after September 11, 2001, President Bush gave secret instructions otherwise to the NSA, removing the restraints.

It seems possible that these new activities of the NSA were violations of either FISA or Fourth Amendment privacy precedents. "There can be no serious question that warrantless wiretaps, in violation of the law, are impeachable [offenses]," wrote John Dean about this secret program ordered by President Bush.[41] Nonetheless, since early 2002, after receiving the order from President Bush, "the technical wizards of the NSA," wrote James Risen, "have been engaged in a program of [foreign and] domestic data mining that is so vast, and so unprecedented, that it makes a mockery of long-standing privacy rules. . . . For the first time since the Watergate-era abuses, the NSA is spying on Americans again, and on a large scale."[42]

In December 2005 the *New York Times* revealed that the NSA was intercepting telephone and other electronic messages sent to persons in the United States from other persons outside the country. According to Jonathan Alter, of *Newsweek,* the president did all he could to kill the story:

> I learned this week that on December 6, Bush summoned *New York Times* publisher Arthur Sulzberger and executive editor Bill Keller to the Oval Office in a futile attempt to talk them out of running the story. The *Times* will not comment on the meeting, but one can only imagine the president's desperation. . . . Bush was desperate to keep the *Times* from running this important story—which the paper had already inexplicably held for a year—because he knew that it would reveal him as a law-breaker. He insists he had "legal authority derived from the Constitution and congressional resolution authorizing force." But the Constitution explicitly requires the president to obey the law. And the post 9/11 congressional resolution authorizing "all necessary force" in fighting terrorism was made in clear reference to military intervention. It did not scrap the Constitution and allow the president to do whatever he pleased in any area in the name of fighting terrorism.[43]

When the story was finally published in the *New York Times,* the White House acknowledged that in October 2001 President Bush had issued an executive order authorizing the NSA to intercept phone calls and e-mails between the United States and overseas in which one of the parties was suspected of some kind of link to al Qaeda. Democrats and Republicans alike condemned the action, saying that Congress did not authorize these actions, for such a program violates the 1978 FISA.

This secret order is but another example of the very broad authority Congress allegedly gave the president when it passed the AUMF Resolution in 2001. According to the president, the NSA program "is constitutional and was *effectively authorized by Congress* when it approved the use of force against al Qaeda after the September 11, 2001, attacks" (my emphasis).[44] The AUMF, however, does *not* authorize the White House to order the NSA to eavesdrop. There was never any discussion of such a policy change authorized by the AUMF. As one scholar noted: "You don't 'effectively' authorize anything. You do or you don't."[45] And Congress, whatever else it did in the terrible days after September 11, most certainly did not authorize the president to allow the NSA to eavesdrop.

One of the eleven federal judges on the secret Foreign Intelligence Surveillance Court resigned in protest of President Bush's secret authorization of the domestic spying program. U.S. District Court Judge James Robertson sent a letter of resignation from the court to the chief justice of the U.S. Supreme Court, John G. Roberts Jr., after the December 2005 revelation in the *New York Times*.[46] One source quoted in the *Washington Post*, who spoke to a number of the judges on the Foreign Intelligence Surveillance Court, said, "What I've heard some of the judges say is they feel they've participated in a Potemkin court."[47]

In April 2006 Attorney General Alberto Gonzales, during an appearance before the U.S. House Judiciary Committee, further enraged critics when he suggested that "the Administration could decide it was legal to listen in on a *domestic* call without supervision or permission if it was a communication relating to al Qaeda. 'I'm not going to rule it out,' Gonzales told Representative Adam Schiff (D–Cal)" (my emphasis).[48] Representative Schiff instantly responded to the attorney general's observation, calling the possibility of a federal agency intercepting domestic calls "disturbing" and stating that it "represents a wholly unprecedented assertion of executive power. . . . No one in Congress would deny the need to tap certain calls under court order, but if the administration believes it can tap purely domestic phone calls between Americans without court approval, there is no limit to executive power. This is contrary to settled law and the most basic constitutional principles of the separation of powers."[49]

President Bush, the same day, haughtily said that he would "absolutely not" apologize for authorizing the October 2001 secret NSA wiretapping program. "You can come to whatever conclusion you want," Bush told a questioner during a North Carolina visit, but "the conclusion is I'm not going to apologize for what I did on the terrorist surveillance program."[50] And Tasia Scolinos, a spokesperson for the Department of Justice, tried to calm the waters: "The Attorney General's comments today should not be interpreted to suggest the existence or nonexistence of a domestic program or whether any such program would be lawful under the existing legal analysis."[51]

Then, in early May 2006, a month after Scolinos's comments, another surprise greeted Americans when they read their morning paper. In the May 11, 2006, edition of *USA Today,* the headline claimed that "NSA Has Massive Database of Americans' Phone Calls": "The NSA has been secretly collecting the phone call records of tens of millions of Americans, using data provided by AT&T, Verizon, and BellSouth, people with direct knowledge of the arrangement told USA TODAY. The NSA program reaches into homes and businesses across the nation by amassing information about the calls of ordinary Americans—most of whom aren't suspected of any crime." According to the *USA Today* article, evidently these tens of millions of "call detail records" enable the NSA and other intelligence agencies "to track who calls whom, and when, but [do] not include the contents of conversations."[52] According to sources who spoke with reporters, intelligence analysts "are seeking to mine their records to expose hidden connections and details of social networks, hoping to find signs of terrorist plots in the vast sea of innocent contacts."[53]

Again, as he did in December 2005, President Bush quickly arranged a press conference to defend the suddenly uncovered secret domestic warrantless wiretap program—in existence since October 2001: "The intelligence activities I authorized are lawful. [We are not] mining or trolling through the personal lives of millions of innocent Americans. Our efforts are focused on links to al Qaeda and their known affiliates." He closed his impromptu conference with reporters with a warning: Any leak about America's "sensitive intelligence [techniques] hurts our ability to defeat this enemy."[54]

In this secret and warrantless domestic wiretapping program, no search warrants were ever asked for by the NSA leaders administering the program.[55] This is the reality for the NSA's foreign wiretapping program as well.

Ironically, in April 2004, one year earlier, in Buffalo, New York, President Bush had told his audience and the world, "Anytime you hear the United States government talking about wiretap, it requires—*a wiretap requires a court order.* Nothing has changed, by the way. When we're talking about chasing down terrorists, we're talking about getting a court order before we do so. . . . Constitutional guarantees are in place . . . *because we value the Constitution*" (my emphasis).[56] It is clear that in the war against terrorism President Bush did not hesitate to lie to the world about the actions of his administration.

In June 2006 another irony unfolded in this particular, once very secret and now quite controversial, presidential policy. Matthew W. Friedrich, chief of staff and principal deputy attorney general, criminal division, testified before the U.S. Senate's Committee on the Judiciary on June 6. After saying, "President Bush has stated that such leaks have damaged our national security, hurt our ability to pursue terrorists, and put our citizens at risk," Friedrich revealed that the Department of Justice's Criminal Division was "committed to investigating and prosecuting leaks of classified information":

> Section 793 of Title 18 USC [of the Espionage Act of 1918], which prohibits the disclosure of information "relating to national defense," [and] Section 798 of Title 18 USC, [which] prohibits the unauthorized disclosure of information relating to communications intelligence activities [may have been violated by reporters from the *Times* and the *Post*]. The Department [of Justice] has never in its history prosecuted a member of the press under Section 793, 798; . . . [furthermore], any decision to proceed against the press in a criminal proceeding is made at the very highest level of the Department.[57]

After he read his statement, Friedrich refused to say whether the Bush administration had considered or was then considering prosecuting journalists for publishing leaked national security information. "You should be ashamed of yourself [for not answering our questions], or your superiors should be ashamed of themselves," a "bristling" Senator Patrick Leahy (D–VT) told Friedrich.[58] In addition to the possibility of prosecutions regarding the publishing of stories about the NSA's warrantless wiretap programs, Senator Leahy, in a statement to the committee on June 6, 2006, noted that "according to the *Washington Times,* reporters for the *Washington Post* and the *New York Times* are being investigated by the Justice Department's [Criminal Division] for publishing stories about the CIA's secret prisons in eastern Europe."[59]

The recent revelations about the secret NSA wiretapping program disturbed many legislators as well as some of the judges on the FISA court. U.S. Senator Arlen Specter (R–PA), a moderate Republican and the chairman of the Senate Judiciary Committee, believes that the secret program ordered by President Bush clearly violates the 1978 FISA legislation. In a letter to Vice President Cheney, dated June 7, 2006, Specter wrote:

The Administration's continuing position on the NSA electronic surveillance program rejects the historical constitutional practice of judicial approval of warrants before wiretapping and denigrates the constitutional authority and responsibility of the Congress and specifically the Judiciary Committee to conduct oversight on constitutional issues. . . . There is no doubt that the NSA Program violates the FISA which sets forth the exclusive procedure for domestic wiretaps which requires the approval of the FISA Court. It may be that the President has inherent authority under Article II to trump the statute but the President does not have a blank check and the determination on whether the President has such Article II power calls for a balancing test which requires knowing what the surveillance program constitutes.[60]

In mid-March 2006 Specter had introduced legislation to authorize the FISA court to rule on the constitutionality of the Administration's electronic surveillance program. The Bush White House refused to stake out a position on the proposed legislation. When the *USA Today* story broke alleging that telephone companies were turning over millions of customer records involving billions of telephone calls, Specter's committee scheduled a hearing of the CEOs of the major telephone companies.

In an effort to quash this investigation, Vice President Cheney met unofficially with the Republican members of the Senate Judiciary Committee on June 6, 2006—without telling Chairman Specter about the meeting or inviting him to attend. In his subsequent letter to the vice president, Specter said, "You had called [them] lobbying them to oppose my Judiciary Committee hearing, even a closed one, with the telephone companies. I was further advised that you told those Republican members that the telephone companies had been instructed not to provide any information to the Committee as they were prohibited from disclosing private information." And for the first time since Bush was elected in 2000, a U.S. senator, a Republican to boot, directly challenged the president to cooperate in order to resolve the disagreement:

It has been my hope that there could be an accommodation between Congress's Article I authority on oversight and the President's constitutional authority under Article II. . . . If an accommodation cannot be reached with the Administration, the Judiciary Committee will consider confronting the issue with subpoenas and enforcement of that compulsory process if it appears that a majority vote will be forthcoming.

Senator Specter closed the strong disparaging letter by voicing a hope that the "matter could be worked out without the necessity of a constitutional confrontation between Congress and the President."[61] Although he said that he could wait a few more days for a resolution, brokered by fellow Republican senator Orrin Hatch (R–UT), he told a reporter that he was "insistent on the protection of civil liberties and insistent on the Congress's right to oversight on constitutional issues."[62]

President Bush's Use of the Presidential Signing Statement to
Thwart the Intent of Congressional Legislation

Another important constitutional controversy, one that goes directly to the heart of the checks-and-balances principle, is whether a presidential "signing statement" can effectively and substantively change the meaning of legislation passed by the Congress. Presidential signing statements are pronouncements made by the president—and printed—after his signing of congressional legislation into law. Probably the most important facet of presidential signing statements is that they provide "[structure for] the initial implementation of the new legislation [within the executive branch]. . . . [The signing statements] include directives to the heads of the responsible agencies in the form of guidance, mandates, and prohibitions issued as part of the signing statements. The admonitions they set forth can be expected to influence [bureaucratic] rulemaking efforts that will further explain and give detailed application to the legislation in question."[63]

Although these signing statements have been employed by presidents since the early nineteenth century, there were only seventy-five presidential signing statements until the administration of President Ronald Reagan (R; 1981–1989). He issued more than a hundred during his two terms. Between 1989 and 2001, Presidents George H. W. Bush (R; 1989–1993) and Bill Clinton (D; 1993–2001) issued a total of 372 signing statements. In the five years since coming to office in January 2001, President George W. Bush has issued over 750 such statements.[64] In a recent examination of the Bush administration's signing statement process, it was discovered that Vice President Cheney's office

> routinely reviews pieces of legislation before they reach the president's desk, searching for provisions that Cheney believes would infringe on presidential power. . . . David Addington, Cheney's legal adviser and chief of staff, is the Bush Administration's leading architect of the 'signing statements' the president has appended to more than 750 laws. [All] the statements assert the president's right to ignore the laws because they conflict with his interpretation of the Constitution.[65]

Generally, these presidential signing statements are "announcements added to a piece of legislation . . . and [they] are perfectly legal."[66] Vice President Cheney is the first vice president in U.S. history to use his power, especially through his continual counseling of the president, "to promote an expansive theory of presidential authority," as the *Boston Globe* put it. According to Cheney's view of the presidency, "Congress cannot pass laws that place restrictions or requirements on how the president runs the military and spy agencies. Nor can it pass laws giving governmental officials [in the executive branch] the power or responsibility to act independently of the president."[67]

This language reflects the commitment of the vice president and his staff to the principle of the "unitary executive." That concept was the paramount reason for reviewing every bill sent to the president for his signature and for drafting the presidential signing statements for Bush when Cheney and Addington believe there is dissonance between the congressional bill and the powers of the president. The Bush White House has always adamantly insisted that "Article II of the Constitution would not permit any interference [by Congress or the federal courts] with the president's control of the unitary executive."[68] In a signing statement attached to the Department of Commerce, Justice, State, Judiciary, and Related Agencies Appropriations Act (Public Law 107-77), President Bush said that any legislation or section of legislation that "raises separation of power concerns by improperly and unnecessarily impinging upon my authority as President to direct the actions of the Executive branch and its employees [will not be followed by me]. I will construe the provision to avoid constitutional difficulties and preserve the separation of powers required by the Constitution."[69]

By the middle of 2002, the Bush administration, as represented by the vice president's office, "was increasingly prepared to issue signing statements that were confrontational and particularly to reject anything that it regarded as interference with its prerogative powers in the areas of national security, foreign affairs, Defense Department matters, intelligence policy or law enforcement."[70] In one signing statement, appended to the Enhanced Border Security and Visa Entry Reform Act of 2002 (Public Law 107-173), the president baldly asserted:

> Sections 2(6); 201 (c) (2), and 202 (a) (3) [of the Act] purport to require the President to act through a specified assistant to the President or in coordination or consultation with specified officers of the United States, agencies, or congressional committees. The President's constitutional authority to supervise

the unitary executive branch and take care that the laws be faithfully executed cannot be made by law subject to [congressional] requirements to exercise those constitutional authorities through a particular member of the President's staff or in coordination or consultation with specified officers or elements of the Government. Accordingly, . . . the executive branch shall treat the purported requirements as advisory.[71]

Critics of the Bush administration's signing statements in the war on terror argue that these little-known devices "reinforce [the president's] claim that both courts and Congress are irrelevant."[72] For example, after President Bush signed the McCain Anti-Torture bill in December 2005 (which made it illegal for Americans to engage in the "cruel, inhuman, and degrading" treatment of detainees), he said in his signing statement that the law would only be followed "in a manner consistent with the constitutional authority of the president to supervise the unitary executive branch . . . and consistent with the constitutional limitations on the judicial power." As one critic observed about this particular signing statement: It was up to Bush (and Cheney), "not Congress or the courts—to determine when the provisions of this bill interfere with his war-making powers, and when they do, he will freely ignore that law."[73]

Other signing statements issued by the president, after Addington prepared them and Vice President Cheney vetted them, include one that claims that the president can bypass the ban on torture, one that ignores a restriction on the use of troops abroad, one that enables the president to go around the oversight provisions of the Patriot Act. In addition a number of signing statements would, at the president's discretion, deny information to Congress.[74]

Senator Leahy has been one of a handful of solons to vigorously object to these presidential actions. They are, he said, "nothing short of a radical effort to re-shape the constitutional separation-of-powers and evade accountability and responsibility for following the law. The President's signing statements are not the law and we [the Congress] should not allow them to become the last word."[75]

In the more than five years of his presidency up to July 2006, President Bush had not vetoed a single piece of legislation. Why? Perhaps he signed legislation disliked by Cheney and Addington and by the lawyers in the Office of Legal Counsel (OLC) (and *presumably* disliked by the president) because of the attachment of a signing statement. Since 2001 Congress has not had a single occasion to debate or discuss the policy enunciated in the signing statements attached to the bill. As the *New York Times* recently editorialized: "President Bush doesn't bother with vetoes; he simply declares his intention [in a signing statement] not to enforce anything he dislikes. . . . [He has] used it so clearly to make the president the interpreter of a law's intent, instead of Congress, and the arbiter of constitutionality, instead of the courts."[76]

The Lack of Ascertainable Standards in Determining
How to Legally Treat Detainees
Since the "crisis" of terrorism began in 2001, "the Bush administration's antiterrorism policies have created a blurring of distinctions between military action and [civilian] law enforcement [actions], along with a resultant uncertainty as to which set of standards applies in certain circumstances."[77] The lawyers in the Department of Justice and the Department of Defense seem to act in a totally arbitrary fashion in "deciding whether to charge terrorism suspects . . . with crimes or hold them in military facilities as enemy combatants."[78] For example, as chapters 4 and 5 will discuss in greater detail, Jose Padilla, an American citizen and a suspected member of al Qaeda, was seized in Chicago under a material witness warrant and then taken to New York City and held in a federal facility. When it was determined that he was a citizen of the United States, he was labeled an enemy combatant by the president and transferred to a military brig in South Carolina, where he stayed, without assistance of legal counsel, from 2002 to 2005.

In November 2005 Attorney General Gonzales announced that Padilla had been indicted for allegedly violating federal criminal law. He was once again moved, this time to the federal detention center in Florida, awaiting his trial in federal court. At no time did Gonzales say anything "about the standards the administration used in deciding whether to charge terrorism suspects like Mr. Padilla with crimes or hold them in military facilities as enemy combatants," possibly subject to trial before a military commission established by the Department of Defense. Furthermore, Jonathan M. Freiman, one of Padilla's attorneys, was told that the Bush administration "reserved the right" to detain Padilla (as an enemy combatant) again should he be acquitted in federal district court.[79]

The flip side of the Padilla story is the case of Ali Saleh Kahlah al-Marri, a student from Qatar detained in the United States. (When arrested, he was attending graduate school at Bradley University, in Peoria, Illinois.) For sixteen months, criminal proceedings against him for alleged fraud were moving along. However, less than one month before his trial was to start in July 2003, President Bush designated al-Marri an enemy combatant. The federal criminal case against him was moot. Al-Marri was moved—immediately—to the navy brig in Charleston, South Carolina, where he presently resides, totally isolated and, until recently, without legal counsel or visitation rights. There has been no explanation for the change in venue.

Although neither charged with a crime nor convicted of anything, al-Marri's detention may be "lifelong." In early 2006 a federal district court judge, Henry F. Floyd, ruled that the Bush administration was authorized to detain al-Marri. Jonathan Hafetz, his lawyer, said, "Al-Marri has been in solitary confinement for two and one half years. He hasn't spoken to or seen his wife and five children since he was designated an enemy combatant. There's no news, no books, nothing."[80]

There are other examples of seemingly arbitrary action by federal lawyers regarding the status of persons detained after September 11, 2001. As Adam Liptak noted, "One American captured on the battlefield in Afghanistan was held in the United States as an enemy combatant. Another was prosecuted as a criminal. One foreigner seized in the United States as a suspected terrorist is being held as an enemy combatant without charges in a Navy brig in Charleston, South Carolina. Others have been prosecuted for their crimes."[81]

Why these switches by administration lawyers in legal venues? Freiman answered the question with a simple observation: "The government continues to be more focused on protecting its strategies than allowing them to be subject to [judicial] review."[82]

Department of Justice Use of the State Secrets Privilege
in U.S. District Courts
By the summer of 2006 the Bush administration found itself facing a number of civil lawsuits regarding treatment of detainees who were held in prisons outside the United States and who were subsequently—after rendition—released because they were innocent victims of the war on terror. The Department of Justice and White House lawyers began to use "a tactic that swiftly torpedoes most lawsuits: the state secrets privilege."[83]

The state secrets privilege was identified and defined by the U.S. Supreme Court in an important 1953 case, *United States v. Reynolds* (345 U.S. 1 [1953]). It is a landmark federal tort claims case that saw the creation of the privilege, an unofficial but judicially recognized extension of presidential power.

In *Reynolds*, the widows of three civilian engineers on board a bomber that had crashed in 1948, preparing possible legal action, sought accident reports on the crash. They were told by the Air Force that to release such details would threaten national security by revealing the bomber's top-secret mission. The air force refused to provide the information.

Absent the report, the U.S. district court and the U.S. court of appeals viewed the question of negligence in the widows' favor and ruled for the plaintiffs. The question of law that was presented to the U.S. Supreme Court by the government was this: If the government invokes the state secrets privilege to withhold information in civil proceedings, must the trial court view the point on which evidence is withheld in the plaintiff's favor?

In a 6–3 opinion written by Chief Justice Fred Vinson, the Court held that cause for privilege must be reasonably demonstrated. As a result, the government may withhold information for reasons of national security even when that information is vital to the plaintiff's case. Vinson wrote:

> When the Secretary of the Air Force lodged his formal "Claim of Privilege," he attempted therein to invoke the privilege against revealing military secrets, a privilege which is well established in the law of evidence. The existence of the privilege is conceded by the court below, and, indeed, by the most outspoken critics of governmental claims to privilege.
>
> Judicial experience with the privilege which protects military and state secrets has been limited in this country. English experience has been more extensive, but still relatively slight compared with other evidentiary privileges. Nevertheless, the principles which control the application of the privilege emerge quite clearly from the available precedents. *The privilege belongs to the Government and must be asserted by it; it can neither be claimed nor waived by a private party. It is not to be lightly invoked.* There must be a formal claim of privilege, lodged by the head of the department which has control over the matter, after actual personal consideration by that officer. The court itself must determine whether the circumstances are appropriate for the claim of privilege, and yet do so without forcing a disclosure of the very thing the privilege is designed to protect. [My emphasis; footnotes omitted][84]

After the remand, the plaintiffs settled their case with the government. (In the mid-1990s the accident reports were declassified and released and were found to contain no secret information. They did, however, contain information about the poor condition of the aircraft itself, which would have compromised the air force's case.)

Since 2005, with the onset of lawsuits brought against Bush and his surrogates for their actions since September 2001, the Department of Justice has "invoked the once rarely cited state secrets privilege to argue that a lawsuit alleging government wrongdoing should be dismissed without an airing."[85] The most recent invocation of the privilege was on May 12, 2006, in a case involving the wrongful detention and rendition by the CIA of a German citizen, Khalid el-Masri. He was mistakenly detained at the Macedonian border, turned over to CIA personnel, flown to Afghanistan, interrogated by the CIA for almost six months, and then released without charge. His erroneous detention was apparently due to a misunderstanding caused by the similarity in spelling of his name and the name of a suspected al Qaeda terrorist, Khalid *al-Masri*.

Assistant U.S. Attorney General R. Joseph Sher told the U.S. district court judge that the "government cannot confirm or deny the allegations" made by el-Masri. The plaintiff brought suit against George Tenet, then the director of central intelligence, and the three companies whose planes had been used by the CIA to move el-Masri from place to place. He sought an apology and financial compensation for having been wrongfully imprisoned in Afghanistan for almost six months by the CIA (December 2003–April 2004).

The allegations, the federal attorney said, "clearly involve clandestine activity abroad [and] there is no way that the case can go forward without causing damage to the national security." The then director of the CIA, Porter J. Goss, said in a declaration filed by the government that secrecy was needed "to protect classified intelligence sources and methods from unauthorized disclosure; they cannot be described in the public record."[86]

El-Masri's attorney, Ben Wizner, said that if the district court judge, T. S. Ellis III (who was appointed by President Reagan in 1987), were to grant the government's motion, it would amount "to giving a broad immunity to the government to shield even the most egregious activities."[87] Ellis, however, did grant the government's motion and dismissed the suit six days later, on May 18, 2006. He wrote that "in the present circumstances, el-Masri's private interests must give way to the national interest in preserving state secrets." If there is a remedy for his wrongful treatment, the judge said that it did not lie with the judiciary to provide it: "Putting aside all the legal issues, if el-Masri's allegations are true or substantially true, then all fair-minded people, including those who believe that state secrets must be protected, that this lawsuit cannot proceed, and that renditions are a necessary step to take in this war, must also agree that el-Masri has suffered injuries as a result of our country's mistake and deserves a remedy." However, sadly, "in times of war," noted the judge, "our country . . . must often take exceptional steps to thwart the enemy."[88]

Another case involving CIA rendition of a person, Maher Arar, a Syrian-born Canadian (subsequently found to be innocent after months of torture in Syria), was also dismissed under the state secrets privilege. The Arar and el-Masri suits are the fourth and fifth times in a year that the government has invoked the state secrets privilege. As other wrongfully detained persons bring suit against the government, the privilege will probably again be invoked, and the lawsuits will, in all probability, be dismissed.

The privilege was created by the U.S. Supreme Court during the cold war to enable the government to press federal courts to dismiss legal cases if, in the eyes of the government's lawyers, continuation of the trial would damage foreign policy or national security. Since the September 11, 2001, attacks, the Justice Department has invoked the state secrets privilege twenty-three times. In the nearly half a century from 1953, when it was first recognized in federal law, to 2001, it was invoked only fifty-five times.[89]

The state secrets privilege has become, for President Bush and the lawyers in the Department of Justice, "a very powerful weapon for the executive branch," according to political scientist William G. Weaver. "Once [the privilege] is asserted, in almost every instance it stops the case cold." What began in 1953 as a mechanism to shield sensitive documents involving national security from being disclosed in a civil suit "is now often used to try to snuff out lawsuits at their inception."[90]

Assertions That Federal Courts Lack Jurisdiction in Enemy Combatants and Terrorism Litigation

Again and again since September 11, 2001, the position of the Bush administration, as expressed by the attorney general and by the U.S. solicitor general in briefs filed with the federal courts and in oral arguments in these venues, has been that judges have no role in reviewing its decisions regarding the war on terror, enemy combatants, and other national security actions. In every argument, the Bush administration has categorically held that the president has "unreviewable authority" to hold individuals any way the Department of Justice and the Department of Defense wanted, "as part of the war on terrorism."[91]

Consider again Padilla's strange case. Many observers believe that the government moved Padilla from a military brig to a federal detention center because the Bush administration did not want the U.S. Supreme Court to consider, a second time, his pending petition. (The change in Padilla's status came just a few days before the solicitor general would have had to file legal papers in the Court. With the change in his status, as will be seen in chapter 5, the Supreme Court, 6–3, denied certiorari in *Padilla v. Rumsfeld*. (*Padilla v. Hanft* is Padilla's second effort to get the Supreme Court to hear his case; the Court's initial opinion was *Padilla v. Rumsfeld*.)

THE CONSTITUTIONAL QUANDARY: THE DRAINAGE OF POWER FROM THE CONGRESS AND THE JUDICIARY

Throughout U.S. history, in times of crisis, that is, war and major economic depressions, the president and his staff exhibited decisive leadership to bring the society through the perilous, and hard, times. President Lincoln (R; 1861–1865) acted decisively during the Civil War. His actions led the Supreme Court to attempt to designate the outer parameters of presidential power in wartime. And after a number of crucial and timely presidential actions, the Congress, post hoc, validated them with the passage of legislation.

During the two world wars, Presidents Woodrow Wilson (D; 1913–1921) and Franklin D. Roosevelt (D; 1933–1945) sought to expand their constitutional powers as far as the judiciary would allow. However, until 2001, these expansions of presidential power were seen as temporary, and most of these expansions of power came with the support of Congress and, generally, the Supreme Court. It was understood that these unusual executive actions were temporary, that there would be a return to the normalcy of separate institutions sharing political power once the crisis ended. And these crises, especially conventional warfare, always had an end in sight.

President Bush's declared war on terror is quite different: It is an open-ended war against fleeting shadows—the fanatical insurgent bent on destroying the "Great Satan" in the name of Muhammad. There is no visible enemy on the battlefield who must be defeated unconditionally. Neither Bush nor Cheney nor others in the Bush administration have addressed a return to constitutional normalcy. There is no perceived or even discussed end to an emergent and necessary state that a few have called a "constitutional dictatorship."[92]

President Bush believes and has been told by his vice president that his power is fundamental to ultimate success in the war on terror. The Bush White House believes the president can override legislation or, as in the case of FISA, ignore legislation signed into law by him or other presidents. He can strategically move prisoners from the jurisdiction of federal courts into military brigs and can argue that courts have no business interfering in any matters relating to the use of these extraordinary powers, whether ceded to him by Congress or taken by him without congressional authorization.

His behavior since September 11, 2001, has concerned and angered only a small number of legislators sitting in Congress, including some Republican leaders. "I have learned of some alleged Intelligence Community activities about which our committee has not been briefed," wrote Congressman Peter Hoekstra (R–MI), chairman of the House Intelligence Committee, to President Bush on May 18, 2006: "If these allegations are true, they may represent a breach of responsibility by the Administration, a violation of law, and, just as importantly, a direct affront to me and the Members of this committee who have so ardently supported efforts to collect information on our enemies. . . . The U.S. Congress simply should not have to play 'Twenty Questions' to get the information that it deserves under our Constitution."[93] These are sharp words from a Republican chairman of a House committee to a Republican president who has not kept the national legislators in the loop regarding the acquisition of intelligence information from detained enemy prisoners.

And this dilemma gets to one of the major issues discussed in this book: the continued importance—and vitality—of the principles of separation of powers and checks and balances in a republic, even one allegedly at war. As Justice Stephen G. Breyer said, in a speech given in New York City in April 2003, "The Constitution applies even in times of dire emergency."[94] The essential problem for a political system built on the principles of separation of powers and checks and balances is that President Bush, for example, in issuing a signing statement, is instructing his subordinates in the executive branch "to refuse to enforce federal law routinely and without any consequences."

The real issue here is whether the proliferation of signing statements signals a significant shift in how the President will treat the other branches in the future. The [dilemma] is that the President is starting to push the limits of his power systematically in order to create a *new status quo* where he is effectively free from oversight [by Congress and the federal judiciary] in a wide range of situations both outside the United States and within it. [My emphasis][95]

Clearly, as the *Washington Post* editorialized on May 14, 2006, there is a "pattern of excess" as, one by one, the president's secret and not-so-secret measures against terrorism have been revealed to a numbed public. Each revelation in the administration's fight against terrorism "raises serious issues of civil liberties or human rights." The *Post* editorial went on to catalog the administration's constitutional transgressions:

> The recently disclosed secret NSA compilations of the telephone data of hundreds of millions of Americans illustrates the contours of the constitutional quandary our society is facing. Before that came the revelation that the CIA has created secret prisons abroad where terrorist suspects are held without charge, due process, or access to the International Red Cross. . . .
>
> We have also learned of the administration's secret decision to subject foreign detainees to torture and other cruel and inhuman treatment, despite United States ratification of a treaty banning such conduct.
>
> We have seen [the Bush administration] assert the right to arrest American citizens in this country, and hold them indefinitely without charges or access to an attorney.
>
> We have learned of its decision to set aside the Geneva Convention in order to hold and interrogate "enemy combatants" indefinitely and try them before special military tribunals with limited rights of appeal.[96]

The remaining chapters examine the specifics of this growing impression of constitutional dictatorship—or, as Jonathan Alter calls it in his *Newsweek* essay, *"just plain dictatorship"*—in the executive branch of government since the war against terrorism began in September 2001.

The picture begins with the men and boys—some assuredly terrorists, others merely Taliban and Iraqi soldiers, and still others, many others, innocent men and boys ensnared in the wars—captured by U.S. forces in Afghanistan and Iraq and detained in Guantánamo Bay and with the countless other captives. (More than 85 percent of the total number of prisoners held by the U.S. military in Afghanistan, Iraq, and Guantánamo Bay were *turned over* by Afghan warlords, the Pakistani secret police, or other foreign governmental agencies.)

The Bush administration's war on terror, as portrayed in this chapter, has weakened the values and virtues that are at the very core of representative government in the United States. Grover Norquist, a leading conservative, spoke to this troublesome issue. He was extremely blunt in his criticism of President Bush: "If you interpret [as President Bush has] the Constitution's saying that the commander-in-chief clause means that the president can do anything he wants and can ignore the laws, you don't have a constitution; you have a king."[97] These presidential threats to democracy's values began as soon as Bush took the nation to war.

The reality of President Bush's expansion of his presidential powers to fight the war on terror is not pretty. What is also not pretty is a question Thomas Ricks raised in his book *Fiasco:* "How could the United States launch wars [on terror, against Afghanistan and Iraq] on false premises? The blame must lie, foremost, with President Bush himself, his incompetence and his arrogance."[98] But blame also has to be shared by both Congress and the federal judiciary (although the Supreme Court began to address some of the White House's axioms in 2003–2004 when captured detainee petitions were received by the court and then granted certiorari). From the beginning of the war on terror in October 2001, the Bush people responsible for gathering intelligence information found very little hard evidence regarding weapons of mass destruction or nation-states working with al Qaeda to attack the United States. Therefore little or no evidence was presented to the coordinate branches, to the public, or to the media about the war. The administration spokespersons' mantra was simply "Trust us."

The reality, as the nation has already found out, is that the war on terrorism "was being guided by little more than the principle of *actionable suspicion*" (my emphasis). The president and his chief lieutenants were "operating in an evidence-free environment." And this executive "reality" was attributed to Vice President Cheney. At one point, in early 2002, after listening to suppositions about Iraqi weapons of mass destruction—suppositions that contained very little evidence—Cheney posited what would become the basis for decision making in the White House: "If *there's a one percent chance* [that the supposition is true], we have to treat it as a *certainty* in terms of our response. It's not about our analyses, or finding a preponderance of evidence. It's about our response" (my emphasis).[99]

This Cheney doctrine of actionable suspicion—the "one percent" doctrine—has evidently been the basis for the majority of the Bush administration's decisions in the war on terror. Decisions were made, as Ricks noted, on the basis of little or no verifiable evidence or on false premises. And Bush and company were able to get away with using these "one percent" decisions because, for five years, most politicians trusted the White House's responses to events.

As the evidence mounted regarding the horrendous errors of judgment made by the White House and the Department of Defense, as well as the reason for such mistakes—actions based only on suspicions, not hard data—even rock-ribbed Bush supporters distanced themselves from such an outlandish methodology of policy making. More openly, things began to change when the justices of the U.S. Supreme Court were asked to examine some of the premises made by the Bush administration regarding the capture, detention, and treatment of these alleged enemy combatants. Chapters 3 and 4 examine some of the basic suppositions of the Bush White House regarding the enemy.

2. Capturing the Enemy

I am only a chicken farmer in Pakistan.[1]

We simply [captured] the slowest guys on the battlefield. . . .
We literally found guys who had been shot in the butt.
LT. COL. THOMAS S. BERG, SEPTEMBER 2002[2]

Early in the war on terror George Bush's understanding of and use of the enemy combatant concept led to the development of a new public policy regarding the treatment of enemy captured by or turned over to U.S. military forces and CIA operatives. By October 2001 American and NATO troops, along with the Northern Alliance troops,[3] were fighting a conventional war in Afghanistan to remove the radical Taliban government because of its policy of providing a safe haven for al Qaeda leaders (Osama bin Laden), for their training camps, and for many hundreds of al Qaeda terrorists. And in November 2001 President Bush signed a military order that called for the creation of military commissions to try those persons suspected of having committed war crimes, an order since overturned by the U.S. Supreme Court in June, 2006.[4]

And President Bush, one year later, in March 2003, used the nation's new national security policy to justify starting a preemptive war against Saddam Hussein and his Iraqi military in order to prevent that nation from developing its weapons of mass destruction (WMDs) arsenal for use by Islamic radicals. The Bush administration took this controversial step because, as President Bush boldly—but falsely—declared in his 2002 State of the Union message to Americans, Hussein was stockpiling WMDs, was seeking uranium from Niger for use in his nuclear weapons–development programs, and was in alliance with al Qaeda to destroy America, the Great Satan. The nation, said Bush, could not wait for the attack from these al Qaeda Islamic terrorists who were armed and supported by Hussein. There was, in the president's eye, an emerging threat to American security. The United States had to attack Iraq in order to prevent other 9/11s from occurring.

One American observer, Kenneth Roth, was gravely concerned about the new, radical national security policy. President Bush, he argued, believed that the war on terror goes beyond battlefield clashes in Afghanistan and Iraq. He quoted the president as saying, on September 29, 2001, "Our war on terror will be much broader than the battlefields and beachheads of the past. The war will be fought wherever terrorists hide, or run, or plan." Roth observed, critically:

> Bush, however, seems to think of the war on terrorism quite literally—as a real war—and this concept has worrisome consequences. . . . The Bush administration has used war rhetoric precisely to give itself the extraordinary powers enjoyed by a wartime government to detain and even kill suspects without trial. In the process, the administration may have made it easier for itself to detain or eliminate suspects. But it has also threatened the most basic due process rights.[5]

Since September 2001, in waging war against international radical Islamic terrorists and the Taliban, President Bush and attorneys general, first Ashcroft and then Gonzales, persistently used the phrase "enemy combatant" to describe the men and boys captured by the U.S. military or handed over to the military by other nations. By February 2002, after a flurry of memoranda had circulated among the White House, the Department of Defense, and the Office of Legal Counsel in the Department of Justice, Bush concluded that all persons captured and held by the U.S. military were "enemy combatants" protected neither by the international laws of war nor by legislation passed in Congress, such as the 1996 War Crimes Act. Most of the over 600 detainees at Guantánamo in 2003 were there because "the United States was paying bounties [of $5,000] for terror suspects," and Northern Alliance Afghanis and Pakistanis were collecting the bounties by turning over to the American military Arab men—Muslims—who happened to be in Afghanistan when the war started in October 2001.[6]

It is worthwhile to look at the term "enemy combatant" as it was first defined in adjudication during World War II because the Bush administration has given it a totally different meaning since September 11, 2001. With the new policy in place, due to incorrect intelligence that the Iraqis had WMDs, President Bush began to implement a radically different philosophy of the role and function of a wartime president.

THE ORIGINAL, INCIDENTAL USE OF "ENEMY COMBATANT" IN AMERICAN POLITICS AND JURISPRUDENCE: *EX PARTE QUIRIN*, 1942

In June 1942 two German submarines each deposited a four-man saboteur group in U.S. waters, one off the coast of Long Island, New York (June 12,

1942) and the other off the coast of Florida (June 16, 1942). By June 26, 1942, all eight men were in the custody of the FBI.[7] The U.S. attorney general, Francis Biddle, asked President Roosevelt to create a secret military commission to try the eight German saboteurs. On July 2, 1942, Roosevelt, "as commander-in-chief of the Army and Navy, . . . appointed a Military Commission and directed it to try petitioners for offenses against the law of war and the Articles of War [created by Congress]."[8] Unlike President Bush after September 11, 2001, in 1942 President Roosevelt "was not claiming inherent or exclusive constitutional authority [to create the military commission]. He acted under a mix of constitutional authority accorded to the president and statutory authority granted by Congress."[9]

Roosevelt issued Proclamation 2561, declaring, "The safety of the United States demands that all enemies who have entered upon the territory of the United States as part of an invasion or predatory incursion, or who have entered in order to commit sabotage, espionage, or other hostile or warlike acts, should be promptly tried in accordance with the law of war."[10]

The trial began on July 8, 1942, in the fifth-floor room 5235 in the Department of Justice building in Washington, D.C. The eight prisoners were charged with one act of violating the (international) law of war, with violating two Articles of War (congressional statute), and with *conspiring* to violate the Articles of War. After the seven-person military commission began to hear the case, the two defense counsels, Col. Kenneth Royall and Col. Cassius Dowell, both officers in the Army Judge Advocate General's Office (JAG), applied for a writ of habeas corpus in the U.S. District Court for the District of Columbia.

Their basic contention was that "the President is without any statutory or constitutional authority to order the petitioners to be tried by military tribunal for offenses with which they are charged; that in consequence they are entitled to be tried in the civil courts with the safeguards, including trial by jury, which the Fifth and Sixth Amendments guarantee to all persons charged in such courts with criminal offenses."[11] While the two officers were presenting their defense of the eight men, the district court denied the habeas corpus request. On July 29, 1942, they appealed directly to the U.S. Supreme Court, and the Court, in special session, heard nine hours of oral arguments by both sides on July 29–30, 1942.

The defense used an 1866 Supreme Court precedent, found in *Ex Parte Milligan* (71 U.S. 2), to argue for the granting of the habeas corpus writ. The case involved Lambdin P. Milligan, a Southern sympathizer who lived in Indiana, a state where the civilian courts were open throughout the Civil War "and their process unobstructed."[12] He was a member of the Sons of Liberty, a group alleged to have links to the Confederacy and thought to be planning attacks against the Union in the North. He was tried, convicted, and sentenced to death by a military commission after President Lincoln suspended the writ of habeas corpus "so that the prisoners could not challenge the legality of their arrest or conviction."[13]

Lincoln's attorney general, in oral argument before the justices, maintained that the legal protections of the Bill of Rights were "peace provisions" that could be set aside in a time of war. The Bill of Rights could be suspended and martial law could be imposed, even though the civil courts of an area under martial law were still functioning. If the federal executive were to make such a determination, the argument concluded, then the commanding military officer in that region would become "the supreme legislator, supreme judge, and supreme executive."

The Court overturned Milligan's conviction and sentence of death. In so doing it established precedent regarding the powers of the president and the scope of the protections afforded all persons by the Bill of Rights—even in wartime:

> The Constitution of the United States is a law for rulers and people, equally in war and peace, and covers with the shield of its protection, all classes of men, at all times, and under all circumstances. . . . Until recently no one ever doubted the right to trial by jury was fortified in the organic law against the power of attack. It is *now* assailed; but if ideas can be expressed in words and language that has any meaning, *this right*—one of the most valuable in a free country—is preserved to every one accused of crime who is not attached to the army, or navy, or militia in actual service.[14]

In *Ex Parte Quirin* (317 U.S. 1 [1942]), however, Biddle, for the government, argued that "the current public danger warrants the substitution of the executive process for the judicial process." He, as attorney general, and the president wanted a military commission to try the eight Nazis because a commission could sentence them to death. Biddle and other government lawyers felt that if the detained Germans were tried in federal court, they would be sentenced, at most, to five years for conspiring to violate the law of war and the Articles of War.[15]

While the defense was presenting its final arguments before the judges of the military commission meeting in the Department of Justice building, the

U.S. Supreme Court, on July 31, 1942, issued a per curiam order validating the creation of the military commission by the president. The justices concluded that the military commission was "lawfully constituted"; therefore, the "motions for leave to file petitions for writs of habeas corpus are denied."[16]

On August 1, 1942, after a nineteen-day trial and one day after the Court's per curiam order was filed, the military tribunal found the eight men guilty on all charges, which meant automatic imposition of the death penalty because some of the charges included spying on the government and planning sabotage against U.S. industrial facilities. Because two of the men, George John Dasch and Ernst Peter Berger, had cooperated with federal authorities, the attorney general and the FBI director asked the president to commute their death sentences. On August 8, 1942, a week later, the other six were electrocuted.

In the extended full opinion of the Court in *Quirin*, filed on October 29, 1942, *almost three months after the sentences were carried out by the government*, the Court distinguished between "lawful combatants" and, as was the case of the eight men on trial in 1942, "unlawful combatants" (such as spies and saboteurs).

In the international laws of war, going as far back as the 1899 and 1907 Hague Conventions and the 1929 Geneva Accord on Prisoners of War,[17] there are two categories of persons: "civilians" and "combatants." In these international laws of war—as well as, beginning with the 1863 Lieber Code, America's own laws concerning the treatment of prisoners, the Articles of War, and, presently in use by the military, the Uniform Code of Military Justice (UCMJ)—"combatants" are divided into two categories: "lawful" and "unlawful" combatants.

According to the laws of war, a lawful combatant is a person who is waging war and who (1) is in uniform, (2) is openly carrying arms, (3) is waging war under a structured military hierarchy, and (4) is waging war according to the customs and laws of war. A combatant not wearing a uniform, captured carrying concealed weapons or engaged in spying or sabotage, is an unlawful combatant, or an unlawful belligerent, is not considered a POW, and is not protected by the laws of war. Such combatants "are likewise subject to capture and detention, but, in addition, they are subject to trial and punishment by military tribunals for acts which render their belligerency unlawful."[18]

Captured lawful combatants, according to the international laws of war, are POWs. Captured unlawful combatants, because of their actions or conspiring to act, are not POWs. They may be dealt with, if the executive so determines, by applicable civilian criminal statutes in a criminal court, or they can be tried by a military commission or court-martial—if Congress has authorized such a proceeding. The *only* time in the *Quirin* opinion the phrase "enemy combatant" appears comes toward the middle of the opinion, after the Court had used the terms "lawful" and "unlawful" "combatants" or "belligerents" a number of times:

> Lawful combatants are subject to capture and detention as prisoners of war by opposing military forces. Unlawful combatants are likewise subject to capture and detention, but in addition they are subject to trial and punishment by military tribunals for acts which render their belligerency unlawful. The spy who secretly and *without uniform* passes the military lines of a belligerent in time of war, seeking to gather military information and communicate it to the enemy, or an *enemy combatant* who *without uniform* comes secretly through the lines for the purpose of waging war by destruction of life or property, are familiar examples of belligerents who are deemed not to be entitled to the status of prisoners of war, but to be offenders against the law of war subject to trial and punishment by military tribunals. [My emphasis][19]

Until President Bush's declaration of the war on terror in September 2001, there were two operative phrases in U.S. Supreme Court precedents and in military law and practice regarding captured enemy prisoners: "lawful" and "unlawful combatants." The "enemy combatant" phrase was used only once by the Supreme Court when Chief Justice Harlan F. Stone wrote describing an example of an unlawful combatant action. *Until the war on terror the phrase had no place in the lexicon of military justice.* It was not used in later Supreme Court opinions. It was not used by military intelligence to describe captured enemies in Korea or in Vietnam.

However, the term was resurrected after September 11, 2001, by lawyers in the Department of Justice, the Department of Defense, and the Bush White House. President Bush's declaration of war on terror ushered in a new kind of warfare. With the declaration of the war on terror, the administration no longer saw a need to distinguish between lawful and unlawful combatants, or between combatants and innocent civilians. *All* those captured or handed over to the U.S. military and held by the United States, whether in Iraq, Afghanistan, or in the special facilities quickly created at Guantánamo Bay Naval Station, were "enemy combatants," and they were not entitled to any of the protections afforded captured enemy prisoners. *There were no innocents and no prisoners of war in the war on terror.*

CAPTURING THE "ENEMY" PRIOR TO THE SEPTEMBER 2001 DECLARATION OF THE WAR ON TERROR

Very rapidly, especially because of the initial military successes in Afghanistan in late 2001, the U.S. military found itself in possession of many hundreds of captured enemy from that war and then, after March 2003, from the second war in Iraq. The question of what to do with these foreign detainees from more than forty nations[20] arose as early as October 2001, when the coalition led by American and NATO military forces began military action in Afghanistan.

The international laws of war (also referred to as International Humanitarian Law)—especially the four 1949 Geneva Conventions and their 1977 Additional Protocols[21]—provide the processes for dealing with and treating captured enemy soldiers and sailors. The language in *Quirin* faithfully followed the concepts found in both the American and the international laws of war. These international laws of war differentiate between lawful and unlawful combatants (and, of course, innocent civilians caught up in the battles and detained). In a war, whether civil, regional, or worldwide, according to the customary international laws of war, there are only lawful and unlawful combatants, not "enemy combatants."

Article 4 of the Third Geneva Convention (see appendix 3) describes the manner in which a belligerent nation may treat its lawful and unlawful captured combatants. Captured lawful combatants—those members of the armed forces of a party at war or those members of an armed group belonging to a party in the conflict who are under an identifiable and responsible command and who are wearing a "fixed distinctive sign," "carrying arms," and respecting international laws of war—are categorized by the convention as POWs and must be treated according to the proscriptions found in that convention and in Protocol I of the 1977 Additional Protocols. As POWs, lawful soldiers cannot be tortured or executed and are only required to give their names, dates of birth, ranks, and serial numbers to their captors. They must be removed from the battle zone and are detained for the duration of the hostilities.

Unlawful combatants—captured spies, saboteurs, or mercenaries—are not POWs and are not under the protection of the convention. Rather, they are subject to trial and punishment by either civilian or military authorities of the party holding them and, if found guilty, under the laws of war, can be executed. Like the lawful combatants held as POWs, these unlawful detainees can be held until the end of hostilities.

A key component of the process, one that became central in the 2004 and 2006 litigation before the U.S. Supreme Court, and one that has *not* been used by the Bush administration in its treatment—either legal or ethical—of what it calls "enemy combatants" is found in Article 5 of the convention (see appendix 3). The article states that if the party holding enemy personnel is uncertain whether a prisoner is a lawful or unlawful combatant—or an innocent civilian—then the detained person must have a hearing by a competent tribunal to determine the individual's status: "Should any doubt arise as to whether persons, having committed a belligerent act and having fallen into the hands of the enemy, belong to any of the categories enumerated in Article 4, such persons shall enjoy the protection of the present Convention until such time as their status has been determined by a competent tribunal."

Until 2001, U.S. military authorities faithfully followed the principles of international law regarding captured enemy personnel, including this article. Indeed, this article is found in U.S. Army Regulation 190-8.[22] The army regulation "provides for military hearings for persons captured on a battlefield to enable them to demonstrate that they are entitled to be held as prisoners of war or that they are in fact innocent civilians."[23] These guidelines were used by military intelligence personnel during the Korean War. In the Vietnam War American forces were constantly capturing people whose status under the Geneva Conventions was in doubt. "Rarely did the Viet Cong wear a recognizable uniform and only occasionally did the guerrillas carry their arms openly. Additionally, some combat captives were compelled to act for the Viet Cong out of fear of harm to themselves and their families."[24]

However, the U.S. Military Assistance Command, Vietnam, issued Directive 381-16, *Military Intelligence: Combined Screening of Detainees*, on December 27, 1967. It called for, after capture of enemy personnel, the "prompt screening and classification of detainees" in order to differentiate lawful from unlawful enemy combatants—that is, it called for Article 5 tribunals. The non-POW classification included (1) "civilian defendants"—those suspected of committing terrorist acts, sabotage, or spying; (2) "returnees"—all persons who "voluntarily submit to the Government of Viet Nam (GVN) control"; or (3) "innocent civilians." Lawful enemy combatants, categorized as POWs, were (1) members of the Vietcong, main force; (2) members of the Vietcong, local force; (3) members of the North Vietnamese Army; or (4) irregulars—organized forces composed of guerillas, self-defense paramilitary forces, and secret self-defense elements (a clandestine Viet Cong organization) "if they were captured while actually engaging in combat or a belligerent act under arms, other than an act of terrorism, sabotage, or spying."

After enemy personnel were screened and classified, the U.S. military directive called for POWs to be "transferred to the ARVM [Army of the Republic of Viet Nam] POW camp" by American forces. However, nonlawful enemy combatants—civilian defendants, saboteurs, spies, and terrorists—were to be "released to the appropriate GVN civil authorities" for subsequent action in accord with GVN military or criminal law.

In the first Gulf War against Iraq, Desert Storm (1992), the Geneva Conventions were followed by American forces, led by the then commander in chief, President George H. W. Bush. The military conducted 1,196 Article 5 hearings to determine the status of detainees, most of whom were released, classified as innocent civilians caught up in the rapidly moving military advances.[25] These hearings "discovered 310 detainees who were entitled to POW status, with the remainder entitled to innocent civilian refugee status."[26]

Until the new post-9/11 asymmetrical war on terror, then, the U.S. military adhered to international laws of war regarding the classification, status determination, treatment, and disposition of captured enemy combatants.

However, a new president, with his lieutenants in the White House and leading the Department of Defense, viewed these questions regarding the status of captured al Qaeda and Taliban fighters (and, after March 2003, captured Iraqi fighters), quite differently. After the invasion of Afghanistan, "the U.S. government refused to hold a single Article 5 hearing because the President declared no one was entitled to POW status,"[27] and no one, argued the lawyers and the policy makers in the administration, was merely an innocent refugee caught up freakishly in the cacophony of war.

Almost as soon as the U.S. military found itself in possession of captured Taliban soldiers, Secretary of Defense Rumsfeld, "ignoring the deeply rooted U.S. military policy of applying the Geneva Conventions broadly," labeled the first detainees to arrive at Guantánamo Bay on January 11, 2002, "as 'unlawful enemy combatants,' automatically denying them possible status [as either] prisoners of war [or innocent civilians]."[28]

Without any classifying taking place to separate lawful from unlawful combatants or to separate combatants from innocent civilians, the administration, from the beginning of the conflict through the first six months of 2004, categorized all of the Guantánamo detainees, at one time nearly 1,000 boys and men, as "enemy combatants" without any due process rights—

whether they were chicken farmers, "shopkeepers or herdsmen,"[29] old men, or members of al Qaeda. (In June 2004, the U.S. Supreme Court, substantively responding to petitions received from foreign detainees and U.S. citizens detained as enemy combatants, did order the Bush administration to modify its policies regarding detainees' efforts to seek habeas corpus review in federal court. More will be said about the federal judiciary's actions and the executive branch's responses in chapters 4 and 5.)

REDEFINING THE CONCEPT OF "THE ENEMY"
AFTER SEPTEMBER 11, 2001

The secretary of defense's pronounced judgment about the captured Taliban soldiers was one of a number of consequences of a "a series of legal memoranda written by the Justice Department's Office of Legal Counsel [that] helped build the framework for circumventing international restraints on prisoner interrogation. These memos argued that the Geneva Conventions did not apply to detainees from the Afghanistan war."[30]

The Reinterpretation of "Enemy Combatant" after 2001
In this fluid time, the notion of enemy combatant as noted in 1942 was transformed into a very different perception by President Bush and the lawyers in the Department of Justice and the Department of Defense.

The very first formal administration document to use the phrase was written in July 2004 by Paul Wolfowitz, then deputy secretary of defense. It followed the Supreme Court's late June 2004 decision in *Rasul v. Bush* (542 U.S. 466). The order he issued created a military tribunal to review the status of each individual held at Guantánamo, the combatant status review tribunal (CSRT). In the order, he defined "enemy combatant" as "an individual who was part of or supporting Taliban or al Qaeda forces, or associated forces that are engaged in hostilities against the United States or its coalition partners. This includes any person who has committed a belligerent act or who has directly supported hostilities in aid of enemy armed forces."[31]

After October 2001 enemy combatants had no protections at all except those the U.S. chief executive and his surrogates opted to give them—which occurred only if the granting of rights served the vital interests of the United

States. They were "held incommunicado without access to an attorney." Furthermore, the Department of Justice argued that anyone classified as an enemy combatant by the president could not challenge this executive decision in federal courts.[32]

The Nazis captured in 1942 were provided counsel and were held under decent jail conditions, and their counsel could bring habeas actions to the federal courts on behalf of their interests. That simply was not the case for all those detained by the United States after the nation went to war against al Qaeda and the Taliban in October 2001. Until the U.S. Supreme Court heard arguments in the spring of 2004 and reached judgments in late June 2004, there were absolutely no due process rights afforded the enemy combatants captured and shipped to Guantánamo after the Afghanistan war began.

After October 2001, all those persons detained by the U.S. military in Afghanistan, Iraq, and Guantánamo who were "not charged in civil courts or taken before a military tribunal"[33] were enemy combatants. Practically speaking, since only a handful of detainees were charged with committing crimes in federal district courts and, as of the spring of 2006, no detainees had been tried before military commissions created by President Bush, that meant that essentially all of those held by the United States were "enemy combatants" and, as such, subject to interrogation by United States interviewers.

Jay S. Bybee, the assistant attorney general in the Office of Legal Counsel, sent a lengthy memorandum, probably drafted by John C. Yoo, to Gonzales, counsel to the president, on August 1, 2002. Its title and subject: "Standards of Conduct for Interrogation under 18 U.S.C. Sections 2340–2340A."[34] The memo used the phrase "enemy combatant":

> As commander-in-chief, the President has the constitutional authority to order interrogations of enemy combatants to gain intelligence information concerning the military plans of the enemy. . . . Any effort [by Congress] that interferes with the President's direction of such core matters as the detention and interrogation of enemy combatants . . . would be unconstitutional. . . . Congress may no more regulate the President's ability to detain and interrogate enemy combatants than it may regulate his ability to direct troop movements on the battlefield.[35]

Bybee's memo, accepted in due course by the president, simply contradicted basic constitutional tenets as well as the specific congressional powers found in Article I of the Constitution. The memo was only revealed to the nation in the spring 2004.

Conversations between the Department of Justice,
the Attorney General, and the President, 2001–2002
The status of these many hundreds of al Qaeda and Taliban suspects, captured
after the battles began in October 2001 in Afghanistan, was the intense focus
of lawyers in the Department of Defense, the Department of Justice, and the
White House. From November 2001 through the spring of 2002, more than
two dozen lengthy memoranda were circulated between the lawyers in these
executive branch agencies in a successful effort to define a policy regarding
the capture and the detention of the enemy in the war on terrorism.

The first question raised was whether these prisoners were protected by
the 1949 Geneva Conventions on the treatment of belligerents. The United
States was among the more than one hundred nations that signed the Geneva
Conventions and the 1977 Additional Protocols. And the United States had incorporated the international laws of war regarding the capture and treatment
of enemy prisoners into the military guides that formed the core of military
behavior for U.S. forces, such as the Rules of Engagement (ROE), the UCMJ,
and domestic legislation passed by Congress (for example, the War Crimes
Act of 1996).

The new detention plan of President Bush and his lieutenants called for
the immediate acquisition of *actionable intelligence* from those al Qaeda terrorists and Taliban military captured or turned over to and detained by the
United States and its allies. Under the Geneva Conventions, however, lawful
combatants were protected from interrogation. Lawful combatants need only
give basic information such as name, rank, serial number, date of birth. If the
United States was bound by the 1949 Geneva Conventions, its special investigators (especially CIA personnel) could not question the detainees in the effort to find out about possible new attacks on innocent civilians living in the
United States.

However, on January 9, 2002—a few weeks before the facility, called Camp
Delta,[36] at Guantánamo Bay was open for long-term detention of the prisoners—William J. Haynes II, the Department of Defense's general counsel, received a memorandum from Deputy Assistant Attorney General Yoo and
Robert J. Delahunty, special counsel, Department of Justice. The title and subject of the memo: "Application of Treaties and Laws to al Qaeda and Taliban
Detainees." Regarding "the treatment of individuals detained by the United
States,"[37] the memo "argued that the Geneva Convention dealt only with state
parties, and al Qaeda was not a state. As for Taliban soldiers, it said that Af-

ghanistan under the Taliban was a 'failed state' to which the convention also did not apply."[38]

> It is clear . . . that members of the al Qaeda terrorist organization do not receive the protections of the laws of war. . . . Taliban militia detainees also do not receive the protections of the laws of war because the Taliban was not the *de facto* government of Afghanistan. . . .
>
> Afghanistan, for the period in question, was a 'failed state' whose territory had been largely overrun and held by violence by a militia or faction rather than by a government.[39]

The president, the memo concluded, has the constitutional authority to determine that neither international laws of war nor congressional statutes (for example, the War Crimes Act of 1996) have any bearing on the treatment of al Qaeda and Taliban detainees. Detention conditions, it stated, are a matter of policy determined by the president and his associates. Furthermore, neither the law of war nor domestic legislation prohibits the president from determining that trial by military commissions of certain al Qaeda and Taliban prisoners is warranted.[40]

The memo was then sent from Haynes to Gonzales, the White House counsel. Days later, on January 18, 2002, President Bush concluded that the Geneva Conventions did not apply to the prisoners detained at Guantánamo and that *all* those held in Cuba were unlawful, enemy combatants.

The president's counsel's memorandum for the president on January 25, 2002, repeated the Yoo/Delahunty conclusions about the international laws of war and congressional statutes. Gonzales also addressed Secretary of State Powell's concerns and effort to have Bush reverse the January 18, 2002, policy. He buttressed the president's earlier pronouncement:

> The nature of this new kind of war places a high premium on other factors, such as the ability to quickly obtain information from captured terrorists and their sponsors in order to avoid further atrocities against American civilians, and the need to try terrorists for war crimes such as wantonly killing civilians. In my judgment, this new paradigm renders *obsolete* Geneva's strict limitations on questioning of enemy prisoners and renders *quaint* some of its provisions. [My emphasis][41]

Although Powell, on January 26, 2002, wrote to the president asking him to reconsider and reverse his decision regarding the status of the detainees, Bush did not relent. Powell pointed out that the new Bush policy "reverses over a century of U.S. policy and practice . . . and undermines the protections of the laws of war for our troops."[42]

On February 7, 2002, President Bush sent a classified memo to his key actors in the war on terror. It ended all discussion in the executive branch regarding the president's constitutional authority to determine that the enemy combatants in this new kind of war did not have the protection of the Geneva Conventions and his ability to create military commissions to try some of the detainees for war crimes. "Our nation," he wrote in the memo (which was not made public until June 2004), "recognizes that this [new kind of war]—ushered in not by us, but by terrorists—requires new thinking in the law of war, but thinking that *should nevertheless be consistent with the principles of Geneva*" (my emphasis).[43]

By 2003, only the first part of the Bush February 7, 2002, message, the "new paradigm" of warfare observation, was getting to the troops guarding the detainees, the military translators, and the hordes of interrogators who descended on Guantánamo in the effort to get intelligence quickly. The last part of Bush's memo, that those new ways of thinking had to be "consistent with the principles of Geneva," never got through to the men and women who were in constant contact with the detainees.

Erik Saar, an army translator assigned to Guantánamo, remembers when the army JAG captain visited Guantánamo Bay in 2003 to talk with the military personnel stationed there about the treatment of the captured detainees:

> [He] spent the next half hour talking not about military tribunals, but the relevance of the Geneva Conventions (GC) at Camp Delta—or irrelevance, in this case. . . . He told us that [the GC] didn't apply to the more than 600 suspected al Qaeda and Taliban figures we had locked up here in the Caribbean. 'These detainees can't be considered prisoners of war, . . . Geneva didn't apply because the war against terrorism ushers in a new paradigm.'[44]

The Bush Military Order, November 2001,
Establishing Military Commissions
President Roosevelt's 1942 proclamation creating the military commission that tried the eight putative saboteurs was not the first time in American military history that such an institution had been created by the chief executive. Presidents from George Washington on have occasionally—during wartime—created such commissions to try individuals who were identified as unlawful combatants, that is, spies and saboteurs.[45] Since September 11, 2001,

President Bush and his aides in the White House have used "FDR's decision [as] the Bush administration's ammunition as it defends court challenges [in 2004 and 2006] to key parts of its legal war on terrorism."[46] There are, however, significant differences between the Roosevelt's 1942 proclamation and Bush's 2001 military order creating military commissions to try enemy combatants. Bush's proclamation calls for trial by military commission of *any* detainee "not a U.S. citizen" who the president "determines that there is reason to believe (i) is or was a member of . . . al Qaeda, (ii) has engaged in, aided or abetted, or conspired to commit, acts of international terrorism, . . . or [iii] has knowingly harbored one or more individuals described in (i) and (ii)." The administration's lawyers had no difficulty extending the logic of the proclamation to U.S. citizens characterized as enemy combatants.

On November 13, 2001, President Bush signed a military order that allowed the government to try certain unnamed enemy combatants, held by the U.S. military, in military commissions rather than in federal district courts or military courts-martial. The military order established basic guidelines for these commissions.

President Bush's authority to establish these military commissions, he wrote, came from Article II of the Constitution and "the laws of the United States of America, including the AUMF Joint Resolution, September 18, 2001 (Public Law 107-40, 115 Stat. 224) and sections 821 and 836 of title 10 U.S.C."[47] The secretary of defense was given the authority to detain possible defendants and, after drawing up specific guidelines for the operation of the military commissions, was also responsible, through the JAG's staff lawyers, for bringing defendants to trial. According to the order, the secretary of defense "shall issue such orders and regulations, including orders for the appointment of one or more military commissions, as may be necessary. . . . [These orders and regulations] shall include, but not be limited to, rules for the conduct of the proceedings of military commissions, including pretrial, trial, and post-trial procedures, modes of proof, issuance of process, and qualifications of attorneys."[48]

Specifics came later, and they were developed by the lawyers in the Department of Defense. On March 21, 2002, Military Commission Order 1 was issued. Secretary of Defense Rumsfeld announced the rules and procedures that would be followed in trials of enemy combatants held before military commissions. The jurisdiction of the commissions was to hear cases involving violations of the laws of war and all other offenses triable by military commission. (A specific list of these "other crimes" was published in February 2003.)

A commission was allowed from three to seven members—the number determined by the severity of the charges—and each member had to be a commissioned officer in the U.S. military. Defense counsels were chosen from among the military JAG offices, or a detainee could use a civilian lawyer if that lawyer was an American citizen. The jurors had to assume innocence until the defendant was proven guilty "beyond a reasonable doubt." And in all trials before a military commission, a two-thirds vote was necessary for conviction, except in death-penalty cases, which required a "unanimous, affirmative vote of all [seven] members" for conviction.

Appeals of guilty verdicts went to a review panel of three persons, one of whom had to have had experience as a judge, appointed by the secretary of defense. The panel had two options: Send its recommendation to the secretary of defense, or return the case to the military commission because a majority of the appeal panel had "formed a definite and firm conviction that a material error of law occurred."[49]

This controversial military order was drafted by a small group of ideologues in the Vice President's Office, especially David Addington (one of the persons who prepared signing statements for President Bush). The decision to issue the military order was taken in secret; when it was issued it

> *stunned* [Secretary of State] Powell; the national security adviser, Condoleezza Rice; the highest-ranking lawyer in the CIA; and many judge advocate generals, or JAG's, the top lawyers in the military services. . . . Rear Admiral Donald Guter, who was the Navy's chief JAG until June 2002, said that he and other JAG's, who were experts on the laws of war, tried unsuccessfully to amend parts of the [plan] when they learned of it, days before the order was formally signed by the President. "But we were marginalized. . . . They didn't want to hear from us." . . . None of them had been consulted. Michael Chertoff, [then] the head of the DOJ's Criminal Division, who had argued for trying terror suspects in the U.S. courts, was also bypassed. . . . *Addington secretly usurped the process.* He and a few hand-picked associates, wrote the [military] order creating the commissions. [My emphasis][50]

Additionally, on February 23, 2003, the Pentagon's legal office released a draft of the rules listing twenty-four categories of specific crimes that could be tried by a military commission. Included on the list were hijacking, terrorism, the use of chemical weapons, attacks on civilians, and the use of "poison or analogous weapons." It also included ordinary crimes such as murder, rape, perjury, and conspiracy.

Since the announcement of these Department of Defense regulations in 2003, Congress has considered legislation that would statutorily authorize these military commissions, but not until the fall of 2006 did it act on the proposals floated in both the House of Representatives and the Senate. As already noted in chapter 1, President Bush, his legal counsel, and the attorney general have all maintained since 2001 that Congress has *already* authorized the president to create the secret military commissions by passing the AUMF.

The military commissions, however, "were stopped before they ever started."[51] Fewer than one dozen detainees have been identified by the secretary of defense as possible defendants in trials before these military commissions. The first detainee scheduled for trial before a military commission was the former car driver for Osama bin Laden, Salim Ahmed Hamdan. In November 2004, a federal district court judge in the District of Columbia, Judge James Robertson (a former Army officer), ruled that the process could not go forward because the Bush administration had totally ignored Article 5 of the Third Geneva Convention, the requirement that a "competent tribunal" had to determine whether a detainee was a lawful combatant, an unlawful combatant, or simply an innocent civilian caught up in the war. (*Hamdan v. Rumsfeld* was argued before the U.S. Supreme Court during its 2005 term. Chapter 5 will discuss the arguments presented to the justices by both parties and analyze the Court's decision. Chapter 6 looks at the implementation and compliance issues.)

DETENTION AND TREATMENT OF THE ENEMY AFTER CAPTURE

This presidential perspective about enemy soldiers captured on the battlefield led, early on, to the development of an administration policy regarding their *treatment during interrogations.* Inexorably, that policy has led to a number of other military policy initiatives in the administration's war on terror. These policies have also, as has been the case in American history, led to vehement criticism and to challenges, both political and legal, by the detainees' families, by critics of the administration, by international human rights organizations such as Human Rights Watch and Amnesty International, by the United Nations, and by many other nations, including American allies in the war on terror.

. Although the international laws of war allow for the detention of lawful and unlawful combatants while hostilities continue, they do require that a detaining power conduct a review of the detainees to determine whether any of them are neither lawful nor unlawful combatants but, instead, innocent civilians—chicken farmers—caught up in the tumult of war. By declaring that *all* captured and detained persons are enemy combatants not subject to the protections of the Geneva Conventions of 1949, especially the Third Geneva Convention—which, like the other three Geneva Conventions, contains Common Article 3, specifying the minimum humane treatment to be applied to "persons taking no active part in the hostilities"—the Bush administration has acted unfairly and, many claim, in violation of domestic legislation, as well as in violation of international humanitarian law.

The terrorist wars in the twenty-first century, according to President Bush and his associates in the executive branch, led to a total revamping of American policy toward detainees held by the U.S. military. Until 2001, both lawful and unlawful combatants were detained until hostilities ended. Then the lawful detainees, the Geneva Convention–protected POWs, were repatriated. Unlawful belligerents, however, faced the possibility of being tried as war criminals before a military commission. Since September 11, 2001, all captured persons have been detained indefinitely in the open-ended war on terror. Deputy Associate Attorney General J. Michael Wiggins, testifying before the Senate Judiciary Committee, bluntly told the senators on June 14, 2006, that "it's [the DOJ's] position that, legally, enemy combatants can be *held in perpetuity*" (my emphasis).[52]

They are also subject to interrogation[53] by the U.S. military and by CIA operatives and their allies across the globe—without the protections of the international laws of war or existing domestic legislation that would punish U.S. personnel for treating captured belligerents in a cruel, demeaning, or humiliating manner. The United States has practiced preventive detention[54] and proactive interrogation of suspected terrorist leaders since late 2001. The administration has offered one fundamental rationale for such treatment: the acquisition of actionable intelligence. Through 2006, however, precious little such actionable evidence has been uncovered by interrogators.

Once the U.S. military began capturing al Qaeda and Taliban soldiers and alleged terrorists in October 2001, America's detention policy quickly followed. This chapter examined the Bush administration's thinking regarding the capture of what they termed enemy combatants and looked at how these thoughts turned into justifications—and policy—for treating all persons captured in Afghanistan and, after 2003, seized in Iraq as unlawful enemy combatants. Chapter 3 examines how, as a consequence of President Bush's war on terror, captured suspected al Qaeda terrorists, Taliban soldiers, and hundreds of innocent civilians have been dealt with by U.S. military personnel, by domestic agencies such as the FBI who have had a role to play in the interrogation of these detained combatants. It also examines the role of the U.S. intelligence-gathering agencies, specifically the Defense Intelligence Agency interrogators, U.S. Army personnel, and the CIA.

3. Treatment of the Enemy

Detention and interrogation are ethically challenging activities.
FINAL REPORT OF THE INDEPENDENT PANEL TO
REVIEW DOD DETENTION OPERATIONS, 2004[1]

We have to work through, sort of the dark side, if you will.
DICK CHENEY, 2001[2]

Do some of these harsh methods really work?
GEORGE BUSH, 2002[3]

In a sharply etched commentary about America's policy toward the men held in American military prisons (including old men and youngsters, according to the International Committee of the Red Cross [ICRC]), Secretary of Defense Rumsfeld, in January 2002, told the world that these captives were *not* prisoners of war. They were enemy combatants and as such were not subject to the protections of the international laws of war—the 1949 Geneva Conventions, the 1984 Convention against Torture, and other laws, domestic and international, that banned "cruel, inhumane or degrading treatment." They would, however, be treated humanely, the defense secretary said, so long as such treatment "was consistent with [the doctrine of] military necessity."[4]

The president was equally blunt about the character of all detainees and terrorists held by U.S. military forces. In his 2003 State of the Union speech, Bush said to Americans and the rest of the world looking on, "All told, more than 3,000 suspected terrorists have been arrested in many countries. *Many others have met a different fate. Let's put it this way—they are no longer a problem to the United States and our friends and allies.* (Applause.)"[5]

In 2006 there were more than 11,000 enemy combatants in U.S. custody in Afghanistan (1,000), Iraq (10,000), and Cuba (600).[6] After capturing the first of these thousands of prisoners, the Bush administration's task was to glean as much information as possible from these unprotected prisoners—as quickly as possible, at whatever the cost. The August 1, 2002, memo from Jay Bybee[7] to Alberto Gonzales (see chapter 2) made it extremely difficult for a military interrogator and his or her superiors to be found criminally liable for engaging in torture in the effort to elicit good intelligence.

The memo spoke to the president's unlimited authority, in time of war, to act in the best interest of the nation's security, stating that in the "current war against al Qaeda and its allies," domestic and international laws prohibiting torture do not apply because they are probably unconstitutional infringements on the president's powers as commander in chief to wage war: "[Any effort by Congress to] regulate the President's power to detain and interrogate enemy combatants, which arises out of his constitutional authority as Commander-in-Chief to determine the interrogation and treatment of enemy combatants would raise serious constitutional issues. Congress may no more regulate the President's ability to detain and interrogate enemy combatants than it may regulate his ability to direct troop movements on the battlefield."[8]

The Bybee memo set the threshold for what is to be defined as torture extremely high:

> Certain acts may be cruel, inhuman, or degrading, but still not produce pain and suffering of the requisite intensity to fall within a [legal] proscription against torture. . . . We conclude that for an act to constitute torture, it must inflict pain that is difficult to endure. Physical pain amounting to torture must be equivalent in intensity to the pain accompanying serious physical injury, such as organ failure, impairment of bodily function, or even death.[9]

The memo's author, one critic observed, "turned intellectual somersaults to find loopholes and excuses for the commission of what a lay observer would surely consider torture."[10] The memo tried to remove criminal liability from those who tortured prisoners: Torturing detainees "may be justified," Bybee wrote, and any law, international or domestic, prohibiting torture "may be unconstitutional if applied to interrogations" conducted in the war against terrorism. The law of war doctrines of "military necessity and self-defense," argued Bybee, "could provide justifications that would eliminate any criminal liability."[11]

These stretches of language are especially understandable in light of existing bars to torture. The 1948 Universal Declaration of Human Rights states that "no one shall be subjected to torture or to cruel, inhuman, or degrading treatment." Such prohibitions are also found—prominently—in the 1949 Geneva Conventions, and the 1984 Convention against Torture and Other Cruel, Inhuman, or Degrading Treatment or Punishment.

This last-mentioned international treaty, ratified by the United States, is "universally regarded as codifying customary international law" prohibiting torture.[12] The first article in the convention defines torture in the following manner:

> For the purposes of this Convention, the term "torture" means any act by which severe pain or suffering, *whether physical or mental,* is intentionally inflicted on a person for such purposes as obtaining from him or a third person information or a confession, punishing him for an act he or a third person has committed or is suspected of having committed, or intimidating or coercing him or a third person, or for any reason based on discrimination of any kind, when such pain or suffering is inflicted by or at the instigation of or with the consent or acquiescence of a public official or other person acting in an official capacity. It does not include pain or suffering arising only from, inherent in or incidental to lawful sanctions. [My emphasis]

The Bybee memo ingeniously interpreted the language of the international laws of war to give the Bush administration's military authorities, from the secretary of defense down, the green light to "engage in practices that the International Committee of the Red Cross has described as 'tantamount to torture.'"[13]

For the interrogators, many very poorly trained for such work, it was bare-knuckles time in prisons in Afghanistan, Cuba, and, after 2003, Iraq. (Until June 2004, when it was repudiated by the new head of the Office of Legal Counsel, Daniel Levin, the Bybee memo was the operative message from the Department of Justice defining the meaning of torture of prisoners.) Although the president distinguished between the treatment of al Qaeda and Taliban prisoners (not subject to the protections of the laws of war) and the treatment of Iraqi prisoners (protected by the Geneva Conventions), in actuality interrogation techniques developed and used in Afghanistan and Guantánamo were soon employed in Iraq.

The president's November 2001 military order establishing the military tribunals further reflects the radically changed nature of the Bush administration's views about the treatment of captured persons in this "new paradigm" of warfare: (1) There is absolutely no mention of the Third Geneva Convention's applicability to the detainees, especially Article 5; (2) due process protections found in American courts and even in military courts-martial is specifically rejected for detainees; (3) Habeas actions to the federal district courts from the decisions of the tribunals created in the order are barred.

Critics, both in the United States and across the globe, argued that although it was "conceptually possible for a president to make a categorical determination that no detainee captured on a particular battlefield qualifies as a POW, [it] is not possible for a president to make a categorical determination that no detainee is an innocent civilian. Such a factual determination can only be made on a case by case basis."[14]

Until the U.S. Supreme Court entered the debates about the treatment of captured detainees in 2004, there were *absolutely* no government efforts to examine and discriminate among the thousands of detainees. However, with the arrival at Guantánamo of the first prisoners, soon to be labeled "enemy combatants," it was clear to some government personnel (experienced interrogators, FBI agents, some DOD and DOJ lawyers, and some in the Department of State) that the prisoners were not what Bush administration leaders had hoped for.

Just prior to the influx of prisoners to Guantánamo in late January 2002, the president, through his White House counsel, Gonzales, ordered Pentagon lawyers to direct interrogation officers at the naval base

> to fill out a one-page form for each prisoner, certifying the president's "reason to believe" their involvement with terrorism. But, within weeks [of the January 22, 2002 presidential request], intelligence officers began reporting back to the Pentagon that *they did not have enough evidence on most prisoners to even complete the forms,* officials said. By March 21, Defense Department officials indicated that they would hold the Guantanamo prisoners indefinitely and on different legal grounds—as "enemy combatants" in a war against the United States. [My emphasis][15]

This chapter, which examines the treatment of the prisoners captured in Afghanistan and Iraq after November 2001, demonstrates (1) that some in government, especially the military services lawyers in the JAG offices, were critical on ethical and legal grounds of the government lawyers' justification for the use of torture techniques; (2) that many of the detainees were either slow-footed soldiers or innocent civilians in the wrong place at the wrong time who, months later, found themselves held in military prisons; and (3) that some in government *knew* of the limited intelligence value of most of the prisoners.

TREATMENT OF WAR PRISONERS
PRIOR TO SEPTEMBER 11, 2001

From the time of the Revolutionary War and

> in that and in subsequent armed conflicts [until 2001] Americans subscribed to
> the laws of war. The United States also promoted efforts to regulate the conduct
> of armed conflict; in 1863, even as it fought a protracted and bloody civil war, it
> promulgated what is known as the Lieber Code, military regulations that have
> formed the cornerstone of many subsequent codifications of the laws of war,
> among them the Geneva Conventions of 1949.[16]

The U.S. Congress, given its constitutional mandate to prepare regulations
for the army and navy (Article I, Section 8), passed the Articles of War and later
the UCMJ—the congressional code of military criminal law applicable to all
members of the U.S. military worldwide. The UCMJ is a lengthy document
that provides the basic parameters of military behavior—in war and during
peace—and the consequences faced by military personnel who disregard its
guidelines. Included in the code are offenses having to do with the cruel treatment of prisoners. All military personnel who treat captured personnel in violation of the international customs and laws of war or in violation of domestic
law are subject to military courts-martial for their behavior.[17]

Treatment of prisoners prior to 2001 was bound by the Geneva Conventions as well as by the U.S. military's own publications. The *U.S. Army Field
Manual, FM 34-52, Intelligence Interrogation,* for example, was published in
May 1987 (revised in 1992) and is still the applicable guide for the military. It
lays out the military rules regarding "intelligence interrogation."[18] In the first
chapter, Section 1 spells out the nature of interrogation and the objectives of
the interrogator: "Interrogation is the art of questioning and examining a
source to obtain the maximum amount of useful information. The goal of
any interrogation is to obtain usable and reliable information, in a lawful
manner, and in the least amount of time, which meets intelligence requirements of any echelon of command."[19] A few paragraphs later Section 3, entitled "Prohibition against the Use of Force," carefully lays out the basic
restrictions on the behavior of interrogators—and the essential reasons for
the prohibition:

> The use of force, mental torture, threats, insults, or exposure to unpleasant and
> inhumane treatment of any kind is prohibited by law and is neither authorized

nor condoned by the U.S. Government. Experience indicates that the use of force is not necessary to gain the cooperation of sources for interrogation. The use of force is a poor technique, as it yields unreliable results, may damage subsequent collection efforts, and can induce the source to say whatever he thinks the interrogator wants to hear.[20]

The reasons for the prohibition are quite fundamental and are understood by experienced interrogators in all of America's wars, including the present war on terror. As a 1943 U.S. Marine report stated, the "successful interrogators all had one thing in common in the way they approached their subjects. *They were nice to them*" (my emphasis).[21]

The author of that 1943 report was U.S. Marine Maj. Sherwood F. Moran. In 2006 his report "remains something of a cult classic for military interrogators." The Marine Corps Interrogator Translator Teams Association has called its message "timeless" in the field, and it has "long been a 'standard read' for insiders."[22] Moran's philosophy is a basic one that, unfortunately, has not been followed by post-2001 military and CIA interrogators: "'Know their language, know their culture, and treat the captured enemy as a human being.'" Strong-arm tactics, psychological and physical, simply do not work, Moran concluded.[23]

Soon after the war against terrorism was declared in September 2001, all bets were off regarding the treatment of the many thousands of prisoners taken into custody by the United States. For a number of reasons—including the impatience of the leaders in the White House and Department of Defense, the Office of Legal Counsel's memos justifying the use of torture in the interrogation of prisoners, and the inexperience of many of the interrogators[24] and almost all of the military guards at the prison camps—the *Army Field Manual*'s protocols were either ignored or categorically rejected.

THE SLIPPERY SLOPE: THE USE OF TORTURE IN AMERICA'S "GULAGS"

Given the green light by lawyers in the Department of Justice and Department of Defense, interrogators have used gruesome techniques to try—unsuccessfully, as it turns out—to acquire useful intelligence about future al Qaeda plans. "Torture lite" is the term coined by observers of the treatment of prisoners in the American "gulags" in Afghanistan, Cuba, and Iraq.[25]

Initially, these harsh techniques were used to acquire information from the prisoners held in Cuba. By the summer of 2003, however, a very frustrated Secretary of Defense Rumsfeld sent the Guantánamo commander, U.S. Army Lt. Gen. Geoffrey Miller, to "'Gitmo-ize' the interrogation techniques in Iraq. . . . So began an era of 'strategic interrogation.' Ordinary military policemen were told by intelligence officials to do things like 'loosen this guy up for us' and 'make sure this guy has a bad night' and 'give him the treatment.'"[26] Clearly, as the 2004 Schlesinger Report indicated, interrogators "found themselves in uncharted ethical ground, with frequently changing guidance from above." And the White House and the Pentagon continued to demand that these persons produce "actionable" intelligence now.[27]

By March 2005, clearly as a consequence of ratcheting up the interrogation techniques, army and navy investigators reported that no fewer than twenty-six prisoners in the gulags died in American custody. More have died since then; some have gone on hunger strikes and many more, at least forty-one, have attempted suicide. In May 2006 three detainees at Guantánamo did succeed in hanging themselves. According to the investigators, many of the deaths were the result of *criminal homicide* committed by the U.S. military—with at least four deaths attributed to rough handling by CIA operatives.[28]

Torture as Bush Administration Policy
after September 11, 2001
"No slope is more slippery, I learned in Iraq," wrote Anthony Lagouranis, a former U.S. Army interrogator, "than the one that leads to torture."[29] Lagouranis had been an interrogator in various places in Iraq, including Abu Ghraib prison. "*Following orders that I believed were legal,* I used military working dogs during interrogations. I terrified my interrogation subjects, but I never got intelligence mostly because 90% of them were probably innocent" (my emphasis).[30] (Another army dog handler, Sgt. Michael J. Smith, on March 21, 2006, was found guilty on six of thirteen counts of tormenting detainees at the Abu Ghraib prison with his Belgian shepherd guard dog.)[31]

Once American forces were introduced into Afghanistan in late October 2001, in Operation Enduring Freedom, they captured many hundreds of Taliban and al Qaeda fighters and others caught in the action. The detainees were held in a number of prisons, including a major one located in Bagram, just north of Kabul, the nation's capital. By January 2002 many hundreds (at one time there were close to 1,000 detainees) of these captured persons had been sent to Guantánamo. And when the coalition led by American forces attacked Iraq, many more thousands of Iraqi and alleged al Qaeda combatants were captured and imprisoned in Iraqi prisons (formerly used by Saddam Hussein), while a smaller number of "high value" prisoners became ghost prisoners in the hands of the CIA operatives.

When Operation Iraqi Freedom began in March 2003, the Bush administration lawyers announced that the Geneva Conventions "applied comprehensively" to prisoners taken in the conflict. They would be detained for interrogation in prisons located in Iraq and they would be protected under the terms of the Geneva Conventions. (In April 2004 the world found out that interrogation techniques intended only for those held in Guantánamo had been transferred by General Miller to Iraq.)[32] However, the administration held that non-Iraqi prisoners captured in Iraq (suspected insurgents) were not entitled to the Geneva protections. Furthermore, a number of these non-Iraqi prisoners, all of whom were under the control of CIA interrogators and operatives, were secretly flown out of Iraq to other nations for further, intensified, torturous questioning.[33]

From the very beginning of these two conventional wars against the Taliban and Iraq, captured detainees were treated cruelly. In the view of many, American military personnel were using torture to try to gather intelligence about the tactics and the future plans of Osama bin Laden and al Qaeda operatives across the globe, but especially information about cells allegedly functioning in the United States.[34] As early as December 2002, the *Washington Post* and other media outlets began to report about the "stress and duress" techniques used by American intelligence agents and military police in Afghanistan and in Cuba. Since late 2001, as a matter of government policy, *all* enemy prisoners have been held in protective detention without legal counsel, subjected to continuous questioning, including torture, and psychological pressure by U.S. military and intelligence personnel:

Sadly, studies of the enemy detainees have revealed that a majority of the people being held at GTMO are innocent. The Seton Hall [University] study found, among other conclusions, that 55% of those being detained have not been determined by the Executive Branch to have committed any hostile acts against the United States or its allies, that only 8% have been characterized by the Executive Branch as having ties to al Qaeda, and 18% have been characterized by the Executive Branch as having no ties to either al Qaeda or the Taliban. The Seton Hall study also found that only 5% of detainees were captured by U.S.

forces (the rest being captured by Pakistani and Afghani forces that were paid by the U.S. to bring in anyone with suspected al Qaeda or Taliban ties.)[35]

The Absence of Policy Debates in the White House
Regarding the Use of Torture, 2002
The slide from adherence to international laws of war to "torture lite" occurred without serious criticism from within the Bush administration. Many pre-2001 laws and treaties restricting cruel, inhuman, degrading treatment and torture techniques—both domestic and international—were creatively reinterpreted throughout 2002 by lawyers in the Bush administration. The new meanings appeared in the legal memos sent to the White House from high-ranking legal and military officials in the Department of Justice and the Department of Defense.

As we now know, there was very little policy debate within the top echelons of the Bush administration regarding the decisions to ignore international laws of war. With the exception of Secretary of State Powell, who sent a memo dated January 26, 2002, to Gonzales, and William Taft IV, a legal counsel for the Department of State, who sent a lengthy one dated February 2, 2002, to Gonzales—both complaining of the impact of American rejection of the Geneva guidelines—none of the major political and military players in the Bush administration expressed public disagreement on the basic issues associated with treatment of detainees. There was absolutely no input from the military services' general counsels or from the four JAGs until well after the detainee interrogation policy was implemented.

Wrote one observer after the memos were declassified and released in 2004:

> What's most striking about these torture memos is their ideological consistency. Almost from the outset the principal ideas were set—that the Geneva Conventions might not apply to some prisoners; that torture could be defined so narrowly so as to permit egregious conduct as long as the intent was not to sadistically violate the law; that conduct prohibited under national and international law could be redefined [by the President] as permissible.[36]

The January 9, 2002, memo from the Department of Justice to the White House and the Pentagon began a year-long round of memo writing regarding the status of persons captured in Afghanistan. The memo recommended that the Geneva Conventions not be followed in the detention conditions and treatment of al Qaeda prisoners. Furthermore, "customary international law has no binding legal effect on either the President or the military." However, the memo noted, as a matter of policy, the detainees should be treated "humanely."

A few weeks later, on January 25, 2002, Gonzales advised President Bush that the Geneva Conventions were "quaint" and "obsolete" and said that if the government were to follow the conventions' restraints on interrogation techniques—and the hoped-for consequences—it would not be able to gather the intelligence information vitally needed to protect U.S. citizens from further terror attacks. Closing this circle of thinking on the matter, on February 7, 2002, President Bush sent a secret memo to his top lieutenants, telling them that Geneva did not apply to al Qaeda and Taliban prisoners captured in Afghanistan and that they would not be classified as POWs.

On August 1, 2002, the Bybee memo defining torture very narrowly—and indemnifying those who used torture in their interrogations—was sent to all concerned parties from the Office of Legal Counsel. This was followed, in December 2002 and April 2003, by memos sent by Secretary of Defense Rumsfeld. In these documents, he approved of between sixteen and twenty-four interrogation techniques—that William J. Haynes II, the Department of Defense general counsel, had euphemistically labeled "counter-resistance techniques" in a November 27, 2002, memo—that could be used on "uncooperative" detainees in Cuba and, afterward, at other prisons run by the U.S. military.

Haynes's memo described a number of categories of techniques to break detainees and get them to provide intelligence. Category I included mild, fear-related techniques. Category II techniques included using stress positions, falsified documents, isolation for up to thirty days, and removal of clothing and preying on the fears of the prisoner. The counterresistance techniques approved by Rumsfeld on December 2, 2002, included enforced prolonged standing, removal of detainees' clothing, sensory deprivation, being hooded during interrogations, prolonged interrogations of up to twenty hours, exposure to detainees' phobias (dogs, women) to induce stress, shaving of beards, good cop/bad cop routines, rapid-fire questioning, grabbing, poking, pushing, sleep adjustment, and exposure to unpleasant smells.[37]

In his April 16, 2002, memo to Gen. James T. Hill, commander, U.S. Southern Command, Secretary of Defense Rumsfeld approved and provided specific details of twenty-four interrogation counterresistance techniques for use on prisoners in Guantánamo (and, eventually, other U.S. gulags). And so, between January 2002 and December 2002, the legal memos sent to the major actors in the Bush administration, including President Bush, Vice President Cheney, Secretary of Defense Rumsfeld, and their legal counsels and political staffers, established the baselines for the treatment of detainees. These presidential declarations regarding the treatment of the detainees, who included not only Afghanis and Iraqis but also persons who had come to Afghanistan or Iraq from more than forty nations, became Bush administration policy until midway through 2004.

The military services lawyers in the respective JAG offices did not participate at all in the discussions surrounding the development of the "'interrogation rules of combat' (IROC) for Operation Enduring Freedom and Operation Iraqi Freedom." The JAGs were "neither consulted nor informed of such issues."[38] When they heard about the new IROC policy, especially when they reviewed the Bybee memo of August 1, 2002, they were flabbergasted to see international laws of war discarded as "quaint" relics.

Although the JAGs did not begin to formally express their concerns until 2003, when the four service branches produced their memos on the issue, Alberto J. Mora, the U.S. Navy's general counsel, began his criticism of the policy in late 2002, soon after it was promulgated. Ironically, his immediate superior in the Department of Defense chain of command was Haynes, the man who prepared the November 27, 2002, memo on appropriate—authorized—interrogation techniques for Secretary of Defense Rumsfeld's signature. Although many of Mora's memos to his boss and others, especially those in the White House, are still secret, there did appear in print a twenty-two-page document addressed to Vice Adm. Albert Church, who led one of ten Pentagon post-2004 investigations into alleged abuses of detainees held in American custody at Guantánamo.

Mora's memorandum to Church, dated July 7, 2004, "is a chronological account, beginning in December 2002, of Mora's criticisms of Administration policy" and of his futile efforts to change the detainee treatment policy of his government.[39] The memo was addressed to the inspector general, Department of the Navy; its title: "Statement for the Record: Office of General Counsel Involvement in Interrogation Issues."

Mora's narrative "largely involves [his] response to the [December 2002] allegations that interrogation abuses were occurring at Guantanamo." His lengthy report is, he wrote, a "chronological narrative of the significant events pertaining to detainee interrogations in which the Office of General Counsel (OGC) or I participated or of which I had knowledge." The first event took place on December 17, 2002, and the last entry is dated June 27, 2003.[40] Some of his entries follow:

18 Dec 02.

. . . [The Navy Criminal Investigation Service (NCIS) chief psychologist] described conditions in GTMO with Army Joint Task Force-170 (JTF-170), who were under pressure to produce results. . . . In contrast to civilian law enforcement personnel [FBI agents] present at GTMO, who were trained in interrogation techniques and limits and had years of professional experience in such practices, the military interrogators were typically young and had little or no training or experience in interrogations.

19 Dec 02.

[Conference between Mora and his general counsel counterparts from the other JAG offices.] The interrogation techniques approved by the Secretary should not have been authorized because some (but not all) of them, whether applied singly or in combination, could produce effects reaching the level of torture. . . . Any such mistreatment would be unlawful and contrary to the President's directive to treat the detainees "humanely."

6 Jan 03.

Detainee mistreatment in GTMO was continuing and the December 2, 2002 Memo had [not] been suspended or revoked. *This came as an unpleasant surprise since I had been confident that the abusive activities would have been quickly ended once I brought them to the attention of higher levels within DOD. I began to wonder whether the adoption [of the interrogation techniques policy] was perhaps a policy consciously adopted—albeit through mistaken analysis—and enjoying at least some support within the Pentagon bureaucracy.*

9 Jan 03.

I met with Mr. Haynes in his office again. He said that some U.S. officials believed the techniques were necessary to obtain information from the few GTMO detainees who, it was thought, were involved in the 9/11 attacks and had knowledge of other al Qaeda operations planned against the United States. I acknowledged the ethical issues were difficult. . . . Even if one wanted to authorize the U.S. military to conduct coercive interrogations [Mora said to Haynes], how could one do so without profoundly altering its core values and character? Societal education and military training inculcated in our soldiers American values adverse to mistreatment. Would we now have the military abandon these values altogether? . . . Mr. Haynes said little during our meeting. Frustrated by not having made much apparent headway, I told him that the interrogation policies

could threaten Secretary Rumsfeld's tenure and could even damage the
Presidency. "Protect your client," I urged Mr. Haynes.

30 Jan 03.
   The OLC [Bybee] paper is fundamentally in error: it spots some of the legal trees,
but misses the constitutional forest.

4 Feb 03.
   I circulated a NCIS Memo entitled "An Alternative Approach to the
Interrogation of Detainees at Guantanamo Bay, Cuba." . . . Mr. Haynes convened
a meeting of the Working Group principals . . . [to discuss the impasse].

6 Feb 03.
   The principal author of the OLC Memo, OLC Deputy Director John Yoo,
glibly defended the provisions of his memo, but it was a defense of provisions
that I regarded as erroneous. [My emphasis][41]

Clearly, Mora was a very big thorn in the side of Haynes and others in the
Pentagon and in the Vice President's Office, including David Addington. As a
consequence of Mora's incessant criticism of the IROC policy, the Pentagon
brought together a working group in late January 2003. At that point, the military service lawyers in the four JAGs drew up their own recommendations regarding the IROC. Memos from the Department of the Navy's JAG, February
6, 2003; from the Department of the Navy, Headquarters, U.S. Marine Corps,
February 27, 2003; and from the Department of the Army's JAG, March 3,
2003, were prepared and sent to their general counsels, who were the principals on the working group. The Marine Corps memo explicitly notes the
common concern expressed in all the JAG memos:

   The common thread among our recommendations is concern for service
   members. OLC does not represent the services; thus, understandably, concern for
   service members is not reflected in their opinion. Notably, their opinion is silent
   on the UCMJ and foreign views of international law. The Working Group [must
   present] the services' concerns that the authorization of aggressive counterresistance techniques by service members will adversely impact the following:

   a. Treatment of U.S. service members by Captors and Compliance with
       international law;
   b. Criminal and Civil Liability of DOD military and civilian personnel in
       Domestic, Foreign, and International Forums;
   c. U.S. and International Public Support and respect of U.S. armed forces;
   d. Pride, Discipline, and Self-Respect within the U.S. armed forces;
   e. Human intelligence Exploitation.[42]

The final report of the working group, entitled "Relating to Interrogation of Detainees Held by the U.S. Armed Forces in the War on Terrorism," was signed by Maj. Gen. Jack L. Rives, deputy JAG, U.S. Air Force. It was extremely critical of the policy on Geneva and on Torture laid out in the Bybee memo:

> Several of the more extreme interrogation techniques, on their face, are violations of domestic criminal law and the UCMJ. . . .
> Other nations are unlikely to agree with DOJ/OLC interpretations of the law. . . .
> Should any information regarding the use of the more extreme interrogation techniques become public, it is likely to be exaggerated/distorted in both the United States and international media. This could have a negative impact on international, and perhaps even domestic, support for the war on terrorism. Moreover, it could have a negative impact on public perception of the U.S. military in general.
> Finally, the use of [these] techniques simply is not the way U.S. armed forces have operated in recent history. We have taken the legal and moral "high road" in the conduct of our military operations regardless of how others operate. . . . We need to consider the overall impact of approving extreme interrogation techniques as giving official approval and legal sanction to the application of interrogation techniques that U.S. forces have consistently been trained are unlawful.[43]

The recommendations of the military services working group were, not surprisingly, rejected by the secretary of defense. The August 1, 2002, Bybee memo remained in effect for over a year, until it was revoked in December 2003.

In January 2006 Mora left the navy. One of his colleagues said of him, "Never has there been a counsel with more intellectual courage or personal integrity."[44] His boss, Haynes, did not attend the retirement party Mora's staff threw for him.

"Torture Lite" in the American Prison Archipelago

What follows are some brief stories that illustrate the general treatment received by many of the detainees held in prisons run by the U.S. military in Afghanistan, Guantánamo, and Iraq.[45]

The men and boys sent to Guantánamo were captured in Afghanistan and Pakistan after Operation Enduring Freedom began in October 2001. Within two months, the first batch of prisoners arrived in Cuba. From the instant the prisoners arrived in late January 2002, they were abused by guards and interrogators. "You won't believe it [the abuses]!" an FBI agent wrote to a colleague in Washington, D.C., in November 2002. He was complaining about the "coercive tactics" being employed indiscriminately on the detainees.[46]

Beginning in 2002 FBI agents were sent to the American prison camps to observe the interrogation process. They were shocked at the treatment of the prisoners and continually criticized the tactics used by the military. One of the ten post-2004 Abu Ghraib scandal reports wrote that the counterresistance techniques implemented at Guantánamo had "migrated"[47] improperly to Afghanistan and Iraq as well. The military leaders, an FBI agent wrote, were "continuing to support interrogation strategies we not only advised against, but questioned in terms of effectiveness."[48]

Torture at Bagram Prison, Afghanistan, 2002–2004

From 2002 to the present, U.S. military and civilian interrogators operating out of Bagram typically "remov[ed] clothing, isolate[ed] people for long periods of time, us[ed] stress positions, exploit[ed] fear of dogs and implement[ed] sleep and light deprivation." In another prison camp, the U.S. Army base at Gardez, detainees "endured repeated beatings, electric shocks, and immersion in cold water."[49]

The U.S. Army's criminal investigation office, the Army Criminal Investigation Command (ACIC), was brought into Bagram to investigate the deaths of some prisoners due to the routine use of counterresistance techniques by military interrogators there. The ACIC investigation led to a 2,000-page confidential report filed in late 2002 (and leaked to the *New York Times* in mid-2005). The file "includes ample testimony that harsh treatment by some interrogators was routine and that guards could strike shackled detainees with virtual impunity."[50]

One of the dead prisoners was a young, frail (five feet four inches, 122 pounds) twenty-two-year-old Afghan taxi driver, known only as Mr. Dilawar. He arrived in Bagram prison on December 5, 2001, and was quickly labeled a "noncompliant" detainee by the guards and the interrogators and had a black hood placed over his head at all times. By December 8, 2001, he had already been interrogated four times. His fifth and last interrogation took place two days later, on December 10, 2001. The report describes the last hours of his life, alone in his cell the morning of December 11, 2001—six days after he arrived:

Dilawar was hauled from his cell at around 2 a.m. to answer questions about a rocket attack on an American base. When he arrived in the interrogation room . . . his legs were bouncing uncontrollably in the plastic chair and his hands were numb. He had been chained by the wrists to the top of his cell for much of the past four days. . . . At the interrogators' behest, a guard tried to force Mr. Dilawar to his knees. But his legs, which had been pummeled by guards for several days, could no longer bend. When he was sent back to his cell, the guards were instructed only to chain the prisoner back to the ceiling. Several hours passed before an emergency room doctor saw Mr. Dilawar. By then, he was dead, his body beginning to stiffen. . . . *Most of the interrogators believed that Mr. Dilawar was an innocent man who simply drove his taxi past the American base at the wrong time.* [My emphasis]

The official autopsy described the reason his heart gave way: "blunt force injury to the lower extremities; [the tissue in his legs] *had basically been pulpified*" (my emphasis).[51]

Torture at Abu Ghraib Prison, Iraq, 2003–2004

The Americans detained prisoners captured during the fighting in Operation Iraqi Freedom in the spring of 2003 and alleged insurgents captured after the "mission was accomplished," to use the words displayed on an aircraft carrier in late spring 2003. Most of the detainees were not shipped out of Iraq, although the CIA did move some "high-value" persons to secret interrogation facilities in eastern Europe (Romania and Poland) and other locations across the globe. Ironically, sadly, according to military estimates reported by the ICRC, 70–90 percent of the Iraqi detainees "had been arrested by mistake."[52] However, these Iraqi detainees, all of whom, said President Bush in his February 2002 memo, would be treated "humanely and, to the extent appropriate and consistent with military necessity, in a manner consistent with" the Geneva Conventions, were subjected to the same counterresistance techniques used in Guantánamo.

These methods included threatening detainees with dogs; shackling them to cell floors in fetal positions for more than twenty-four hours; leaving them without food, water, or medical treatment; forcing them to urinate and defecate on themselves; leaving them naked in extreme heat or cold; shackling them upright to keep them awake; placing lit cigarettes into their ear openings; covering them with hoods and subjecting them to "extremely loud rap music"; placing a loaded 9 mm pistol to the head of a bound detainee; shocking detainees with wires from an electric transformer. Other agent-observers "found prisoners with burn marks on their backs and complaining of kidney pain."[53]

In February 2004 the ICRC presented to the U.S. government another of their regular confidential reports on conditions in American prisons in Iraq. Entitled *Report of the International Committee of the Red Cross (ICRC) on the Treatment by Coalition Forces of Prisoners of War and Other Protected Persons by the Geneva Conventions in Iraq during Arrest, Internment, and Interrogation,* this report charged that "psychological and physical coercion *tantamount to torture*" was employed by coalition forces on some of the Guantánamo detainees, especially "in the early stages of the internment process" (my emphasis).[54] Months later the ICRC report was leaked to the media and was made available on the *New York Times* Web site on November 30, 2004.[55]

Desperation: A Shared Experience for the Detainees
A cruel consequence of the many years of imprisonment in the American prison archipelago is the detainees' increased sense of desperation, a desperation born of helplessness and isolation. Most of the more than 3,000 detainees presently held across the American gulags have spent more than four years in these camps—without proper medical treatment[56] and in isolation for most of their time in prison—and have lost hope. For the most part, until very recently the prison system had no psychiatric treatment personnel or facilities for the many mentally disturbed patients. Death certificates were falsified by doctors. Dirty medical equipment abounded, amputations have been performed by nonmedical personnel,[57] and medical doctors and nurses have been used as accomplices in the poor treatment of the prisoners and have been charged as accessories in criminal homicide cases that have emerged in the past two years.

Mourad Benchellali was a prisoner in Guantánamo for almost three years before being released in July 2004. He had been seized by Pakistani military forces in November 2001 and turned over to the Americans. He was nineteen years old at the time. Within a few months he was flown to Guantánamo where he stayed until his release. "The worst aspect of being at the camp," he wrote in 2006,

> was the despair, the feeling that whatever you say, it will never make a difference. . . . I am a quiet Muslim—I've never waged war, let alone an asymmetrical one. . . . In Guantanamo, I did see some people for whom *jihad* is life itself, people whose minds are distorted by extremism and whose souls are full

of hatred. *But the huge majority of the faces I remember—the ones that haunt my nights—are of desperation, suffering, incomprehension turned into silent madness.* [My emphasis][58]

Another prisoner at Guantánamo, a thirty-two-year-old Bahraini national, Junah al-Dossari, was depressed enough to plan his suicide. (He has tried to kill himself more than one dozen times since his imprisonment in 2002.) In his suicide note he wrote:

> [We] are suffering from the bitterness of despair, the detention humiliation and the vanquish of slavery and suppression [*sic*]. I hope you will always remember that you met and sat with a "human being" called "Junah" who suffered too much and was abused in his belief, self, dignity, and also in his humanity. He was imprisoned, tortured, and deprived from his homeland, his family, and his young daughter who is the most need of him for four years . . . with no reason or crime committed.

He was saved from death only because his lawyer, Joshua Colangelo-Bryan, "found him bleeding and hanging limp in an interrogation cell."[59]

Of course, say observers about the despair and depression of the prisoners, "that's exactly what the interrogators wanted them to feel"[60]—even if these depressed prisoners are farmers or taxi drivers. The often-brutal treatment of the detainees continued—even in the face of worldwide condemnation. In the summer and fall of 2005, over 110 Guantánamo detainees began a hunger strike to protest their indefinite detention. "More than two dozen were being kept alive only by force-feeding." And Secretary of Defense Rumsfeld denied the UN human rights investigators permission to meet with detainees at Guantánamo.[61]

Torture: "A Policy That Spun Out of Control"
The legal memos sent from the Department of Defense and the Department of Justice in 2002 on torture validated its use throughout the American archipelago prison system. Whereas experienced interrogators, men and women in the FBI, NCIS, ACIC, and DIA, knew how ineffective such "counterresistance techniques" were, the policy was followed by aggressive military commanders and by military police officers called up from the Reserves and National Guard to perform prison tasks they had never been trained to do.

Megan Ambuhl had been in the Army Reserves for about a year before her military police unit was called up and shipped to Iraq. Their first mission was in a small village, Hilla, Iraq, where the unit "conducted neighborhood searches for insurgents, in what the military calls 'law and order missions.'" Ambuhl was a Humvee driver. The unit was then assigned guard duty at Abu Ghraib prison. They "received no training in dealing with enemy prisoners of war, were never specifically instructed about the Geneva Conventions, and were presented with no standard operating procedures for the prison. In the middle of a war, a world away from Northern Virginia, Ambuhl did not question her superiors."[62]

Ambuhl was, like so many hundreds of others, a "good American soldier": She obeyed orders. After the Abu Ghraib horrors hit the media, she and other low-level soldiers were charged under the UCMJ. Because she agreed to testify against her colleagues at their courts-martial, she left the army after receiving the punishment of a reduction in rank and a fine for "dereliction of duty" but did not receive any jail time. She said, mournfully, in 2006, "I wish I had done more to stop it."[63]

THE ROLE OF THE CIA IN THE WAR ON TERRORISM[64]

Also, since 2001, U.S. CIA's Counterterrorism Center (CTC) operatives have been and are still secretly shipping "high value" detainees to the CIA's own covert prison archipelago. The CIA has also sent some detainees to a number of nations for harsh and cruel aggressive interrogations in order to generate actionable intelligence and, at the same time, to evade media spotlighting this top-secret operation.[65]

Interrogating "High Value" Suspects in
CIA-Operated "Black Sites"
About the time ground forces engaged the Taliban military in late October 2001, President Bush

> chose the CIA, over the FBI and the Pentagon [DIA operatives], to take the lead in handling senior al Qaeda prisoners. . . . In choosing the CIA over the FBI, Bush was rejecting the law enforcement approach to fighting terrorism that had been favored during the Clinton administration. Bush had decided that al Qaeda was a national security threat, not a law enforcement problem, and he did not want al

Qaeda operatives brought back to face trial in the United States, where they would come under the strict rules of the American legal system.[66]

Unwilling to provide suspected terrorists with even minimal due process rights, Bush gave the task of interrogating the major al Qaeda suspects to America's top-secret federal intelligence gathering agency, the CIA. The assignment came with the understanding that "the CIA [would be] allowed to operate under different rules" than those followed by the FBI, the DIA, and other intelligence gathering agencies of the federal government.[67] Like their counterparts in Afghanistan, Iraq, and Cuba, the CIA operatives relied on torture techniques to try to elicit good intelligence from their detainees.

Under this September 2001 Bush mandate, the CIA planned, said one CIA source, "how to make people disappear." Very quickly, the CTC began to establish secret CIA prison sites in third-world countries in Africa and on the Pacific Rim, "with dubious human rights records," who were more than happy to accommodate the CIA's needs. Two major CIA prisons were established secretly: Bright Light (a still-secret location) and Salt Pit (Afghanistan). The view held by CIA operatives was that "once you get sent to Bright Light, you never came back."[68]

Not only were the CIA operatives working secretly, but their clandestine interrogation facilities were also top secret. The name given to these interrogation centers across the globe speaks volumes about their character: "Black Sites." The CIA coveted secrecy. It "needed complete control over the interrogation and debriefings, free from the prying eyes of the international media, free from monitoring from civil rights groups, and, most important, far from the jurisdiction of the American legal system."[69]

Eastern Europe, a secret interrogation center in the Bagram prison, ships at sea, Diego Garcia (an atoll in the Indian Ocean), Jordan, and Thailand are other black site locales that have been used to interrogate these high-level suspects.[70] Another secret prison run by the CIA was in Guantánamo itself. (After the June 2004 Supreme Court decisions regarding the jurisdictional status of Guantánamo, that particular CIA black site was shuttered.)

To further avoid detection by the media and by nongovernmental organizations (NGOs) opposed to the use of cruel, degrading, or humiliating techniques on detainees, the CIA flew prisoners from one secret CIA prison to another in their clandestine global prison network. In February 2005

Newsweek published a table that illustrated the complexities of this movement. Entitled "Aboard Air CIA," it followed the flight plan of a Boeing 737, tail number N313P, chartered by the CIA in January 2004. It made thirteen stops to pick up and drop off alleged high-value suspects for interrogation by the CIA. The multistop flight began on January 16, 2004, and ended twelve days later on the twenty-eighth. Its itinerary:

1. Washington, D.C., to Shannon, Ireland
2. Ireland to Larnaca, Cyprus
3. Cyprus to Sale, Morocco
4. Morocco to Kabul, Afghanistan
5. Afghanistan to Algeria
6. Algeria to Palma, Majorca
7. Majorca to Skopje, Macedonia
8. Macedonia to Baghdad, Iraq
9. Iraq to Kabul, Afghanistan
10. Afghanistan to Timisoara, Romania
11. Timisoara to Bucharest, Romania
12. Romania to Palma, Majorca
13. Majorca to Washington, D.C.[71]

Such frequent and highly secret CIA flights have taken, so far, as many as 200 allegedly high-value prisoners to secret interrogation centers in these and other countries.

"This agency does not torture," asserted former CIA director Porter J. Goss in November 2005.[72] Although the CIA has denied torturing the detainees, these assertions "were undercut by the fact that the FBI decided that the [CIA's] tactics were so severe that the bureau wanted no part of them, and FBI agents were ordered to stay away from the CIA-run interrogations."[73] At least six of the controversial CIA interrogation techniques were leaked to ABC News in late 2005 by anonymous CIA personnel. The first three include shaking and striking prisoners.

The fourth consists of forcing a prisoner to stand, handcuffed and with shackled feet, for up to 40 hours. Then comes the "cold cell": Detainees are held naked in a cell cooled to 50 degrees, and periodically doused with cold water. Last is "waterboarding," where the prisoner is bound to an inclined board, feet raised and head slightly below the feet. Cellophane is wrapped over the prisoner's face and water is poured over him. Unavoidably the gag reflex kicks in and a terrifying fear of drowning instantly leads to almost instant pleas to bring the treatment to a halt.[74]

Still another practice employed by the CTC, especially since September 11, 2001, is the extraordinary rendition of detainees to other nations whose own military intelligence personnel and police would interrogate them.

Outsourcing Torture: "Extraordinary Rendition"
of Detainees by the CIA
Until recently, rendition—the outsourcing of certain high-value detainees to third-party states, such as Egypt and Syria, that use torture for "aggressive interrogation"—occurred regularly after 9/11.[75] This top-secret U.S. intelligence policy was "beyond the reach of United States law and [until 2004] the press."[76] Rendition "transfers individuals from one country to another, by means that bypass all judicial and administrative due process," in order to have these high-value detainees questioned by the intelligence and military communities of the receiving nation. "Renditions involve multiple layers of human rights violations."[77]

The nations that receive these detainees from the CIA for questioning—Egypt, Syria, Thailand, Morocco, Saudi Arabia, South Africa, Jordan, and Pakistan, among others—use torture (not the army's "torture lite" techniques approved by Secretary of Defense Rumsfeld) as one of the mechanisms to gather intelligence information. After 9/11 the CIA secretly began sending high-value detainees to their home nations for further questioning, that is, "torture heavy."

The policy is encapsulated in what the U.S. military and the CIA have labeled the Special Access Program (SAP).[78] "Where outsourcing is impractical," wrote one critic of the U.S. rendition policy, "[the U.S.] imported qualified interrogators from abroad: in September 2002 a visiting Chinese "delegation" was invited to participate in the "interrogation" of ethnic Uighur detainees held at GTMO."[79]

Soon, because of leaks within the Bush administration from opponents of the policy, stories were published in the *Washington Post,* the *New York Times,* and other papers about "secret CIA interrogation centers at Guantanamo Bay and at other undisclosed locations around the world."[80] And in late 2005 it was disclosed that the CIA

> has been hiding and interrogating some of its most important al Qaeda captives at a Soviet-era compound in Eastern Europe. The secret facility is part of an overt prison system set up by the CIA nearly four years ago that at various times has included sites in eight countries, including Thailand, Afghanistan, and several democracies in Eastern Europe, as well as a small center at Guantanamo Bay prison in Cuba, according to current and former intelligence officials from three continents. . . . The hidden global internment network is a central element in the CIA's unconventional war on terrorism.[81]

More recently, an April 2006 report issued by the European Parliament concluded that Air CIA "had flown 1,000 undeclared flights over European territory since 2001." Many times these planes "stopped to pick up terrorism suspects who had been kidnapped to take them to countries that use torture," the report concluded.[82]

One example of this kind of CIA activity was revealed in Italy. In early July 2006 the prosecutor in Milan, Italy, arrested two individuals who worked in the Italian government's intelligence agency because of their 2002 involvement "in an American-led operation to detain and interrogate [the cleric Hassan Mustafa Osama Nasr]. Prosecutors also sought the arrest of three operatives of the CIA and an employee of the American military airbase at Aviano, Italy." The imam was picked up by the operatives while walking near his home in Milan, taken to an Italian air base, and then flown to Egypt by Air CIA. In July 2006 the imam was "apparently still in Egypt,"[83] although he was finally released February 11, 2007. In late February 2007, the Italian government indicted twenty-six Americans and five Italians—military personnel, CIA operatives, and Italian security agents—for Nasr's abduction from Italy to Egypt. He was held for four years in Egyptian custody. Nasr claimed that Egyptian officials regularly tortured him during those years in captivity. [84]

Such secret, heavy-handed policies made it impossible to obtain due process, humane treatment, or the release of innocent civilians. Indeed, many persons "swept up by rendition *simply vanish*" (my emphasis).[85] Blunt-speaking Secretary of Defense Rumsfeld put the Bush administration policy in sharp focus: America's "interest is in—during this global war on terror—keeping [these captured unlawful enemy combatants] off the streets, and so that's what's taking place."[86]

TREATMENT OF PRISONERS AFTER THE ABU GHRAIB
PRISON SCANDAL, MARCH–MAY 2004

Although the ICRC, the United Nations, and international NGOs knew about the mistreatment and torture taking place behind prison walls, there was no widespread media attention to this reality until March–April 2004, when the *New Yorker* magazine published a "damning report by investigative reporter Seymour Hersh,"[87] as well as photographs of prisoner abuse at Abu Ghraib prison near Baghdad.

Hersh's shocking account of the events at Abu Ghraib revealed that between October and December 2003 there were numerous instances of sadistic, blatant, and wanton criminal abuses by American GIs at the prison, a "systematic and illegal abuse of detainees . . . perpetrated by soldiers of the 372nd Military Police Company, and also by members of the American intelligence community." A confidential army report, obtained by the reporter, listed some of the army reservists' wrongdoings:

> Breaking chemical lights and pouring the phosphoric liquid on detainees; pouring cold water on naked detainees; beating detainees with a broom handle and a chair; threatening male detainees with rape; allowing a military police guard to stitch the wound of a detainee who was injured after being slammed against the wall in his cell; sodomizing a detainee with a chemical light and perhaps a broom stick, and using military working dogs to frighten and intimidate detainees with threats of attack, and in one instance actually biting a detainee.

Furthermore, Hersh wrote, there was stunning evidence to support the allegations: "detailed witness statements and the discovery of extremely graphic photographic evidence." Photographs and videos taken by the soldiers as the abuses were happening were not included in army report because of their "extremely sensitive nature."[88]

The photographs—several of which were broadcast on CBS's *60 Minutes* in late April 2004—show leering GIs taunting naked Iraqi prisoners who are forced to assume humiliating poses.

> The photographs tell it all. In one, Private England, a cigarette dangling from her mouth, is giving a jaunty thumbs-up sign and pointing at the genitals of a young Iraqi, who is naked except for a sandbag over his head, as he masturbates. Three other hooded and naked Iraqi prisoners are shown, hands reflexively crossed over their genitals. A fifth prisoner has his hands at his sides. In another, England

stands arm in arm with Specialist Graner; both are grinning and giving the thumbs-up behind a cluster of perhaps seven naked Iraqis, knees bent, piled clumsily on top of each other in a pyramid. There is another photograph of a cluster of naked prisoners, again piled in a pyramid. Near them stands Graner, smiling, his arms crossed; a woman soldier stands in front of him, bending over, and she, too, is smiling. Then, there is another cluster of hooded bodies, with a female soldier standing in front, taking photographs. Yet another photograph shows a kneeling, naked, unhooded male prisoner, head momentarily turned away from the camera, posed to make it appear that he is performing oral sex on another male prisoner, who is naked and hooded.[89]

The Consequences of the New Yorker's *Abu Ghraib Story*

To an observer of these hundreds of shocking pictures,[90] it is clear that the military guards, interrogators, and some medical personnel violated the stipulations of the Third Geneva Convention (see appendix 3), which directs that all prisoners "must at all times be protected, particularly against acts of violence and intimidation and against insults and public curiosity" (Article 13) and states that they are "entitled, in all circumstances to respect for their persons and their honor" (Article 14).

The revelation of mistreatment and torture was followed by a firestorm of protest, in America and across the globe, about American use of techniques against the captured detainees that clearly seemed to violate international humanitarian law. Clearly, American treatment of the detainees went beyond the bounds of civil treatment and violated both the Geneva Conventions and the Convention against Torture ratified by the United States and most of the world's nations.

Pentagon and Military Investigations, 2004–

One consequence of this huge embarrassment for the United States was immediate investigations by the Pentagon and the military branches into these incidents. By 2005 at least ten different groups of military investigators had finished interrogating military personnel and presented their final reports to the secretary of defense. Interestingly, but not surprisingly, all reports "stopped short of leveling serious blame against high ranking military and civilian officials like Defense Secretary Donald Rumsfeld; Lieutenant General Ricardo Sanchez, former U.S. commander in Iraq; Major General Geoffrey Miller, former commander of the detention facility at GTMO, and General Daniel McNeill, commander of allied forces in Afghanistan."[91] The focus, instead, was on troopers and low-level officers who had immediate command and control of the soldiers.

Release of 2002 Secret Memos on Detainee Policy
Released about the same time as the Abu Ghraib torture photos were all the 2002 secret internal memos justifying the rejection of the Geneva Conventions and other international laws of war that protected detainees in war. These were the memos written by the legal ideologues in the Department of Defense, the Office of Legal Counsel, and the White House. They were released in April 2004 because of Freedom of Information Act requests by the American Civil Liberties Union (ACLU) to the Department of Justice and the Department of Defense. These events, especially the Abu Ghraib photos, led to a worldwide firestorm of protest from America's allies as well as its enemies. Both the memos and the photos were immediately used in a new wave of anti–United States propaganda across the globe, especially in Middle Eastern Muslim countries.

President Bush's Condemnation of Torture, July 2004
On July 5, 2004, partly in response to the global anti–United States propaganda campaign, President Bush issued a statement on UN International Day in Support of Victims of Torture. He said, "America stands against and will not tolerate torture. We will investigate and prosecute all acts of torture . . . in all territory under our jurisdiction. Torture is wrong no matter where it occurs, *and the United States will continue to lead the fight to eliminate it everywhere*" (my emphasis).[92] Given the president's awareness of the use of torture by military personnel and the CIA, as early as 2002, on enemy detainees, his public pronouncement was simply another lie uttered by the "trust us" chief executive.

The December 2004 Definition of Torture
The August 1, 2002, Bybee memo on torture was also changed. On December 30, 2004, the Office of Legal Counsel issued a new order concerning torture: "Legal Standards Applicable under 18 U.S.C. §§ 2340–2340A, Memorandum Opinion for the Deputy Attorney General." On the very first page, the opinion reads,

> Questions have since been raised, both by this Office and by others, about the appropriateness and relevance of the non-statutory discussion in the August 2002

Memorandum, and also about various aspects of the statutory analysis, in particular the statement that "severe" pain under the statute was limited to pain "equivalent in intensity to the pain accompanying serious physical injury, such as organ failure, impairment of bodily function, or even death." *Id.* at 1. We decided to withdraw[93] the August 2002 Memorandum, a decision announced [earlier] in June 2004. . . . Because of the importance of—and public interest in—these issues, . . . This memorandum [was] prepared in a form that could be released to the public so that interested parties could understand our analysis of the statute. This memorandum supersedes the August 2002 Memorandum in its entirety. . . . We disagree with statements in the August 2002 Memorandum limiting "severe" pain under the statute to "excruciating and agonizing" pain, *id.* at 19, or to pain "equivalent in intensity to the pain accompanying serious physical injury, such as organ failure, impairment of bodily function, or even death." . . . Although Congress defined "torture" under sections 2340–2340A to require conduct specifically intended to cause "severe" pain or suffering, we do not believe Congress intended to reach only conduct involving "excruciating and agonizing" pain or suffering [as its definition of torture].[94]

New Policy Debates about Geneva and Torture, July 2004–2005

After Bush's July 2004 speech condemning torture, a new policy debate began within the White House, the Department of Justice, and the Pentagon over whether or not Department of Defense standards for handling terror suspects "should adopt language from the Geneva Conventions prohibiting 'cruel,' 'humiliating,' and 'degrading' treatment."[95] *All* the military JAG lawyers and some of the lawyers in the State Department believed "Geneva" language should be incorporated into the new guidelines.

After the initial Bybee memo regarding treatment of detainees became policy in 2002, the uniformed military services JAGs, in particular, were extremely critical of the Bush administration's rejection of the Geneva protections, although they remained silent in public. However, in their frustration and concern about the 2002 IROC policy, since 2005 they have gone public with their criticism of the Bush administration's IROC protocols. These top lawyers for the armed forces, as recently as March 2006, went before Congress to say that "a number of aggressive techniques used by military investigators on detainee[s] were not consistent with the guidelines in the Army field manual [32-54] on interrogations."[96] The military service lawyers' views, however, have steadfastly been rejected by the White House, the Pentagon, and the Department of Justice.

The U.S. State Department's lawyers also wanted the Geneva standards included in the new guidelines on detainee treatment. They have "fiercely opposed the military's decision to exclude Geneva Convention protections and [they have] been pushing for the Pentagon and White House to reconsider."[97] However, until the Supreme Court's opinion in June 2006 in *Hamdan v. Rumsfeld,* the administration ignored all such requests.

On the other side of the debate were the conservative ideologues in the Bush White House, the Pentagon, and the Department of Justice. High-level staff members, such as David Addington and other aides to Vice President Cheney, as well as some senior Pentagon officials, including Stephen A. Cambone, Department of Defense undersecretary for intelligence, form the core of the opposition to Geneva-like changes in the documents. They insisted that the proposed moderate changes in Defense Department document 23.10, titled "DOD Program for Enemy Prisoners of War and Other Detainees," and in the army's field manual on interrogation would wreak havoc on America's efforts in the war on terror. The Geneva Conventions' Common Article 3, they argue, creates "'an unintentional sanctuary' that allows al Qaeda members to keep information from interrogators."[98]

Their basic argument is that the proposed moderate language is vague and "would tie the government's hands in combating terrorists and still would not satisfy America's critics."[99] In one clash between Addington and Matthew C. Waxman, Rumsfeld's chief adviser on detainee matters, Waxman "left bruised and bloody. He tried to champion Article 3, and Addington just ate him for lunch."[100] (It should be noted that however the documents are changed, they will not "cover the treatment of detainees held by the Central Intelligence Agency.")[101] In June 2006 the Cheney-Rumsfeld-Addington-Cambone team won out. After more than a year of internal debate, the Pentagon "has decided to omit from new detainee policies a key tenet of the Geneva Convention that explicitly bans 'humiliating and degrading treatment,' a step that would mark a further, potentially permanent, shift away from strict adherence to international human rights standards."[102]

The June 2006 victory for the IROC hard-liners, however, seemed short-lived. On July 7, 2006, about a week after the U.S. Supreme Court handed down its decision in *Hamdan v. Rumsfeld,* Gordon England, deputy secretary of defense, sent a memorandum titled "Application of Common Article 3 of the Geneva Conventions to the Treatment of Detainees in the Department of Defense" to all the military branches. The two-page memo seemed to signal a major policy change by the Bush administration regarding the treatment of

detainees held by American military forces in Afghanistan, Iraq, and Guantánamo. England's memo contained the complete text of Common Article 3 of
the Geneva Conventions, included to make sure all reporting organizations
and their leaders within the Department of Defense got the message. England's memo said,

> The Supreme Court has determined that *Common Article 3 of the Geneva
> Conventions of 1949 applies as a matter of law to the conflict with Al Qaeda.* . . . You
> will ensure that all DOD personnel adhere to these standards. In this regard, I
> request that you promptly review all relevant directives, regulations, policies,
> practices, and procedures under your purview to ensure that they comply with
> the standards of Common Article 3. [My emphasis]

For the first time since the beginning of the post-9/11 wars in Afghanistan
and Iraq, the White House "conceded . . . that terror suspects held by the
United States had a right under international law to basic human and legal
protections under the Geneva Conventions."[103] The memo—and the
Supreme Court decision in *Hamdan* that preceded it—had the effect of nullifying that part of President Bush's February 7, 2002, executive order to his key
subordinates that al Qaeda and Taliban detainees were *not* covered by the
Geneva Conventions.

The England memo, according to most reporters covering these events,
"reversed a position" held by the White House since 2002 and represented "a
victory for those within the administration who argued that the United
States' refusal to extend the Geneva Conventions to al Qaeda prisoners was
harming the country's standing abroad."[104] The initial euphoria of the president's critics quickly ended when they saw the White House's actions in the
months preceding the passage of the Military Commissions Act in September
2006. With the passage of the act, the hard-liners were once again in charge of
detainee policy. The England memo had a very short life span as Bush policy.
(Chapter 6 discusses these events in more detail.)

However, as the events of late summer and early fall of 2006 illustrated,
President Bush aggressively challenged the U.S. Supreme Court's majority decision in *Hamdan v. Rumsfeld* (see chapter 6 and the epilogue).

Status of Guantánamo Detainees, 2006

In February 2006 the Pentagon announced that the United States "was ready
to repatriate more than 150 of the [almost 600] detainees once arrangements

could be made with their home countries." But, continued the Department of Defense spokesman, U.S. Navy Lieutenant Commander Jeffrey Gordon, "the Pentagon has no plans to release any detainees in the immediate future," because negotiations with foreign nations "have proven to be a complex, time-consuming and difficult process."[105] The reason for the alleged difficulty: The State Department was pushing for "human rights assurances" for the repatriated detainees from their home nations![106]

In April 2006, when the Department of Defense was ordered[107] to release the names of all enemy detainees held at Guantánamo, an outcry arose from many of the nations whose citizens had been held, without charges ever filed, since 2001: "A chorus of complaints [from Great Britain, China, Pakistan, Afghanistan, Egypt, Jordan, Bahrain] against the Bush administration erupted Thursday [April 20, 2006] after the Pentagon released a previously secret list of the names and nationalities of 558 people held at the U.S. military prison in Guantanamo Bay."[108]

For many diplomats and government leaders in these nations, the American attitude in 2006 regarding repatriation smacked of hypocrisy. They saw the U.S. demand that they treat their repatriated citizens humanely as another example of Bush administration chutzpah. "It is kind of ironic that the United States government is placing conditions on other countries that it would not follow itself in Guantanamo or Abu Ghraib [Iraq]," said a Middle Eastern diplomat to *New York Times* reporter Tim Golden.[109]

Since 2002, the ICRC has determined that the treatment of these detainees by U.S. military personnel "amounts to torture."[110] And in a report issued in mid-February 2006, the UN Human Rights Commission called on the United States to either release all enemy detainees held at Guantánamo or bring them to trial. The UN report, based on a three-year investigation by five UN investigators, called on the Bush administration "to close down the Guantanamo Bay detention center and to refrain from any practice amounting to torture, or cruel, inhuman, or degrading treatment."[111] But based on recent actions taken by the Pentagon on Guantánamo—the building of an ultramodern prison facility and the recent opening of a state-of-the-art medical facility there—it does not seem that Guantánamo will be closing down in the near future.

The U.S. Supreme Court Enters the Picture, 2003–2004

As the horrid story of torture and mistreatment of Abu Ghraib detainees by American soldiers unfolded in the media in early 2004, the nine justices of the

U.S. Supreme Court were reading the briefs and hearing oral arguments in the first of two sets of enemy combatants cases they heard during the 2003 term: *Rasul v. Bush* and *Al Odah v. United States* (see chapter 4). These two cases involved questions of jurisdiction (and justiciability) of the federal courts to hear habeas corpus petitions from foreign nationals held at Guantánamo.

Two other petitions were granted certiorari by the justices shortly thereafter. These cases involved the question of what due process rights American citizens have who are held as "enemy combatants" by the government in military brigs in America: *Rumsfeld v. Padilla* (03-1027) and *Hamdi v. Rumsfeld* (03-6696). Chapter 4 examines these appeals to the federal courts from detained suspected enemy combatants.

4. Bush versus the U.S. Supreme Court, Round One, 2003–2004

I don't care what the international lawyers say, we are going to kick some ass.

PRESIDENT GEORGE W. BUSH[1]

We cannot permit the executive branch to declare unilaterally that a U.S. citizen [is] an enemy combatant [who can be] whisked away, detained indefinitely without charges, denied legal counsel, and prevented from arguing to a judge that he is wholly innocent.

ROBERT A. LEVY, CATO INSTITUTE[2]

In American jurisprudence, the term "enemy combatant" was first used in obiter dicta during the early days of World War II, in *Ex Parte Quirin* (see chapter 2). The *Quirin* case was not the first time federal courts had been asked to determine whether presidential acts during wartime were constitutionally valid. From the very beginning of the Republic to the middle of the twentieth century the U.S. Supreme Court heard war-power cases and decided them on the merits—at times for the president (the 1944 decision in *Korematsu v. United States*) and at times against him (*Youngstown Sheet and Tube Co. v. Sawyer*, the 1952 steel seizure case).[3]

During the era of litigation over the Vietnam War, 1963–1975, however, the Court—much to the chagrin of Justice William O. Douglas—generally deferred to the executive by not hearing cases that challenged the constitutionality of President Johnson's conduct of the Vietnam War. Using the "political question" doctrine[4] and other judicially created and imposed self-restraints, Court majorities regularly deferred to the executive or Congress.[5] Either the majority favored nonjusticiability rulings or ruled in favor of the government in cases such as *United States v. O'Brien* (391 U.S. 367, a 1968 case in which the Court ruled that burning one's draft card was not protected free speech).

Almost a year after the 9/11 terrorist attacks, the federal courts began to receive petitions from persons and organizations claiming that the Bush administration, in "kick[ing] some ass," was denying civil and due process rights to immigrants seized in the United States and was also denying these rights to foreign detainees held in the prison at Guantánamo Bay and to U.S. citizens held in military brigs in the United States.

When the certiorari petitions came to the Supreme Court in 2003 and early 2004 regarding the Bush administration's treatment of "enemy combatants," most observers believed that the Court, a somewhat conservative one (with at least five Republican jurists sitting on the High Bench), would not grant certiorari. After all, many reasoned, this was the Court that, 5–4, had "elected" George W. Bush president in December 2000.[6] This was a Court led by the redoubtable Chief Justice William H. Rehnquist and his quartet of conservative justices, Associate Justices Antonin Scalia, Clarence Thomas, Anthony Kennedy, and Sandra Day O'Connor. This was a Court that had trumpeted the concept of a strong executive since the 1980s. And these requests, if the certiorari petitions were granted, would "raise fundamental questions about the judges' ability to check presidential power" in wartime.[7]

However, although the Court denied certiorari in petitions from immigrants who were seized by the INS, it did, surprisingly, grant the petitions from the foreign-born Guantánamo detainees and from U.S. citizens detained as "enemy combatants." In November 2003 and January and February 2004, the justices granted certiorari in the three cases involving enemy combatants.

On November 10, 2003, the Court granted certiorari in *Rasul v. Bush* and *Al Odeh v. United States.* The cases involved petitions from foreign detainees held at Guantánamo. *Rasul* was consolidated with the *Al Odah* petition, and they were argued together in April 2004.

In early January 2004 the Court granted certiorari in *Hamdi v. Rumsfeld,* involving a U.S. citizen captured in Afghanistan and held in a Navy brig as an enemy combatant. In February 2004 the justices granted certiorari in *Rumsfeld v. Padilla,* a second case involving the question of due process rights for an American citizen, this time a man seized in Chicago and held in a military brig as an al Qaeda terrorist.

Oral arguments for the three cases were held on April 20 (*Rasul*) and 28 (*Hamdi* and *Padilla*), 2004. On June 28 the Court handed down its judgments in these three enemy combatants cases.

In addition to the question of whether the federal courts had jurisdiction to hear petitions from the foreign detainees being held at Guantánamo, there was also the "status determination for foreign detainees" matter. The lawyers for the detainees argued that there had been no (Geneva) Article 5 hearings held to determine the status of the detainees. Were they POWs, or spies, or simply innocent civilians? And another legal and moral question emerged in the briefs and in oral argument before the Court in the spring of 2004: Can U.S. citizens, picked up in Afghanistan (*Hamdi*) and in Chicago (*Padilla*), allegedly members of the Taliban and al Qaeda, respectively, be held indefinitely—without any due process rights—in military brigs because they were labeled enemy combatants by President Bush?

THE ENEMY COMBATANTS CASES: A PRISM FOR VIEWING THE EXPANSION OF PRESIDENTIAL POWER IN AMERICA'S WAR ON TERROR

When, in November 2003, the Supreme Court granted certiorari to detainees held in Guantánamo and, in early 2004, it accepted cases from "enemy combatants" who were citizens and held in military brigs on U.S. soil, "the Court moved from the sidelines to the center of the debate over whether the administration's response to the terrorist attacks of September 11, 2001, reflects an appropriate balance between national security and individual liberty."[8] In the international laws of war, especially Common Article 3 of the Geneva Conventions, protections are afforded *all* enemy prisoners. However, following President Bush's exhortation to his generals to "kick some ass" after his September 11, 2001, speech to a shocked nation, lawyers in the Department of Justice, the Department of Defense, and the White House "translated these words into formal directives."[9]

The blizzard of memos circulated for most of 2002 among high-level politicians and lawyers in the executive branch contained at least four constitutional arguments:

1. As commander in chief, President Bush has the power to override all laws and treaties, whether domestic or international.
2. The "U.S. anti-torture laws can be stretched to provide a winning legal defense for any CIA interrogator accused of torture."
3. The Guantánamo detainee prison was beyond the jurisdiction of federal courts.
4. In time of war, especially asymmetrical wars between bands of terror-

ists and a sovereign nation-state, courts must defer or accede to decisions of the president as commander in chief.[10]

For the first time since September 11, 2001, a coordinate branch of the federal government, the U.S. Supreme Court, was being asked to enter the controversy surrounding the scope of presidential powers in a time of war. For more than two years, presidential actions had gone unchallenged or had simply been hidden from federal legislators and judges. Congress, with its two AUMF resolutions, had given the president nearly unlimited authority to fight the war against terrorism any way he wanted. There was very little oversight—or criticism—of presidential actions abroad and at home. What there was came from JAG lawyers and from a very small number of State Department lawyers. The Court's entry into the political controversy was unexpected. Its decision to grant certiorari was greeted warmly by defense lawyers, but not by the White House, the Department of Justice, the Department of Defense, or the Vice President's Office.

RASUL V. BUSH AND AL ODAH V. UNITED STATES (CONSOLIDATED) BEFORE THE JUSTICES

On November 10, 2003, the Court rejected the arguments of the Bush administration and granted certiorari in two cases: *Rasul, Shafiq, et al. v. Bush, President of the United States, et al.,* Case 03-334, and *Al Odah, Fawzi, et al. v. United States, et al.,* Case 03-343. These two cases, soon to be consolidated by the Court, were petitions from sixteen British, Australian, and Kuwaiti detainees at Guantánamo who were captured allegedly fighting for the Taliban government in the short Afghanistan war. In January 2002 they were shipped to Guantánamo, labeled "unlawful enemy combatants," and were thereafter held captive in Camp X-Ray. Lawyers for *Rasul et al.* (retained by the parents of the two British detainees, joined by two Australian prisoners) and for *Al Odah et al.* (retained by relatives of the twelve Kuwaiti prisoners), sixteen in all, filed habeas corpus petitions with the federal district court in Washington, D.C.

The federal Habeas Corpus Statute (28 *U.S. Code,* sec. 2241) gives federal courts the *discretion* to hear arguments by petitioners who claim to be held "in custody in violation of the Constitution or laws or treaties of the United

States." Only Congress has the power to suspend the writ of habeas corpus. Article I, Section 9, Clause 2 of the U.S. Constitution states, "The Privilege of the Writ of Habeas Corpus shall not be suspended, unless when in cases of Rebellion or Invasion the public Safety may require it."

The petitioners argued that they were all innocent civilians who had been illegally seized by bounty hunters,[11] turned over to American military forces, arrested by the United States, and then detained at Guantánamo. Further, the briefs argued,

> it is not for the executive branch to define the jurisdiction of the federal courts. . . . The United States has created a prison on GTMO that operates entirely outside the law. The conditions that make this "war" unique are the same conditions that make it essential for the government to provide some process by which innocent people can secure their release. Someone impartial must have authority to examine the executive's actions. That is the traditional role of the judiciary.[12]

The two separate lawsuits were combined by the federal district court judge, Colleen Kollar-Kotelly, who then ruled against the plaintiffs. She based her decision on a 1950 case, *Johnson v. Eisentrager* (339 U.S. 763), which stated that federal courts lack jurisdiction over the military trials and imprisonment of foreign nationals outside *sovereign* U.S. territory. (The German nationals who were the subjects of the case had been captured in China after the German surrender in World War II, detained, tried by a military commission in China, and found guilty of war crimes. They were imprisoned in a U.S. military prison in Landsberg, Germany.) On March 11, 2003, a three-judge panel of the U.S. Court of Appeals for the District of Columbia Circuit affirmed the judgment of the district court. A rehearing was denied on June 2, 2003.

On September 2, 2003, petitions for writs of certiorari were filed in the U.S. Supreme Court by the detainees' lawyers. Three questions were presented for Court responses: (1) Did the lower courts erroneously hold that *Eisentrager* denied petitioners a "judicial forum in which to question the factual basis for their detention or its legality under the Constitution and international law"? (2) Did the lower courts err "in holding categorically that the Constitution gives 'no constitutional rights under the due process clause or otherwise,' to foreign nationals"? (3) Did "the Due Process clause of the Fifth Amendment permit the United States to detain foreign nationals indefinitely, in solitary confinement, without charges and without recourse to any legal process, so long as they are held outside the 'ultimate sovereignty' of the United States"?[13]

On October 3, 2003, the brief for the respondents, George W. Bush et al., in opposition to the granting of certiorari was filed. In it, the Bush administration's then U.S. solicitor general, Theodore B. Olson, argued that the federal judiciary must stay out of these wartime matters. In the briefs and again during oral argument, the president's legal spokespersons in the Solicitor General's Office insisted that federal judges "must avoid judicial interference with military affairs." Allowing "unlawful" enemy combatants confined on Cuba access to the federal courts would "directly, and perhaps gravely, [interfere] with the executive's conduct of the war and divert attention of the military from on-going hostilities abroad to courtrooms at home. . . . This litigation challenges the President's military detentions while American soldiers and their allies are still engaged in armed conflict against an unprincipled, unconventional, and savage foe." Solicitor General Olson's brief asked the Court not to grant certiorari because the lower federal court had properly applied the 1950 Supreme Court precedent and held "that aliens detained by the military abroad [only have rights] *determined by the executive and the military, and not the courts*" (my emphasis). Under *Eisentrager,* the reply brief in opposition argued, "United States courts lack jurisdiction over claims filed by or on behalf of aliens, like the Guantanamo detainees, who are detained outside of the sovereign territory of the United States." The Guantánamo detainees "lack[ed] capacity and standing to invoke the process of federal courts," the government's brief concluded.[14]

There were, in addition to the two briefs filed by the parties to the dispute, an additional eight amicus curiae (friends of the court) briefs filed.[15] All focused on whether or not the Court should grant certiorari, thereby getting into the political thicket surrounding the issue of enemy combatants.

On November 10, 2003, much to the chagrin and dismay of many in the Bush administration, the petitions for certiorari were granted, "limited to the following question": "Whether the United States courts lack jurisdiction to consider challenges to the legality of the detention of foreign nationals captured abroad in connection with hostilities and incarcerated at the Guantanamo Bay Naval Base, Cuba. The cases [*Rasul,* 03-334, and *al Odah,* 03-343] are consolidated and a total of one hour is allotted for oral argument."[16]

The petitioners' brief on the merits was filed with the Court on January 14, 2004. It was accompanied by twenty amicus curiae briefs filed in support of the plaintiff detainees by such groups as Retired Military Officers, Fred Korematsu,[17] Hungarian Jews and Bougainvilleans, Center for Justice and Accountability, 175 Members of Both Houses of the Parliament of the United Kingdom of Great Britain and Northern Ireland, and Former American Prisoners of War.[18]

There were two major arguments presented in the *Rasul* merits brief: First, that "the Habeas Statute Gives the District Court Jurisdiction," and second, that "The Government Offers No Persuasive Reason to Ignore the Unambiguous Command of the Habeas Statute."[19]

> The government is mistaken [when it] argues that the Federal courts are powerless to review these prisoners' indefinite detentions because they are foreign nationals brought by the military to a prison beyond the "ultimate sovereignty" of the United States. . . . This country has rejected imprisonment without legal process, even during times of war, and the Court should not interpret the habeas statute in a manner that permits the creation of an off-shore prison for foreign nationals that operates entirely outside the law.

Clearly, the lawyers wrote, habeas is the universal remedy when prisoners—regardless of nationality or status—are in executive detention and believe they are wrongly held: "The Court has long recognized that federal courts have the power to review *every* species of Executive imprisonment, wherever it occurs and whatever form it takes" (my emphasis).[20]

"The Executive," the brief's second argument began, "argues that current hostilities demand indefinite detention without legal process, and [relying heavily on *Eisentrager,* maintains that] . . . No court may inquire into the lawfulness of the detentions on Guantanamo. . . . This reliance is misplaced."[21]

On March 3, 2004, the president's brief on the merits was deposited in the Supreme Court. It was accompanied by seven amicus curiae briefs supporting the Bush administration's position on the question of enemy combatants. Included among those filing these briefs were such organizations as Citizens for Common Defense, Former Attorneys General of the United States, and the Washington Legal Foundation. The solicitor general's brief on the merits focused on the continued validity of the *Eisentrager* opinion: "The fundamental jurisdictional question presented in this case is governed by this Court's decision in *Johnson v. Eisentrager*. . . . [It] controls the outcome in this case. . . . [The 1950 opinion] makes clear that *sovereignty*, not mere control, is the touchstone of its jurisdictional rule. . . . There is no basis in law for carving a 'Guantanamo Exception' out of *Eisentrager's* sovereignty-based rule" (my emphasis).[22]

This was the essential legal argument of the Bush administration. *Eisentrager* held that all U.S. courts lacked jurisdiction over suits filed by aliens "detained abroad." And, the government's brief noted, the opinion has "only been reinforced" since 1950 by federal court rulings, including orders of the U.S. Supreme Court. It was "settled law" that all federal courts lack jurisdiction in these cases.[23]

The government's second major argument stated that if the Supreme Court of the United States were to depart from its own precedent, it "would raise grave separation-of-powers concerns." Any "exercise of federal court jurisdiction over habeas actions filed on behalf of the Guantanamo detainees would directly interfere with the Executive's conduct of the military campaign against al Qaeda and its supporters." Such judicial action in the middle of an ongoing war, "would *thrust* the federal courts into the *extraordinary* role of reviewing the military's conduct of hostilities overseas, second-guessing the military's determination as to which captured aliens pose a threat to the United States or have strategic intelligence value, and, in practical effect, superintending the Executive's conduct of an armed conflict—even while American troops are on the ground in Afghanistan and engaged in daily combat operations" (my emphasis).[24]

This, then, was the essence of the government's argument in all the 2004 enemy combatants cases: There was strong precedent for barring federal courts from granting habeas petitions. For a court to grant such a petition would be a violation of the separation-of-powers concept embedded in the U.S. Constitution. Finally, the courts must stay out of the executive's conduct of the war on terror.

The petitioners filed their reply to the government brief on April 7, 2004. It must surely have caught the eyes of the justices and their law clerks with its very first sentence: "The government has submitted an extraordinary brief." The brief continued,

> What is truly astounding is that the government attempts to persuade the Court that it has employed a fair and legitimate process for determining whether

petitioners are enemy combatants while simultaneously declaring that courts have no authority to examine that process and, indeed, that national security would be threatened if they did. . . . The government animates its apocalyptic vision of the harms resulting from judicial review with repeated mischaracterizations of what petitioners seek, stating that [they] are asking the courts to second-guess military judgments about the conduct of the war on terrorism, [etc.].[25]

The twenty-page brief focused in part on the government's arguments that judicial review of the Guantánamo detainees' claims would do violence to the concept of separation of powers.[26] However, "ensuring that the government adheres to procedures ratified by Congress [habeas corpus] and adopted in executive regulations cannot plausibly be said to interfere with the President's war powers or threaten national security."[27]

The brief also argued that the proposition put forward by the solicitor general that the president could evade judicial review "by detaining individuals outside the Nation's borders is anathema to international law." The conclusion was unusually blunt: "The Executive argues that it had absolute immunity from judicial examination whenever it elects to hold foreign nationals outside U.S. sovereign territory. It claims Guantanamo as a judicial-free zone for the people it captures in the war on terrorism. . . . That position has no precedent in our history; it contravenes the fundamental ideals upon which this nation was founded and which it has come to symbolize around the world."[28]

With the receipt of the lower courts' opinions, the *Rasul; al Odah* docket was complete, and the lawyers for both sides then turned to the task of preparing for oral argument in the U.S. Supreme Court.

The oral argument took place on April 20, 2004. For the plaintiffs, John J. Gibbons, of Newark, New Jersey, spoke. The U.S. solicitor general, Theodore B. Olson, argued for the Bush administration. It was a classic confrontation between two unalterably opposed sides in the dispute, one of between ten and twenty such confrontations that occur in the Court annually.[29]

On its face, the question raised in the foreign detainees consolidated case was a jurisdictional one: Do the federal courts have the constitutional authority to hear habeas corpus petitions from foreign nationals detained as enemy combatants in Guantánamo? However, as all observers noted in their commentaries, the fact that the Court granted certiorari in the face of the Bush administration's rhetoric—about the need for the president to have a judicially and congressionally unfettered ability to fight his wars—was in itself a very *substantive* action. For the very first time, a coequal branch of the federal government, the U.S. Supreme Court, was going to examine the complex issue of the treatment of enemy combatants. The Court's examination began when the thousands of pages of briefs were received by the Clerk's Office. It continued with the oral arguments that took place in the Court's small courtroom.

There was another hint about the focus of the justices: In his brief on the merits, Solicitor General Olson had phrased the question he believed the Court must confront thus: Whether federal courts have jurisdiction to decide the legality of detaining "aliens captured abroad in connection with ongoing hostilities and held outside the sovereign territory of the United States at [Guantánamo]." In contrast, the Court worded the question quite differently: "Whether the United States courts lack jurisdiction to consider challenges to the legality of the detention of foreign nationals captured abroad in connection with hostilities and incarcerated at [Guantánamo]." The Court's phrasing of the question of law "incorporated no assumption about whether the base was or was not 'outside the sovereign territory of the United States.'"[30]

That question was one the Court would decide for itself. The justices ignored the "Judges Keep Out" messages the Bush administration legal spokespersons sent in the legal briefs and in oral argument. As one astute observer wrote at the time: "[Nothing can] diminish the importance of what happened Monday, when the Supreme Court could have turned away but decided, instead, to decide."[31]

The justices heard oral arguments in the two foreign detainees cases on April 20, 2004. Gibbons, the lawyer for the plaintiffs and a former judge for the U.S. Court of Appeals for the Third Circuit, started the argument. "What is at stake in this case is the authority of the Federal courts to uphold the rule of law." Guantánamo, he intoned, is "a lawless enclave, insulating the executive branch from any scrutiny now or in the future."[32] The chief Justice, William Rehnquist, interrupted Gibbons to ask a question. "Suppose your clients were detained for only six months. Does that weaken your case?"

Gibbons: "It wouldn't weaken it at all."

Rehnquist: "So they would have a habeas corpus entitlement, in your view, within weeks after their detention?"

Gibbons: "They would have had entitlement to the process."

Justice Anthony M. Kennedy, one of two key swing voters on the Supreme Court since the late 1980s (the other was Justice O'Connor), wanted Gibbons to tell him what substantive rights, beyond the right to enter a courtroom, should be conferred on these detainees. "What happens when the person comes before the court? What is a judge supposed to do?" Kennedy asked.

Gibbons: "[He] determines first whether or not the government's response that the detention is legal is in fact an adequate response."

The questioning then turned to the issue of jurisdiction of federal courts given the 1950 *Eisentrager* precedent that denied convicted German prisoners held abroad the right to seek habeas relief in federal courts.

Justice Breyer's question brought the focus back to what substantive rights enemy prisoners are entitled to under the laws of war. Couldn't the Geneva Conventions be used to flesh out the basic due process rights of detainees? he inquired. Gibbons, seeing this opening, immediately agreed. Breyer responded, "You're not simply being polite?"

The next set of questions dealt with the question the Court wanted addressed by both parties in the briefs and in oral argument: What is the legal status of Guantánamo?

Gibbons: "GTMO, as I can attest from a year of personal experience [he was an officer in the navy], is under complete United States control and has been for a century."

Ginsburg: "We don't need your personal experience. That's what it says in the treaty. It says complete jurisdiction."

Gibbons: "That's exactly what it says in the lease, yes."

Rehnquist: "Now, it also says Cuba retains [ultimate] sovereignty."

Gibbons: "It does not say that. It says that if the United States decides to surrender the perpetual lease, Cuba has ultimate sovereignty. . . . Cuban law doesn't apply there. Cuban law has never had any application inside that base."

Justice Antonin Scalia interrupted to point out that, in his view, ultimate sovereignty resides with Cuba. Guantánamo is foreign territory, and *Eisentrager* is applicable: "The treaty recognizes the continuance of the ultimate sovereignty of the Republic of Cuba over the leased area. . . . It's the law of the land, as you say."

Gibbons responded by noting, again, that the United States maintains de facto control over Guantánamo: "If one of the detainees [in Guantánamo] assaulted another detainee in GTMO, there's no question they'd be prosecuted under American law." He added an afterthought: "A stamp with Fidel Castro's picture on it couldn't get a letter off base." In his closing moment, Gibbons

reminded the Court that the Bush administration had created in Guantánamo "a no-law zone, not accountable to any judiciary, anywhere." He sat
down, having used up his thirty minutes.

Solicitor General Olson began his argument by reminding the justices that
"the United States is at war. Over 10,000 American troops are in Afghanistan
today, in response to a virtually unanimous Congressional declaration of an
unusual and extraordinary threat to our national security, and an authorization to the President to use all necessary and appropriate force to deter and
prevent acts of terrorism against the United States." Furthermore, given *Eisentrager*, there was *absolutely* no federal court jurisdiction. No judge, including
the justices of the U.S. Supreme Court, had the constitutional authority to entertain a petition for habeas corpus from a foreign-born detainee held at
Guantánamo.

Justice John Paul Stevens interrupted with a question: Would the government argument be different if the war on terror was over? No, quickly answered the solicitor general. Justice O'Connor asked Olson whether the
government argument would be different if the petitioners were American
citizens. Yes, he responded. Justice Kennedy, however, was not happy with the
answer: "This is a prisoner, detained by the United States," he said, and the
federal habeas corpus statute seemed to give that prisoner the right to seek
habeas corpus relief in a federal court.

Justice Breyer then opined that there had to be a middle way between the
President's "lock-'em-up forever" position and the "sweeping-rights for detainees" position. The Bush administration's belief leaves "the executive free to
do whatever they want" without any check "and gets in the way" of more than
200 years of American legal history. While he understood that the Bush administration did not want "undue court interference," what would be wrong
with the Supreme Court "helping you shape" the substantive rights of these
enemy prisoners? Olson took umbrage at Breyer's view that the executive
branch had unchecked power regarding the treatment of enemy detainees.
There *is* a check on the president, he said: the Congress. That coordinate
branch had had fifty-four years to change the federal habeas corpus statute in
light of the *Eisentrager* ruling but had chosen not to act. Justice Scalia agreed
with Olson's response. He said, "If the people think that this is unfair, if Congress thinks it's unfair, [they] can change [the law] with a stroke of a pen."
Turning to Breyer, he said that courts, including the Supreme Court, "don't
exist to legislate the rights of enemy combatants."

Olson: "That's precisely correct. Congress has also dealt with the habeas statute in a variety of ways and has seen fit in no way to change the decision required by this Court with respect to the statute." However, Justice Souter was moved to respond to Scalia's comments. "In bringing people from Afghanistan to GTMO, we are doing in functional terms exactly what we would do if we brought them to the District of Columbia, leaving aside the metaphysics of ultimate sovereignty."

Olson: "The Court . . . specifically addressed that [question], and held that the United States did not have sovereignty for the enforcement of its laws in Guantanamo."

Souter: "We've been doing a pretty good job of it since then, am I right?"

Justice Breyer, at the end of Olson's thirty minutes, said that he was still "honestly most worried about the fact that there would be a large category of unchecked and uncheckable actions dealing with the detention of individuals that are being held in a place where America has power to do everything."

At the close of the oral argument, the case was submitted to the Court for decision. The decision came down on June 28, 2004, along with the other two enemy detainee cases, *Hamdi* and *Padilla*.

HAMDI V. RUMSFELD AND RUMSFELD V. PADILLA
BEFORE THE JUSTICES

The second set of enemy combatants cases that came to the Supreme Court involved U.S. citizens who were captured in Afghanistan (*Hamdi v. Rumsfeld*)[33] and in Chicago (*Rumsfeld v. Padilla*),[34] labeled "enemy combatants," and confined in naval brigs in the United States without any charges being filed and without even the minimum due process between 2002 and the filing of the 2004 petitions for certiorari. As one libertarian critic wrote, these two cases raise the following question: "Can the President . . . override the ancient writ of *habeas corpus* [for an American citizen]?"[35]

Hamdi v. Rumsfeld
Yaser Esam Hamdi is a Saudi national who was captured as an alleged enemy combatant during ongoing military operations in Afghanistan. Like so many others captured there, he was shipped to Guantánamo. During his initial interrogation, it was revealed that he was born in the United States and was an

American citizen. Hamdi was immediately flown to the United States and transferred to Norfolk Naval Station Brig, where he was held incommunicado without any charges being filed against him and without a legal hearing of any kind. The federal public defender for the Eastern District of Virginia and Christian Peregrim, a private citizen, filed petitions for a writ of habeas corpus as "next friend" of Hamdi.

Robert G. Doumar, senior district judge, sitting in the U.S. District Court for the Eastern District of Virginia, at Norfolk, Virginia, heard the case and concluded that the public defender had properly filed his case as next friend, and he ordered the government to allow him unmonitored access to Hamdi.[36]

The U.S. Court of Appeals for the Fourth Circuit, on January 8, 2003, ruled that Hamdi was not entitled to an attorney and had no legal basis to challenge his confinement. The three-judge panel of appellate judges determined that "the Constitution gives the executive branch the responsibility to wage war and that courts must yield to the military." The appeals court, sitting en banc on July 9, 2003, voted 8–4 to uphold the panel's ruling.

On October 1, 2003, Hamdi's father, Esam Fouad Hamdi, asked the U.S. Supreme Court to grant certiorari to determine whether an American citizen labeled as "enemy combatant" and held in a military brig in America could be held without charges and without due process of law. The Court docketed the case one day after Hamdi's petition for certiorari and motion was filed for leave to proceed in forma pauperis.[37] Two amicus curiae petitions were filed on October 3, 2003.

The Hamdi petition for certiorari was prepared and filed by Frank W. Dunham Jr., the federal public defender of the Eastern District, U.S. District Court, Virginia. It presented three questions for the justices to consider:

1. "Does the Constitution permit executive officials to detain an American citizen indefinitely in military custody in the United States, hold him essentially incommunicado and deny him access to counsel, with no opportunity to question the factual basis for his detention before any impartial tribunal, on the sole ground that he was seized abroad in a theatre of the War on Terrorism and declared by the Executive to be an 'enemy combatant'"?
2. "Is the indefinite detention of an American citizen seized abroad . . . permissible under applicable congressional statutes and treaty provisions?"

3. "In a habeas corpus proceeding, . . . does the separation of powers doctrine preclude a federal court from following ordinary statutory procedures and conducting an inquiry into the factual basis for the Executive branch's asserted justification of the detention?"[38]

In petitioning the Supreme Court for the granting of a writ of certiorari, the petitioner must show some very clear and important reasons why the Court should grant the request. Of the more than 9,000 petitions for certiorari received by the Court in a given year, only between 70 and 80 are granted by the Court.[39] Rule 10, Considerations Governing Review on Certiorari, of the Court's own rules, modified most recently in May 2005, lays out what the Court looks for and *must* find in order to grant the writ of certiorari:

> *Review on a writ of certiorari is not a matter of right, but of judicial discretion. A petition for a writ of certiorari will be granted only for compelling reasons.* The following, although neither controlling nor fully measuring the Court's discretion, indicate the character of the reasons the Court considers:
>
> (a) a United States court of appeals has entered a decision in conflict with the decision of another United States court of appeals on the same important matter; has decided an important federal question in a way that conflicts with a decision by a state court of last resort; or has so far departed from the accepted and usual course of judicial proceedings, or sanctioned such a departure by a lower court, as to call for an exercise of this Court's supervisory power;
>
> (b) a state court of last resort has decided an important federal question in a way that conflicts with the decision of another state court of last resort or of a United States court of appeals;
>
> (c) a state court or a United States court of appeals has decided an important question of federal law that has not been, but should be, settled by this Court, or has decided an important federal question in a way that conflicts with relevant decisions of this Court.
>
> *A petition for a writ of certiorari is rarely granted when the asserted error consists of erroneous factual findings or the misapplication of a properly stated rule of law.* [My emphasis]

More important than the questions believed to be at the heart of the litigation are the *reasons presented* for granting the petition. Dunham followed the guidelines in Rule 10. The brief stated that the case "presents issues of *fundamental importance,*" that "the Court of Appeals' ruling *conflicts*" with prior decisions of the Supreme Court, and that "review is warranted because the ruling is *contrary to constitutional protections and congressional limitations against indefinite detention without due process*" (my emphasis).[40]

On December 3, 2003, the brief in opposition to the granting of certiorari was filed on behalf of the respondent, Secretary of Defense Rumsfeld, by the solicitor general. The solicitor general's brief, whether as respondent (in this case), as petitioner (as in *Padilla*), or even as an amicus curiae (in cases it either chooses to file or is asked to file by the Supreme Court), carries gargantuan weight as the Court determines—throughout the year—which petitions for certiorari will be granted. Four justices must vote to grant a certiorari petition. While less than 1 percent of the total number of certiorari petitions are granted, the statistics change dramatically if the government is involved. Whether in getting certiorari granted (when the government is a petitioner or files an amicus curiae brief) or in convincing the Court not to grant certiorari (when the solicitor general is respondent), the government has 75–80 percent success at the initial stage of the Court's decision-making process.

For Solicitor General Olson, who prepared the government's brief for the respondents in opposition to the granting of certiorari, the issue was clear:

> After careful consideration and multiple appeals, the court of appeals concluded that respondents have established the legality of Hamdi's detention, and that Hamdi therefore is not entitled to habeas relief. *That decision is correct and does not conflict with any decision of this Court or of any other court of appeals.* To the contrary, the military detention at issue in this case is consistent with this Court's precedents recognizing the President's authority to capture and detain combatants in wartime, Congress's express statutory backing of the President's use of all necessary and appropriate military force in connection with the current conflict, and the time-honored laws and customs of war. Petitioners devote the bulk of their petition to re-airing their objections to the legality of Hamdi's detention. The court of appeals correctly rejected those objections, and they provide no basis to grant further review in this Court.[41]

On December 17, 2003, the Court received the reply brief of the petitioners. It presented a number of arguments to counter Olson's position. Dunham argued that "the . . . incommunicado imprisonment of a citizen solely on the authority of the military, with no opportunity for any hearing to test the factual basis for the prolonged detention, offends the nation's first and most enduring principles." He maintained, in opposition to the Olson brief, that this case turns on whether the Executive has the power to detain a citizen without explicit sanction from Congress far from any theater of conflict and more than two years after any exigency has grown stale. What separates the parties is a competing view of the separation of powers—one in which the Judiciary is entrusted to review, and the Legislature is empowered to limit, the detention of citizens by the Executive, and another in which all power over citizens declared by the military to be "enemy combatants" is held exclusively by the Executive branch and is subject to only cursory judicial review. Reversing the decision below will ensure constitutional protection in the handful of cases in which the Executive claims that an American citizen is an "enemy combatant" but chooses not to prosecute for a criminal offense or an offense against the laws of war. An affirmance will unleash a new and far-reaching executive power to imprison citizens indefinitely that cannot be restrained by the other two branches of government.[42]

On January 9, 2004, the Court granted the certiorari petition and leave to file in forma pauperis. By this time, given that the Court had already granted certiorari in the Guantánamo detainees cases, the Bush administration was angered, but not surprised, by the decision to grant certiorari in *Hamdi.* The Court asked the parties to address the following questions in their briefs on the merits and in oral argument:

1. Does the Constitution permit Executive officials to detain an American citizen indefinitely in military custody in the United States, hold him essentially incommunicado and deny him access to counsel, with no opportunity to question the factual basis for his detention before any impartial tribunal, on the sole ground that he was seized abroad in a theater of the War on Terrorism and declared by the Executive to be an "enemy combatant"?

2. Is the indefinite detention of an American citizen seized abroad but held in the United States solely on the assertion of Executive officials that he is an "enemy combatant" permissible under applicable congressional statutes and treaty provisions?

3. In a habeas corpus proceeding challenging the indefinite detention of an American citizen seized abroad, detained in the United States, and declared by Executive officials to be an "enemy combatant," does the separation of powers doctrine preclude a federal court from following ordinary statutory procedures and conducting an inquiry into the

factual basis for the Executive branch's asserted justification of the detention?

During February, eleven amicus curiae briefs supporting the plaintiffs were filed with the Court. Some of the groups filing were the ACLU, ABA, Cato Institute, Experts on the Law of War, Certain Former Prisoners of War, and Global Rights.[43]

In February Dunham presented Hamdi's brief on the merits to the justices. In the fifty-page document, the lawyers for the petitioner argued that Bush went beyond the authority he had as commander in chief when he labeled Hamdi an enemy combatant and shipped him to a navy brig, where, for two years, he was held incommunicado, without the benefit of counsel and without a hearing regarding his status. "Although 'the powers of the three branches are not always neatly defined,' . . . the power to authorize the indefinite detention of citizens by the federal government is . . . firmly entrusted to Congress. The court of appeals therefore erred by recognizing an illegitimate power of the Executive to make its own law."[44]

On March 29 the brief on the merits of the case was filed by the Bush administration lawyers. The government's argument had four major themes.

First, the government's brief held that the petitioners' legal challenges to Hamdi's wartime detention were without merit because the challenged wartime detention fell squarely within the commander in chief's war powers; Hamdi's detention was bolstered by and was by no means contrary to the actions of Congress, in particular the 2001 AUMF; and Hamdi's detention was consistent with Article 5 of the 1949 Geneva Conventions and the military's own regulations. "In our constitutional system," the government's brief maintained, "the responsibility for waging war is committed to the political branches. In time of war, the President, as Commander in Chief, has the authority to capture and detain enemy combatants for the duration of hostilities. That includes enemy combatants presumed to be United States citizens."

Second, under any constitutionally appropriate standard, the record demonstrates that Hamdi was an "enemy combatant":

> The scope of judicial review that is available concerning the military's determination that an individual is an enemy combatant is necessarily limited by the fundamental separation-of-powers concerns raised by a court's review or second-guessing of such a core military judgment in wartime. Applying an appropriately deferential standard of review, the court of appeals correctly

concluded that the record adequately demonstrates that Hamdi is indeed an enemy combatant. The sworn declaration accompanying the government's return explains that Hamdi surrendered with an enemy unit in a theater of combat operations while armed with an AK-47, and that he is therefore a prototypical enemy combatant.

Third, the necessarily limited scope of review in this extraordinary context comported with the Constitution and the federal habeas statutes; neither the suspension clause, the habeas statutes, nor the common law required additional proceedings for Hamdi: "A captured enemy combatant who is being detained during the conflict—and has not been charged with any crime—has no right under the law of war to meet with counsel to plot a legal strategy to secure his release. The Due Process Clause—which is interpreted in the light of that long-settled rule—does not supply any different guarantee."

And finally, the government held that the alternative proceeding envisioned by the district court and petitioners could not be supported constitutionally: "Any attempt at further factual development concerning the military's enemy-combatant determination would *present formidable constitutional and practical difficulties.* Attempting to recreate the scene of Hamdi's capture is inconsistent with the practical reality that the troops in Afghanistan are charged with winning a war and not preparing to defend their judgments in a U.S. courtroom."

The reply brief from Hamdi's lawyers was filed on April 20. Their brief response to the government's arguments was essentially a replay of their earlier arguments: (1) The due process clause guarantees Hamdi the right to be heard in federal courts; (2) Congress can, and has, limited the executive's authority to detain enemy belligerents who are American citizens; (3) only Congress possesses the authority to permit the president to detain citizens for an indefinite period, and Congress has not done so.

Rumsfeld v. Padilla

On May 8, 2002, Jose Padilla, a U.S. citizen, was arrested at O'Hare Airport in Chicago on "suspicion of plotting acts of espionage in the United States on behalf of al Qaeda." (According to the government, he arrived in Chicago after months of training with al Qaeda terrorists in Pakistan. He was accused of plotting to build and detonate a radiological dirty bomb.) He was quickly taken to New York for detention in regular criminal custody after federal agents apprehended him while executing a material witness warrant issued by the U.S. District Court for the Southern District of New York (Southern District) in connection with its grand-jury investigation into the September 11, 2001, al Qaeda terrorist attacks.

While Padilla's motion to vacate the warrant was pending, the president, on June 9, 2002, issued an order to Secretary of Defense Rumsfeld designating Padilla an enemy combatant and directing that he be detained in military custody. Padilla was then moved to a navy brig in Charleston, South Carolina, where he was held until the government, in late 2005, charged Padilla and others with criminal actions in a federal district court in Florida and moved Padilla to a federal facility in that state to await trial there.

His counsel, Donna Newman, filed a habeas petition in the U.S. District Court for the Southern District of New York (Southern District). The petition, as amended, alleged that Padilla's military detention violated the Constitution and named as respondents the president, the secretary of defense, and Cdr. Melanie Marr, the brig's commander. Two days before he was to appear in federal district court in New York on Newman's motion to free him by dropping the material witness warrant, President Bush classified him as an enemy combatant and placed him in protracted, incommunicado military detention. Like Hamdi, Padilla was isolated in a navy brig and was not allowed to speak to an attorney or his family. Nor was the ICRC allowed to visit him.

The government moved to dismiss the habeas petition, arguing that Commander Marr, as Padilla's immediate custodian, was the only proper respondent and that the district court lacked jurisdiction over her because she was located outside the Southern District. The district court held that the secretary's personal involvement in Padilla's military custody rendered him a proper respondent and that it could assert jurisdiction over the secretary under New York's so-called long-arm statute, notwithstanding his absence from the district. On the merits, the district court accepted the government's contention that the president has authority as commander in chief to detain as enemy combatants citizens captured on American soil during a time of war.

On December 18, 2003, another federal appeals court, the U.S. Court of Appeals for the Second Circuit, in the case of *Jose Padilla and Donna R. Newman, as Next Friend of Jose Padilla v. Donald Rumsfeld* (352 F. 3rd. 695 [2nd Cir., 2003]) ruled against the Bush administration. The divided appeals court concluded that President Bush lacked the authority to indefinitely detain a U.S. citizen arrested on American soil on suspicion of terrorism by declaring him an enemy combatant.

Even the sole dissenter on the three-judge federal appellate panel, Richard Wesley, agreed with his colleagues that Bush did not have any constitutional authority to deny Padilla access to an attorney. "No one," said Wesley in his opinion, "has suspended the Great Writ," and therefore Padilla was entitled to an attorney to file the papers in a federal court. Furthermore, Wesley also noted, while the Congress had the power to legislate in this area, the president, on his own authority and absent congressional authority, did not: "The President, acting alone, possesses no inherent constitutional authority to detain American citizens seized within the United States, away from the zone of combat, as enemy combatants. . . . Presidential authority does not exist in a vacuum, and this case involves not whether those responsibilities should be aggressively pursued, but whether the president is obligated . . . to share them with Congress."[45]

The judges on the second circuit court gave the Department of Defense thirty days to either release Padilla or charge him criminally in federal court. The administration immediately appealed the ruling of the federal appeals court to the U.S. Supreme Court. Bush's press secretary, Scott McClellan, told reporters, "The President's most solemn obligation is protecting the American people. We believe the Second Circuit ruling is troubling and flawed. The President has directed the Justice Department to seek a stay, and further judicial review." The petition for an *expedited* writ of certiorari was filed by Solicitor General Olson on January 16, 2004. That motion to expedite consideration was granted by the Court four days later, on January 20, 2004. On February 4, the brief of Jose Padilla and Donna Newman in opposition was filed with the Court. In it Newman, still Padilla's lawyer, wrote:

> The Government's assertion of Executive power in this case is raw and stark. After 20 months, the Government has not brought any charges against Padilla stemming from his alleged participation in a plot to commit a terrorist act. . . . There is a profound difference between the historical practice of detention of prisoners of war on the field of battle, and the new power the President claims here to deem the entire nation a battlefield in which any person may be seized and held without trial for the indefinite future. The risk of error, and the potential for abuse, are much greater in this new context, for the Executive's novel argument would allow it to exile any citizen from the protection of our Constitution and laws simply through the artifice of labeling him—without any visible standards—as an "enemy combatant."[46]

Finally, in short order, on February 11, the response brief of the petitioner (the Bush administration) was submitted.

Because the *Hamdi* case was already scheduled for oral argument on April 28, 2004, both parties moved swiftly to file their briefs with the Court in order to argue the case alongside *Hamdi*. On February 20, 2004, one month after the Court had granted the motion to expedite, the certiorari petition was granted, and the Court set oral argument in the *Padilla* case on the same day as *Hamdi*'s. All briefs on the merits were due in the Court by April 21, 2004. Oral argument was set for the following week.[47]

The Oral Argument in Hamdi v. Rumsfeld

On April 28, 2004, the oral arguments in *Hamdi* and *Padilla* took place—one week after the oral arguments in *Rasul*. During the hour of oral argument allotted to each case, "the justices probed both sides with tough questions, expressing concerns about detention with so little oversight, about infringing on presidential war powers, and—in Padilla's case—about whether the Supreme Court has jurisdiction to decide the matter at all."[48]

There were two issues that stood out in the two oral arguments involving American citizens labeled as enemy combatants and held indefinitely without any due process rights: "Hamdi is saying," said Marcia Coyle, Washington, D.C., bureau chief at the *National Law Journal,* "that as an American citizen, he has a right to full [due] process in American courts. And he and Padilla are both challenging the authority of the President to hold them indefinitely as enemy combatants."[49]

Frank Dunham, the lead counsel for petitioner Hamdi, spoke first and zoomed in on the habeas corpus relief issue: The "historical core of habeas corpus is to challenge extrajudicial executive detention. It cannot be a violation of the separation of powers for a [federal district] court to perform its judicial function of inquiry into long-term, indefinite detention of a citizen in a habeas corpus proceeding."[50]

Justice O'Connor began the questioning, asking whether habeas relief is available to every American citizen caught while fighting with the enemy: "What precedents do we look to?"

Dunham replied that that allegation at the core of her question has never been proved in court, for there have been no court proceedings regarding Hamdi's incarceration since his arrival in Guantánamo in January 2002. In response to tough questions from the chief justice and from Justice Scalia, Dunham again pointed out that Hamdi "has never been allowed to give any kind of explanation of his side of the story."

On another tack, Dunham argued that Congress never authorized the Guantánamo detentions. When O'Connor pointed out that Congress had passed the September 2001 AUMF Resolution and said that it affected "this very conflict," Dunham replied, "[The AUMF] doesn't have the word 'detention' anywhere in it. It talks about the use of force and it is the equivalent, in our view, of a declaration of war. . . . When Congress passed the AUMF, it did not say we suspend habeas. Habeas corpus statutes are still on the books."

Justice Kennedy noted that the AUMF was authorization for the president "to use his judgment. It was not a list of things he can do."

Dunham: "If that [AUMF] is interpreted to mean that he can impose detention on anybody that he thinks is necessary in order to fulfill [the AUMF's] command, we could have people locked up all over the country tomorrow without any due process, without any opportunity to be heard, because we know that this war that we're talking about here is going on worldwide and it's going on within our borders."

Dunham reserved the balance of his thirty minutes for rebuttal after the government argument concluded.

On this day in open court, Deputy Solicitor General Paul Clement (who became the solicitor general after Olson left the office) argued the government's case. He began by pointing out, as had Olson one week earlier, that a reason for the detention of Hamdi was to keep him "from rejoining the battlefield" while the United States still had 10,000 American troops "remain[ing] on the field of battle in Afghanistan."

Justice Ginsburg asked Clement to explain why the government chose to try certain enemy detainees in federal courts while holding Hamdi and Padilla in navy brigs indefinitely without any due process rights whatsoever:[51] "How does the government justify some going through the criminal process and others just being held indefinitely?"

Clement: "Well Justice Ginsburg, I think that reflects a sound exercise of prosecutorial and executive discretion. There are some individuals who may be captured in a situation where they do not have any particular intelligence value [and therefore] can be dealt with in the [judicial system]. But there are plenty of individuals who either have a paramount intelligence value [so] that putting them into the [judicial system] immediately and providing them with counsel, whose first advice would certainly be to not talk to the government is a counterproductive way to proceed in these cases." (One commentator noted the surrealism of this argument: "The notion that the government will learn more from interrogating Hamdi, a Taliban foot soldier, than Moussaoui, a man who ate ice cream with ranking al Qaeda members, is so preposterous that it cannot just be left on this page to die.")[52]

Souter raised the issue of the appropriateness of 18 *U.S. Code*, sec. 4001 (the statute that prohibits the incarceration of American citizens without congressional authorization) in this case: "I take it it's the government's position that 4001 has absolutely no application to the situation. That it simply refers to the normal circumstances of the criminal law. Is that right?"

Clement: "That's right, Justice Souter." He added that the September 18, 2001, AUMF authorized such presidential actions.

Souter: "It doesn't follow that it is adequate for all time. . . . The question I would be interested in is this. Is it reasonable to think that the [AUMF] was sufficient at the time it was passed, but that at some point, it is a Congressional responsibility, and ultimately a constitutional right on this person's part, for Congress to assess the situation and either pass a more specific continuing authorization or at least to come up with the conclusion that its prior authorization was good enough. . . . It's two and a half years later. . . . Does the AUMF, like Wrigley's gum, just last an extra, extra, extra long time?"

Justice Breyer then asked a very substantive question. "The operative words in the 2001 AUMF are 'necessary and appropriate,' and also the words in the Constitution are 'due process of law.' And also the words in the Magna Carta were 'according to law.' And whatever form of words in any of these documents there are, it seemed to refer to one basic idea that's minimum. *That a person who contests something of importance is entitled to a neutral decision maker and an opportunity to present proofs and arguments.* . . . I want a practical answer. I don't want a—yes" (my emphasis).

Clement: "The practical answer that you are looking for assumes a process that's never been provided."

Clement insisted that Hamdi had been screened at least two times, on the battlefield and in Guantánamo. "The interrogation process," he said, "also provides an opportunity for him to say this has all been a mistake." The justices, seemingly stunned by this outlandish retort, were silent for a moment. Then they began peppering Clement with more questions.

Justice Ginsburg: "Doesn't he have a right to tell some tribunal, in his own words?"

Clement: "He does have a right to say, in his own words. . . ."

Souter: "When? During interrogation?"

Clement: "During interrogation. During the initial screening. During the screening in GTMO. . . . The interrogation process itself provides an opportunity for an individual to explain that this has all been a mistake."

Justice O'Connor then raised the issue of the open-endedness of the Bush administration's war on terror: "We've never had a situation where this war could last 25 years or 50 years."

Breyer: "Let's say it's the 100 Years' War. Is there no opportunity for a court, in your view, to say that this violates, for an American citizen, the elementary due process that the Constitution guarantees?"

Clement: "The Courts remain open."

Souter: "But your answer to Justice Breyer's and Justice O'Connor's questions, I thought, was, we don't have to worry or a court should not be worrying about the indefiniteness of the time because it may well be that the President or the Congress will at some point say that the war in Afghanistan is no longer a matter of concern and, therefore, we don't have to hold the Hamdis. Am I wrong?"

Clement: "I mean, can you imagine a situation where the evidence and the government's own affidavit shows that somebody's only detained with regard to the war in Afghanistan. And then you could imagine that that has been signed, sealed, and delivered—it's over, the president says so, the Congress says so—and there's an effort to continue to detain that individual."

Souter: "Well, I can imagine it and I can also imagine that the concern about Afghanistan will go on as long as there is concern about al Qaeda, and there is no end point that we can see at this point to that. So that it seems to me your answer boils down to saying, 'Don't worry about the timing question, we'll tell you when it's over.'"

In a brief four-minute rebuttal period, essentially an impassioned soliloquy (for no justice asked a question), Dunham said to the justices that Clement

is a worthy advocate who is able to make the unreasonable sound reasonable. But when you take his argument at its core, it is: "Trust us." And who's saying, "trust us"? The executive branch. And why do we have the great writ? *We have the Great Writ because we didn't trust the executive branch when we founded this government. That's why the government saying "trust us" is no excuse for taking away and driving a truck through the right of habeas corpus and the Fifth Amendment that "no man shall be deprived of liberty except upon due process of law."* . . . [My emphasis]

We have a small problem here. One citizen. . . . Is it better to give him rights, or is it better to start a new dawn of saying there are circumstances where you can't file a writ of habeas corpus, and there are circumstances where you can't get due process? I think not. I would urge the Court not to go down that road. I would urge the Court to find that citizens can only be detained by law. . . . And here there is no law. Until Congress acts, these detentions are not lawful. And I would respectfully ask this court to step up to the plate and say so.

Dunham sat down and the case, intoned the chief justice, "is submitted."

The Oral Argument in Rumsfeld v. Padilla

The *Padilla* case was argued immediately after the *Hamdi* argument ended. The government's advocate, Paul Clement, spoke first. As he had in *Hamdi*, throughout this argument Clement repeated the Bush administration's mantra that neither Congress nor the federal courts can put any limits on executive power in wartime. The September 2001 AUMF resolution gave the president the power to make "discretionary judgments in finding out what is necessary and appropriate force."

He started off by distinguishing this case from the *Hamdi* petition: "This case raises only two relatively discrete questions. First, whether the habeas petition in this case, challenging Padilla's present physical confinement in South Carolina, was properly filed in Manhattan. . . . Second, whether the President has the authority to detain a citizen who travels abroad, affiliates and then associates with the enemy abroad, . . . and then returns to the United States at the direction of the enemy to commit hostile and warlike acts."[53]

After some moments were spent discussing the venue matter, Justice Breyer interrupted: "Let me ask you a question to get you to the merits, if I can. . . . Why would it be necessary and appropriate in a country that has its courts open, that has regular criminal proceedings, . . . to proceed [against a citizen] by other than the normal court procedure?"

Clement: "Why? It is precisely because, in this war on terrorism, the government can confront an individual who is . . . guilty of past war crimes."

Ginsburg: "Can we punish him?"

Clement: "Certainly we could punish him."

Ginsburg: "Would you shoot him when he got off the plane? . . . If the law is what the Executive says it is, so what is it that would be a check against torture? . . . Suppose the executive says mild torture we think will help get this information?"

Clement: "In situations where there is a war—where the Government is on a war footing, . . . you have to *trust* the executive to make the kind of quintessential military judgments that are involved in things like that" (my emphasis).

Justice O'Connor, evidently perturbed by Clement's categorical argument, asked him why "a neutral decision maker of some kind" could not determine whether a detainee was being illegally held. Clement instantly responded: "For all intents and purposes, the government's own process of deciding who should be held was a neutral decision maker."

Justice Scalia had been uncharacteristically quiet until about this time in the oral argument.

Scalia: "I understand the commander-in-chief power to be a power over the military forces, when they're being used as military forces, [but] it doesn't mean that he has power to do whatever it takes to win the war."

Clement: "No, but . . . you have the authority to detain individuals, even if they're not formal military officers."

Jennifer Martinez, a law professor at Stanford Law School, next argued on behalf of Padilla. She opened with a razor-sharp observation:

> Even in wartime, America has always been a nation governed by the rule of law. Today the government asks this court for a broad ruling that would allow the president unlimited power to imprison any American anywhere at any time without trial simply by labeling him an enemy combatant. . . . We simply ask this Court to hold that at a minimum Congress would have to clearly and unequivocally authorize such a departure from our nation's traditions. And since Congress has not done so, Mr. Padilla is entitled to be charged with a crime and to have his day in court.

Interestingly, perhaps because the justices had poured themselves out in the *Hamdi* oral arguments, there were only a handful of substantive questions addressed to Martinez during her thirty minutes in front of the justices.

During the *Padilla* oral argument, one jurisdictional problem was discussed at length: the standing/jurisdiction issue. Had Padilla's habeas corpus petition been filed in the right venue? Newman filed the petition in a federal district court in New York City one day after Padilla had been moved to a navy brig in South Carolina. As it turned out, for five justices—a majority—the venue matter became the critical determinant in their resolution of the case.

Once Rehnquist declared *Padilla* "submitted to the Court," the justices had to vote in chambers and then write their decisions on these two American citizen/enemy combatant cases. It was clear from the oral arguments heard in all three cases that the justices would be writing a number of majority, plurality, concurring, and dissenting opinions.

A few days after the oral arguments concluded, the hundreds of shocking Abu Ghraib photos were released.

THE THREE JUNE 28, 2004, SUPREME COURT DECISIONS

On June 28, 2004, the Court began to answer some—*but not all*—of the questions raised in these cases. In two of three opinions handed down that day, Court majorities forcefully acted to limit the actions of President Bush in his war on terror. And in those two opinions, *Rasul* and *Hamdi,* every justice except Justice Clarence Thomas criticized Bush's actions. The justices told President Bush that he could not ignore domestic and international law in the government's handling of enemy combatants captured in Afghanistan and in Iraq after September 11, 2001. However, because there were ten opinions written in the three cases, the Court's message was not as clear as the detainees' lawyers wished.

Rasul v. Bush

In *Rasul v. Bush* the Court decided in favor of the plaintiffs, overturning the U.S. Court of Appeals for the District of Columbia Circuit. Justice Stevens wrote the opinion for the five-person majority. Justice Kennedy wrote a concurring opinion. There were three dissenting votes: Chief Justice Rehnquist, and Justices Scalia and Thomas.

In the two cases, the district court had construed the suits as habeas petitions and dismissed them for want of jurisdiction, holding that under *Eisentrager* aliens detained outside U.S. sovereign territory may not invoke habeas relief. The court of appeals affirmed. The Stevens majority opinion held that U.S. courts have jurisdiction to consider challenges to the legality of the detention of foreign nationals captured abroad in connection with hostilities and incarcerated at Guantánamo Bay:

> At its historical core, the writ of habeas corpus has served as a means of reviewing the legality of Executive detention, and it is in that context that its protections

have been strongest. . . . The question now before us is whether the habeas statute confers a right to judicial review of the legality of Executive detention of aliens in a territory over which the United States exercises plenary and exclusive jurisdiction, but not 'ultimate sovereignty.' . . . Application of the habeas statute to persons detained at [Guantanamo] is consistent with the historical reach of the writ of habeas corpus. At common law, courts exercised habeas jurisdiction over the claims of aliens detained within sovereign territory of the realm. . . . In the end, the answer to the question presented is clear. Petitioners contend that they are being held in federal custody in violation of the laws of the United States. Section 2241 [the Habeas Corpus Statute], by its terms, requires nothing more. . . . We therefore hold that §2241 confers on the District Court jurisdiction to hear petitioners' habeas corpus challenges to the legality of their detention at the Guantanamo Bay Naval Base.[54]

Stevens's majority opinion rejected the government's "primary submission that these cases are controlled by *Eisentrager*'s holding." *Rasul, al Odah* and the other petitioners differed from the *Eisentrager* detainees in important respects: They are not nationals of countries at war with the United States; they deny they have engaged in or plotted acts of aggression against this country; they have never been afforded access to any tribunal, much less charged with and convicted of wrongdoing; and for more than two years they have been imprisoned in territory over which the United States exercises exclusive jurisdiction and control. The opinion concluded with a final paragraph of judicial parsimony:

> *Whether and what further proceedings may become necessary after respondents make their response to the merits of petitioners' claims are matters that we need not address now.* What is presently at stake is only whether the federal courts have jurisdiction to determine the legality of the Executive's potentially indefinite detention of individuals who claim to be wholly innocent of wrongdoing. Answering that question in the affirmative, we reverse the judgment of the Court of Appeals and remand for the District Court to consider in the first instance the merits of petitioners' claims. It is so ordered. [My emphasis]

Justice Kennedy concurred with the majority opinion, but his analysis differed from the Stevens factual assessment in

> two critical ways. . . . First, Guantanamo Bay is in every practical respect a United States territory, and it is one far removed from any hostilities. . . . The second critical set of facts is that the detainees at Guantanamo Bay are being held indefinitely, and without benefit of any legal proceeding to determine their status. In *Eisentrager*, the prisoners were tried and convicted by a military commission of

violating the laws of war and were sentenced to prison terms. Having already been subject to procedures establishing their status, they could not justify "a limited opening of our courts" to show that they were "of friendly personal disposition" and not enemy aliens. Indefinite detention without trial or other proceeding presents altogether different considerations. It allows friends and foes alike to remain in detention. . . . In light of the status of Guantanamo Bay and the indefinite pretrial detention of the detainees, I would hold that federal court jurisdiction is permitted in these cases. This approach would avoid creating automatic statutory authority to adjudicate the claims of persons located outside the United States, and remains true to the reasoning of *Eisentrager*. For these reasons, I concur in the judgment of the Court.[55]

There were three dissenters in *Rasul/al Odah:* Chief Justice Rehnquist and Justices Scalia and Thomas. Scalia wrote the dissent, joined by his two colleagues. It was an angry dissent, typical of Scalia. He labeled the majority and the concurring opinions "irresponsible," "monstrous," "clumsy," and "counter-textual" and called them "judicial adventurism." His dissent asserted that the majority "overturned settled law [*Eisentrager*] in a matter of extreme importance to our forces currently in the field," and rejected statutory stare decisis when it "changed the habeas statute," which only Congress could have modified—if it wanted to in a time of war:

This case turns on the words of §2241, a text the Court today largely ignores. Even a cursory reading of the habeas statute shows that it presupposes a federal district court with territorial jurisdiction over the detainee. Section 2241(a) states: "Writs of habeas corpus may be granted by the Supreme Court, any justice thereof, the district courts and any circuit judge *within their respective jurisdictions*." (Emphasis added). It further requires that "[t]he order of a circuit judge shall be entered in the records of *the* district court of *the district wherein the restraint complained of is had*." (emphases added). . . . No matter to whom the writ is directed, custodian or detainee, the statute could not be clearer that a necessary requirement for issuing the writ is that *some* federal district court have territorial jurisdiction over the detainee. Here, as the Court allows, the Guantanamo Bay detainees are not located within the territorial jurisdiction of any federal district court. One would think that is the end of this case.

Scalia argued that because the majority all but ignored *Eisentrager*, it had jettisoned the statutory stare decisis principle:

Departure from our rule of *stare decisis* in statutory cases is always extraordinary; it ought to be unthinkable when the departure has a potentially harmful effect upon the Nation's conduct of a war. The Commander in Chief and his subordinates had every reason to expect that the internment of combatants at Guantanamo Bay would not have the consequence of bringing the cumbersome machinery of our domestic courts into military affairs. Congress is in session. If it wished to change federal judges' habeas jurisdiction from what this Court had previously held that to be, it could have done so. And it could have done so by intelligent revision of the statute, instead of by today's clumsy, countertextual reinterpretation that confers upon wartime prisoners greater habeas rights than domestic detainees.

Scalia's concluding words were as caustic and critical as his opening comments: "For this Court to create such a monstrous scheme in time of war, and in frustration of our military commanders' reliance upon clearly stated prior law, is judicial adventurism of the worst sort. I dissent."[56]

Hamdi v. Rumsfeld

Justice O'Connor wrote for a Court plurality in *Hamdi v. Rumsfeld*. The justice announced the judgment of the Court and delivered an opinion, in which Chief Justice Rehnquist and Justices Kennedy and Breyer joined. Justice Souter filed an opinion concurring in part, dissenting in part, and concurring in the judgment, in which Justice Ginsburg joined. Justice Scalia filed a dissenting opinion, in which Justice Stevens joined. Justice Thomas filed a separate dissenting opinion.

Justice O'Connor, after reviewing the facts and the earlier federal court decisions in *Hamdi,* raised the threshold question: "whether the Executive has the authority to detain citizens who qualify as 'enemy combatants.'"

O'Connor did accept the government's argument that the 2001 AUMF congressional resolution gave President Bush the authority to detain enemy combatants: "The Government maintains that no explicit congressional authorization is required, because the Executive possesses plenary authority to detain pursuant to Article II of the Constitution. We do not reach the question whether Article II provides such authority, however, because we agree with the Government's alternative position, that Congress has in fact authorized Hamdi's detention, through the AUMF."

The next question was whether Hamdi's detention, although authorized by Congress, nevertheless, by denying the petitioner access to counsel, denied Hamdi due process of law:

> Even in cases in which the detention of enemy combatants is legally authorized, there remains the question of what process is constitutionally due to a citizen

who disputes his enemy-combatant status. Hamdi argues that he is owed a meaningful and timely hearing and that "extra-judicial detention [that] begins and ends with the submission of an affidavit based on third-hand hearsay" does not comport with the Fifth and Fourteenth Amendments. The Government counters that any more process than was provided below would be both unworkable and "constitutionally intolerable." Our resolution of this dispute requires a careful examination both of the writ of habeas corpus, which Hamdi now seeks to employ as a mechanism of judicial review, and of the Due Process Clause, which informs the procedural contours of that mechanism in this instance. . . . We reaffirm today the fundamental nature of a citizen's right to be free from involuntary confinement by his own government without due process of law, and we weigh the opposing governmental interests against the curtailment of liberty that such confinement entails.

After engaging in the balancing of the competing interests, O'Connor concluded that due process due citizens outweighs the government's argument that in wartime presidential judgments are primary. Although Congress authorized the detention of combatants in the narrow circumstances alleged in the case, "we hold that a citizen-detainee seeking to challenge his classification as an enemy combatant must receive notice of the factual basis for his classification, and a fair opportunity to rebut the Government's factual assertions before a neutral decision-maker."

She could not let another core argument of the government—that courts had no role to play in assessing the judgments of the president in wartime—pass without comment:

> In so holding, we necessarily reject the Government's assertion that *separation of powers principles mandate a heavily circumscribed role for the courts in such circumstances.* Indeed, the position that the courts must forgo any examination of the individual case and focus exclusively on the legality of the broader detention scheme cannot be mandated by any reasonable view of separation of powers, as this approach serves only to condense power into a single branch of government. *We have long since made clear that a state of war is not a blank check for the President when it comes to the rights of the Nation's citizens.* [My emphasis]

Hamdi, the O'Connor judgment concluded, "has received no process. An interrogation by one's captor, however effective an intelligence-gathering tool, hardly constitutes a constitutionally adequate fact-finding before a neutral decision-maker. . . . The judgment of the United States Court of Appeals for the Fourth Circuit is vacated, and the case is remanded for further proceedings."[57]

Justice Souter, joined by Justice Ginsburg, concurred in part, dissented in part, but concurred with the O'Connor opinion's remand of the case back to the lower federal court. He believed that Hamdi's detention was unauthorized but joined with the plurality to conclude that on remand Hamdi should have a meaningful opportunity to offer evidence that he is not an enemy combatant:

> The plurality rejects any limit on the exercise of habeas jurisdiction and so far I agree with its opinion. The plurality does, however, accept the Government's position that if Hamdi's designation as an enemy combatant is correct, his detention (at least as to some period) is authorized by an Act of Congress as required by §4001(a), that is, by the Authorization for Use of Military Force. Here, I disagree and respectfully dissent. The Government has failed to demonstrate that the AUMF Resolution authorizes the detention complained of here even on the facts the Government claims. If the Government raises nothing further than the record now shows, the Non-Detention Act [Section 4001(A)] entitles Hamdi to be released. . . . The threshold issue is how broadly or narrowly to read the Non-Detention Act, the tone of which is severe: "No citizen shall be imprisoned or otherwise detained by the United States except pursuant to an Act of Congress."

Souter read the scope of the 1971 Non-Detention Act very broadly and therefore could not join the O'Connor opinion. In his final paragraphs, he explained his position:

> Because I find Hamdi's detention forbidden by §4001(a) and unauthorized by the AUMF Resolution, I would not reach any questions of what process he may be due in litigating disputed issues in a proceeding under the habeas statute or prior to the habeas enquiry itself. *For me, it suffices that the Government has failed to justify holding him in the absence of a further Act of Congress, criminal charges, a showing that the detention conforms to the laws of war, or a demonstration that §4001(a) is unconstitutional.* I would therefore vacate the judgment of the Court of Appeals and remand for proceedings consistent with this view. Since this disposition does not command a majority of the Court, however, the need to give practical effect to the conclusions of eight members of the Court rejecting the Government's position calls for me to join with the plurality in ordering remand on terms closest to those I would impose. Although I think litigation of Hamdi's status as an enemy combatant is unnecessary, the terms of the plurality's remand will allow Hamdi to offer evidence that he is not an enemy combatant, and he should at the least have the benefit of that opportunity. I join with the plurality in a judgment of the Court vacating the Fourth Circuit's judgment and remanding the case. [My emphasis][58]

"The very core of liberty secured by our Anglo-Saxon system of separated powers has been freedom from indefinite imprisonment at the will of the

Executive," wrote conservative—and libertarian—justice Antonin Scalia, joined by Justice Stevens, in his dissenting opinion in *Hamdi*. He wrote:

> Where the Government accuses a citizen of waging war against it, our constitutional tradition has been to prosecute him in federal court for treason or some other crime. Where the exigencies of war prevent that, the Constitution's Suspension [of the writ of habeas corpus] Clause, Art. I, §9, cl. 2, allows Congress to relax the usual protections temporarily. Absent suspension, however, the Executive's assertion of military exigency has not been thought sufficient to permit detention without charge. No one contends that the congressional AUMF, on which the Government relies to justify its actions here, is an implementation of the Suspension Clause. Accordingly, I would reverse the decision below.

Scalia continued to note that O'Connor's opinion was incorrect regarding the way in which the government has treated United States *citizens* fighting against their country when captured:

> Justice O'Connor, writing for a plurality of this Court, asserts that captured enemy combatants (other than those suspected of war crimes) have traditionally been detained until the cessation of hostilities and then released. That is probably an accurate description of wartime practice with respect to enemy *aliens*. The tradition with respect to American citizens, however, has been quite different. Citizens aiding the enemy have been treated as traitors subject to the criminal process.

"Hamdi," concluded Scalia after a lengthy historical account of habeas and the laws of war, "is entitled to a habeas decree requiring his release unless (1) criminal proceedings are promptly brought, or (2) Congress has suspended the writ of habeas corpus." In hard-boiled, acerbic language, he said of the O'Connor plurality opinion that

> having *distorted* the Suspension Clause, the plurality finishes up by *transmogrifying* the Great Writ—disposing of the present habeas petition by remanding for the District Court to "engag[e] in a fact-finding process that is both prudent and incremental. In the absence of [the Executive's prior provision of procedures that satisfy due process], . . . a court that receives a petition for a writ of habeas corpus from an alleged enemy combatant must itself ensure that the minimum requirements of due process are achieved." This judicial remediation of executive default is unheard of. The role of habeas corpus is to determine the legality of executive detention, not to supply the omitted process necessary to make it legal. [My emphasis]

His concluding remarks were somber "Scalia-isms":

Many think it not only inevitable but entirely proper that liberty give way to security in times of national crisis—that, at the extremes of military exigency, *inter arma silent leges.* Whatever the general merits of the view that war silences law or modulates its voice, that view has no place in the interpretation and application of a Constitution designed precisely to confront war and, in a manner that accords with democratic principles, to accommodate it. Because the Court has proceeded to meet the current emergency in a manner the Constitution does not envision, I respectfully dissent.[59]

The only justice who accepted the argument of the Bush administration was Justice Thomas. He dissented from the rest of the justices on the core, foundational, issues raised in *Hamdi.* Very bluntly, in his opening paragraph, he staked out his position:

The Executive Branch, acting pursuant to the powers vested in the President by the Constitution and with explicit congressional approval, has determined that Yaser Hamdi is an enemy combatant and should be detained. This detention falls squarely within the Federal Government's war powers, and we lack the expertise and capacity to second-guess that decision. As such, petitioners' habeas challenge should fail, and there is no reason to remand the case. . . . The plurality utterly fails to account for the Government's compelling interests and for our own institutional inability to weigh competing concerns correctly. I respectfully dissent.[60]

By a vote of 8–1, the Supreme Court concluded, for a number of different and conflicting reasons, that Hamdi had been denied due process. The case was remanded to the lower federal courts for action consistent with the order of the Supreme Court.

Rumsfeld v. Padilla

Chief Justice Rehnquist delivered the opinion of the five-person Court majority, in which Justices O'Connor, Scalia, Kennedy, and Thomas joined. Justice Kennedy also filed a concurring opinion, in which Justice O'Connor joined. Justice Stevens filed a dissenting opinion, in which Justices Souter, Ginsburg, and Breyer joined.

For the five-person majority, Rehnquist concluded that there was no federal district court jurisdiction to hear Padilla's habeas petition, and therefore there was no need to reach the substantive question of whether the president has authority to detain Padilla militarily:

We confront two questions: First, did Padilla properly file his habeas petition in the Southern District of New York; and second, did the President possess authority to detain Padilla militarily. We answer the threshold question in the negative and thus do not reach the second question presented. . . . The District of South Carolina, not the Southern District of New York, was the district court in which Padilla should have brought his habeas petition. We therefore reverse the judgment of the Court of Appeals and remand the case for entry of an order of dismissal without prejudice. It is so ordered.[61]

Justice Kennedy wrote a separate concurring opinion, joined by Justice O'Connor. Kennedy concluded that

both Padilla's change in location and his change of custodian reflected a change in the Government's rationale for detaining him. He ceased to be held under the authority of the criminal justice system and began to be held under that of the military detention system.[62] Rather than being designed to play games with forums, the Government's removal of Padilla reflected the change in the theory on which it was holding him. Whether that theory is a permissible one, of course, is a question the Court does not reach today. The change in custody, and the underlying change in rationale, should be challenged in the place the Government has brought them to bear and against the person who is the immediate representative of the military authority that is detaining him. That place is the District of South Carolina, and that person is Commander Marr. The Second Circuit erred in holding that the Southern District of New York was a proper forum for Padilla's petition. With these further observations, I join the opinion and judgment of the Court.[63]

Justice Stevens wrote a strong dissent from the Court's jurisdiction-framed nondecision in *Rumsfeld v. Padilla:* "The petition for a writ of habeas corpus filed in this case raises questions of profound importance to the Nation. The arguments set forth by the Court do not justify avoidance of our duty to answer those questions. . . . This is an exceptional case that we clearly have jurisdiction to decide."

The four dissenting justices saw the fundamental importance of the issues at the core of *Padilla:*

At stake in this case is nothing less than the essence of a free society. Even more important than the method of selecting the people's rulers and their successors is the character of the constraints imposed on the Executive by the rule of law. Unconstrained Executive detention for the purpose of investigating and preventing subversive activity is the hallmark of the Star Chamber. Access to counsel for the purpose of protecting the citizen from official mistakes and mistreatment is the hallmark of due process. Executive detention of subversive citizens, like detention of enemy soldiers to keep them off the battlefield, may sometimes be justified to prevent persons from launching or becoming missiles of destruction. It may not, however, be justified by the naked interest in using unlawful procedures to extract information. Incommunicado detention for months on end is such a procedure. Whether the information so procured is more or less reliable than that acquired by more extreme forms of torture is of no consequence. For if this Nation is to remain true to the ideals symbolized by its flag, it must not wield the tools of tyrants even to resist an assault by the forces of tyranny. I respectfully dissent. [My emphasis][64]

As already noted, *Padilla* made its way back to the Court in December 2005—*but with totally different legal questions raised.* However, because of other actions of the Bush administration, the Court majority, in April 2006, denied certiorari in *Padilla II.* (Much more will be said about this turn of events in chapter 5.)

For the most part, the media coverage of the decisions was positive. Linda Greenhouse, senior *New York Times* legal correspondent, wrote that "although divided in its rationale, the court was decisive in rejecting the administration's core legal argument that the executive branch has the last word in imposing open-ended detention on citizens and non-citizens alike. The justices' language was occasionally passionate, reflecting their awareness of the historic nature of this confrontation between executive and judicial authority."[65]

Other journalists, however, wrote about the "harmful rulings" of the Supreme Court. "Let's start with the bad news," wrote Matthew J. Franck in the *National Review,*

and then move to the worse news. The Bush administration has been dealt a serious setback by the Supreme Court's rulings in two out of three cases decided on June 28 regarding the government's enemy-combatant-detention policies. . . . Far worse [than the political impact of these rulings] are the effects these rulings will have on the rule of law and the conduct of the war. In that respect, the nation, and not just the Bush administration, has been harmed by the Supreme Court.[66]

Justices—all judges, whether local, state, or federal—know that the issuance of an order is not the end of the matter; rather, it is only the beginning of a new issue, the *compliance* matter. Will the adversely affected party comply with the ruling of the appellate court? Or will there be either unintended noncompliance or deliberate noncompliance with the ruling of the court? The constitutional history of the United States is replete with example after example of both kinds of noncompliance, although generally there is compliance because there is a respect for the rule of law.

In these legal challenges to the treatment of persons detained by the U.S. military, the Bush administration stridently argued for the maintenance of unalloyed and absolute presidential power if he were to fight the war *successfully* against the forces of international terrorism bent on attacking Americans. The Court majority's rulings, however cautious, adversely affected presidential power to wage war.

The inexorable question facing the president and his advisers, political, military, and legal, was how to react to these Supreme Court decisions that intruded on the powers and prerogatives of the American president.

Chapter 5 lays out the Bush administration's efforts to outflank and, at best, minimally comply with the Court's orders. The ideologues in the administration were committed to do all they could to *not comply* with the Court's general messages, messages that, for the first time since the war on terror began, attempted to constrain the president.

5. Bush versus the U.S. Supreme Court, Round Two, 2004–2006

This guy Padilla's a bad guy.

GEORGE W. BUSH, 2004[1]

In the June 2004 enemy combatants cases, the justices of the U.S. Supreme Court concluded that foreign aliens and American citizens held as enemy combatants could petition federal courts for habeas grants to challenge their detentions. However, they "coyly refrained from commenting one way or another"[2] on what the *content* of these challenges should look like.

The Court's restraint is not unusual; throughout American history, in most cases the justices have entered an issue carefully and have usually decided on very narrow grounds. Further actions on questions not answered by the justices have been predicated on reaction and response from the parties to the dispute and from the lower federal court judges themselves. Only when the justices believe, based on new filings with the Court, that these new questions should be addressed, in the light of Rule 10's guidelines, will they further "clarify matters."[3]

Given the Bush administration's almost instantaneous *minimally compliant* responses to the June 2004 decisions of the Court, it was not too long before the Supreme Court reentered this controversial political arena to try to spell out matters.

For two years after the 2004 opinions were announced, a flurry of Bush administration activity—regarding the fates of Hamdi, Padilla, and the detainees at Guantánamo—reiterated the position of the president and his chief lieutenants, Vice President Cheney and Secretary of Defense Rumsfeld. To avoid further hearings and legal appeals in the federal courts, the administration shipped Hamdi back to Saudi Arabia in late 2004. And, wishing to avoid further legal challenges to Padilla's treatment as an enemy combatant, it indicted him on criminal conspiracy charges in federal district court in Florida in 2005. He was charged with the far-less-serious crime of conspiring with a number of others to send money overseas to assist terrorist activities.

And in a startling and transparent action in early January 2006, the Bush lawyers in the Solicitor General's Office filed briefs asking federal judges to drop the many dozens of habeas petitions they had been receiving from Guantánamo detainees. The solicitor general argued that the controversial Detainee Treatment Act of 2005 *abolished* the jurisdiction of *all* federal courts—including the U.S. Supreme Court—except the U.S. Court of Appeals for the District of Columbia Circuit to hear such appeals.

In another major development involving the Guantánamo detainees, the Supreme Court, in November 2005, granted certiorari in the case of *Hamdan v. Rumsfeld* in order to hear a case involving the constitutionality of the military commissions created by the November 2001 Bush military order. The March 28, 2006, oral argument in the case was a testy, almost raucous one, in part because of the Bush administration's refusal to comply with the Court's 2004 opinions.

The two years after the June 2004 Supreme Court decisions came down were turbulent ones for detainees, the petitioners' attorneys, and the judges involved in the litigation that followed. The Court's personnel changed dramatically. Justice O'Connor announced her retirement from the Court in late June 2005 and was replaced by Samuel Alito. Chief Justice Rehnquist died in September and was replaced by John Roberts. Probably the only parties involved in the dispute that did not experience the tension were President Bush and his nonattorney colleagues in the executive branch.

CALCULATED DE MINIMUS COMPLIANCE

When a coordinate branch of the federal government rules against the executive branch, observers may wonder whether or not the president will accept the adverse judgment. In the case of a Supreme Court order going against the government, the question becomes *how* or *whether* the executive will implement the ruling of the Court. The Court has no mechanisms for enforcing its orders; no formal sanctions attach to a president's noncompliance. However, political and normative sanctions do come into play when and if a president decides to ignore an order of the highest court in the United States.

A week after the June 2004 decisions of the Court came down, the administration's lawyers, press secretaries, and "spinners" were portraying the Court decisions as a victory for President Bush "that incidentally raised 'some concerns' that needed to be addressed."[4] In the case of the enemy combatants orders, the Bush administration immediately tried to find ways *not to comply* with the Court's orders: The lawyers at the Department of Justice, the Department of Defense, and the White House tried tactically to maintain the administration's tight, unilateral control over the substantive issue of treatment of enemy prisoners detained across the globe by American military forces and CIA operatives.

The White House, ironically, was greatly helped by the fact that there were ten Court opinions written in the three cases. This plethora of opinions was not unusual for the Court in such a controversial area of constitutional law. However, so many opinions meant that if the adversely affected party—in these cases, the Bush administration—wanted to obfuscate and otherwise minimally comply with the orders of the Court, it could do so with relative ease. At no time did the Bush administration lawyers and political managers acknowledge that their legal views of presidential power had been rejected by the Court majorities.

Compliance or noncompliance with a court order is generally in the hands of the parties involved in the litigation. Only rarely can a party to a dispute be forced to comply or face serious consequences. In civil rights cases involving the ending of the segregated dual school system in Virginia, for example, the members of county school boards faced fines if they did not comply with the federal court order to desegregate the schools. The federal judiciary, however, generally does not have any mechanism for ensuring compliance, or even for knowing if there has been compliance. If there are no clear Court orders, if there is only a plurality opinion for the court, accompanied by a few concurring opinions, then there is give and flexibility in the implementation—or nonimplementation—of these decisions.

In these 2004 enemy combatants cases, given the divisions on the Court, the justices knew that they were merely scratching the surface of the controversial legal issues. For example, it was unclear who could challenge their detention through habeas corpus filings. Justice Scalia, in his stinging dissent in *Rasul,* said, "From this point forward, federal courts will entertain petitions from these prisoners, and others like them around the world, challenging actions and events far away, and forcing the courts to oversee one aspect of the executive's conduct of a foreign war."

And the *Rasul* majority opinion did not provide any clear guidelines regarding the next steps in the legal processes for foreign nationals detained at Guantánamo. Justice Stevens, who authored the narrow five-person majority opinion in *Rasul,* admitted as much when he wrote, "Whether and what further proceedings may become necessary after the respondents make their response are matters we need not address now." Stevens's statement is a classic example of the Court's tendency not to overreach and answer questions that were not properly before them. They avoided taking the next steps, avoided answering questions that were not raised in the petitions and in the briefs. If the Bush administration did not comply with the orders, then there would surely be additional challenges to the president's response. As law professor Douglas W. Kmiec, of the Pepperdine University School of Law, noted, the *Rasul* ruling was "written in a deliberately incomplete manner so that it found a right to habeas review but left the nature of that review to some district court [judge]."[5] Implicit in this observation is the reality that if the president did not comply, there would be new petitions filed in the federal courts.

As most observers expected, the Bush administration remained obdurate and unyielding. By November 2004, defense lawyers for the hundreds of Guantánamo detainees were beyond frustration because "the Bush administration [was] purposely ignoring the justices' mandate and ruling." Outraged defense lawyers cited the government's refusal to acknowledge and to tell detainees that they could have free access to lawyers to make their cases in federal district court, the Department of Defense and Department of Justice lawyers' re-arguing of issues in federal district court that the administration had lost in the 2004 decisions, and administration lawyers' use of the same language used two years earlier in a case the administration lost in the Supreme Court.[6] Some angry lawyers compared these Bush administration actions to the "massive resistance" of white segregationists after the Supreme Court's "Black Monday" decision of May 17, 1954, *Brown v. Board of Education of Topeka, Kansas* (347 U.S. 483), ended the segregated dual school system.

One professor of law, Anthony G. Amsterdam, of New York University School of Law, argued that the government lawyers' resistance to recognizing detainee rights bordered on the unethical: "It is simply amazing that they are proceeding as if those cases had not been heard before the Supreme Court and that those arguments had not been heard and rejected by the Court. I would not expect a reputable lawyer to split nonexistent hairs that way and treat what was plainly a decision that these people had a right to be in court as if it were nothing."[7] However, the Bush lawyers' noncompliance continued unabated. If any of these detainees were released, said the Department of Justice, "it will be only when the government itself decides they should be free to go because they no longer present a terrorist threat, or no longer have any intelligence value."[8]

AVOIDING HABEAS REVIEWS

One of the first minimally compliant consequences of the *Rasul* decision was the Department of Defense's announcement that it would provide *all* Guantánamo detainees with military hearings similar to those described in Army Regulation 190-8.[9] That regulation required status reviews at the outset of detention. Two orders were issued by the Pentagon in July 2004. On July 7, 2004, an order "Establishing Combatant Status Review Tribunals" was issued. On July 29, 2004, an order entitled "Implementation of Combatant Status Review Tribunal Procedures for Enemy Combatants Detained at Guantanamo Bay naval Base, Cuba," was issued.[10] Under these procedures, a detainee's status review hearing was to be conducted by three military officers not involved with his capture or interrogation or any subsequent reviews of his status. A personal representative could assist the detainee in the hearing. Every hearing conducted under these new procedures made a *rebuttable presumption*[11] in favor of the government's evidence.

At the time the June 2004 decisions of the Court were announced, dozens of habeas corpus petitions from Guantánamo detainees had already been filed in federal district courts around the nation. After three months of delaying tactics by the Department of Justice and Department of Defense lawyers, a federal district court judge, Joyce H. Green, who had been designated by her colleagues in the U.S. District Court for the District of Columbia to "coordinate and manage" all Guantánamo habeas corpus cases filed in that court, set a deadline of October 4, 2004, for the Bush administration to respond to challenges by over sixty detainees.[12] Judge Green also fixed a second deadline, October 18, 2004, by which the Department of Justice would have to have submitted the facts gathered during the status review process conducted by the Department of Defense.

Nevertheless, not until December 2004 did the Department of Defense announce that it would begin to formally notify the sixty-odd Guantánamo detainees of their right to file habeas corpus claims in federal courts challenging their incarcerations.[13] The carefully crafted three-paragraph notice told them that they were considered a member or supporter of al Qaeda or the Taliban and were classified as enemy combatants, and that they had the right to contest the lawfulness of the Department of Defense's judgment about their status as enemy combatants. The letter ended with an address to which they could mail their legal challenges: the U.S. District Court courthouse in the District of Columbia.

However, most of the more than 500 enemy detainees at Guantánamo were not immediately scheduled to be told of their right to file habeas corpus petitions with the district court. When they were notified, the Department of Defense letter instructed them to have relatives or friends file the petition or to file the petition themselves. Almost immediately after the Supreme Court announced its *Hamdi* opinion, "dozens of pro bono lawyers of every persuasion, those from tony white-shoe firms and those from left-wing civil liberties groups," stood ready to assist the Guantánamo detainees.[14] They soon had a name for themselves: the Guantánamo Bay Bar Association.[15] However, the Department of Defense stubbornly refused to tell the detainees about this unique bar association and took its time allowing the detainees to meet with its members.

In January 2005 lawyers for sixty detainees challenged the new special military status review tribunal process. (On January 19, 2005, another U.S. district court judge, Richard J. Leon,[16] ruled that the Guantánamo detainees had no due process rights and therefore could not be granted habeas writs by the federal courts to have their detentions reviewed in them.)

On January 31, 2005, Judge Green ruled in a seventy-five-page opinion that the Bush administration had to allow those detainees to contest their detention through habeas appeals in U.S. district courts. The Department of Defense "has largely denied plaintiffs these most basic fundamental rights [the right to the assistance of counsel and the right to confront the evidence against them in legal proceedings]." She concluded that the Pentagon creation, the combatant status review tribunal, was unconstitutional. She ruled, in part, that "although this nation unquestionably must take strong action under the leadership of the commander in chief to protect itself against enormous and unprecedented threats, that necessity cannot negate the existence of the most basic fundamental rights for which the people of this country have fought and died for well over two hundred years." Reading her opinion, one sees her frustration at the Bush administration's argument that federal courts could not issue habeas writs for Guantánamo petitioners. The Supreme Court ruling in *Rasul,* she reminded the Bush administration lawyers, "definitively" ruled that Guantánamo was under the umbrella of American law. "American authorities are in full control at Guantánamo Bay, their activities are immune from Cuban law."[17] There was no reason to argue, as the Bush lawyers had repeatedly done *since Rasul,* that American law does not apply to the detainees there.

While these federal trial court rulings were being appealed, the Department of Defense developed another artifice to evade the Court's directive regarding habeas rights for detainees: administrative review boards (ARBs). Created after the Green ruling that the combatant status review tribunals were unconstitutional, ARBs are panels of three military officers who conduct a hearing at which a detainee—*without the assistance of counsel*—tells his story and tries to dispute accusations that he was part of the Taliban forces or somehow connected to al Qaeda. First a prosecutor spells out the facts that led to the person being detained at Guantánamo. Then, in order to be released from Guantánamo, the detainee has to convince the board members that he is not a threat to the United States or its allies. (The constitutionality of this Pentagon creation would be examined by the Supreme Court during its 2005 term.)

The delaying tactic employed by the Department of Justice was to work closely with the Department of Defense and "intertwine" the habeas cases with the output from the combatant status review tribunals. The "facts" culled from these status review boards became "the facts that the government [would] be allowed to put forward in court to explain any given individual's detention, and thus to resist his release."[18]

THE *HAMDI* DEAL, SEPTEMBER 2004

In late September 2004, just months after the Supreme Court decision, a deal was reached regarding Hamdi's status. The Bush administration, unwilling to give Hamdi a hearing as called for by the Court, decided to strike a bargain that would give Hamdi a "get out of jail" card. After many weeks of negotiation, lawyers for the Department of Justice and Hamdi and his attorneys announced an agreement whereby, after he renounced his U.S. citizenship, he would be freed from the brig and allowed to return to Saudi Arabia. According to the official Department of Justice statement:

Like many other enemy combatants captured and detained by U.S. armed forces in Afghanistan who have been subsequently released, the United States has determined that Mr. Hamdi could be transferred out of United States custody subject to strict conditions that ensure the interests of the United States and our national security. As we have repeatedly stated, the United States has no interest in detaining enemy combatants beyond the point that they pose a threat to the United States and our allies.[19]

The release contract signed by Hamdi requires him to abide by strict travel restrictions. He is prohibited from leaving Saudi Arabia for a certain period of time and he is prohibited for the rest of his life from traveling to the United States, Afghanistan, Iraq, Israel, Pakistan, Syria, the West Bank, or the Gaza Strip. The contract also stipulates that Hamdi cannot sue the government for his lengthy detention. It was not clear how these restrictions would be enforced. Dahlia Lithwick summed up the general media response to the agreement in her inimitable manner:

If you've followed the government's claims in the Hamdi case, you would think the guy was some unstoppable, lethal killing machine, the Taliban's own Hannibal Lecter—a man so evil, he requires permanent warehousing down a bottomless hole. So the Bush administration's decision to release Hamdi is stunning, given that only months ago he was so dangerous that the government insisted in front of the U.S. Supreme Court and the world that he could reasonably be locked up for all time, without a trial or criminal charges. . . . Did Hamdi spontaneously stop being dangerous? Or was he never really a danger in the first place?[20]

By the end of 2004 the level of the Bush administration's compliance with the enemy combatants litigation seemed clear. Although, to the surprise of many, the Supreme Court had granted certiorari in these hard cases, the messages it sent to the president and his lawyers were somewhat unclear and therefore open to misinterpretation. To almost no one's surprise, after the Court's imprecise decisions were announced, the Bush administration very quickly began efforts to disembowel the Court's judgments.

The administration was not going to tolerate any interference with the powers of the president to conduct the war on terror as Bush believed it should be conducted. Even though the justices had rebuked the White House and the Department of Justice lawyers' categorical message about the powers of the president in time of war, the Bush administration continued to act unilaterally—without any interference from Congress or the Supreme Court.

JOSE PADILLA'S ODYSSEY CONTINUES,
2004–2007

Jonathan Freiman, one of Padilla's lawyers, saw the 2004 jurisdictional nonde-cision of the Court as just a nominal loss. "The Court says it wants a do-over, so we'll file in South Carolina and do it over."[21] As it turned out, Freiman was way off the mark: The Padilla saga was to take a number of Byzantine turns worthy of a Dan Brown novel.

In February 2005 a U.S. district court in South Carolina granted Padilla's new petition for habeas corpus. The judge held that Congress's September 2001 AUMF Resolution had not given the president the authority to detain Padilla. Padilla was detained not on a battlefield carrying arms against Ameri-can troops but at O'Hare Airport and was initially held as a material witness in an unidentified federal case.

Padilla's indefinite detention, observed the judge, is a "betrayal of this na-tion's commitment to the separation of powers that safeguards our demo-cratic values and individual liberties." The judge concluded that Padilla had been held in a military brig in clear violation of the Non-Detention Act. The Bush administration must either charge Padilla with a crime or release him.

The Bush lawyers in the Solicitor General's Office immediately appealed the district court decision to the U.S. Court of Appeals for the Fourth Circuit. Oral arguments in that federal appellate court were scheduled for July 19, 2005. Padilla's lawyers filed a brief with the U.S. Supreme Court, asking the Court for an expedited grant of certiorari. They wanted an immediate ruling from the Supreme Court before the federal appellate court heard oral argu-ments. In mid-June 2005, however, the Supreme Court denied expedited cer-tiorari.[22]

On September 9, 2005, the court of appeals three-judge panel reversed the federal district court judge who had ordered the government to either charge Padilla or release him:

> The exceedingly important question before us is whether the President . . . possesses the authority to detain militarily a citizen of this country who is closely associated with al Qaeda, an entity with which the United States is at war; who took up arms on behalf of that enemy and against our country in a foreign combat zone of that war; *and* who thereafter traveled to the United States for the avowed purpose of further prosecuting that war on American soil, against

American citizens and targets. We conclude that the President does possess such authority pursuant to the AUMF Joint Resolution enacted by Congress in the wake of the attacks on the United States of September 11, 2001. Accordingly, the judgment of the district court is reversed.[23]

The trio of federal appeals court judges considered the 2001 AUMF broad enough to allow the president to detain indefinitely American citizens labeled enemy combatants. They asserted that Padilla's indefinite detention constituted "necessary and appropriate force," the operative language of the AUMF Resolution, by President Bush.

On October 26, 2005, Donna Newman, Padilla's lead attorney, filed a petition for certiorari with the U.S. Supreme Court. Newman's brief essentially asked the justices "when and how long the government can jail people in military prisons. The government's position is not only can we do it, we can do it forever."[24]

However, less than one week before the solicitor general's response in opposition to the granting of certiorari petition was to be filed, the Bush administration surprised and shocked the federal judges and the nation. On November 17, 2005, it released a federal indictment charging Padilla and four other persons—allegedly members of a "North American support cell"—with eleven counts of conspiracy, including for "murder, maiming, [and] kidnapping" individuals overseas and providing financial support for terrorists: "The defendants, along with other individuals, operated and participated in a North American support cell that sent money, physical assets, and mujahideen recruits to overseas conflicts for the purpose of fighting violent jihad."[25]

President Bush immediately signed an order transferring Padilla into the custody of the Department of Justice. "I hereby determine that it is in the interest of the United States that Jose Padilla be released from detention by the Secretary of Defense and transferred to the control of the Attorney General for the purpose of criminal proceedings against him."[26] Padilla's enemy combatant status was not addressed in the Bush order or in subsequent statements issued by the government.

For the government, U.S. Attorney General Alberto Gonzales said that the criminal indictment should make Padilla's appeal to the Supreme Court "irrelevant" because Padilla's certiorari petition asked that he be either charged or released. "Since he has now been charged in a grand jury in Florida," said Gonzales, "we believe that the petition is moot and that the petition should not be granted."[27]

Critics of the Bush administration saw the indictments as another strategy to avoid and evade the 2004 Supreme Court orders. Bush, and more specifically, his lawyers in Department of Defense and Department of Justice, "hope[d] that the indictment will effectively derail the possibility of an adverse ruling from the Supreme Court in the Padilla case, which could decide to limit the government's ability to detain U.S. citizens as enemy combatants," suggested a *Washington Post* reporter.[28] A *Post* editorial entitled "Three Years Late" observed, "It's about time" criminal charges were brought against Padilla. The Bush administration was *only* three and one half years late.[29]

Many lawyers agreed with the conclusion reached by Eugene Fidell, the president of the private National Institute for Military Justice, who called this development in the Padilla litigation "a remarkable game of musical courtrooms."[30] A few days after the firestorm, government spinners were again at work justifying yanking Padilla from military custody and thrusting him back, once again, into the federal criminal justice system. According to anonymous current and former senior administrative sources, the Bush administration charged Padilla "with less serious crimes because it was unwilling to allow testimony from two senior members of al Qaeda who had been subjected to harsh questioning. . . . They could not be used because their testimony could expose classified information and open up charges from defense lawyers that their earlier statements were a result of torture, officials said."[31]

Freiman, speaking for Padilla, said that they would continue to seek Supreme Court review even though the government's position was that the enemy combatant case was moot. He said that "the government could redesignate Mr. Padilla as an enemy combatant if he was found not guilty at his criminal trial. As long as the government does not disclaim that right, the case is, in the legal jargon, 'capable of repetition yet evading review,' and so not moot. 'It's a power [the government] claims to have not only over my client, but every American citizen.'"[32]

On December 21, 2005, in another surprise for Padilla case watchers, the U.S. Court of Appeals for the Fourth Circuit, probably the most conservative federal appellate court in the nation, denied the Bush administration's request to move Padilla from military custody to civilian Department of Justice authorities. What was so startling was the fact that it was the very same conservative three-judge panel of appeals court judges that had ruled in favor of the Bush administration's continued military detention of Padilla that issued the order.

The three judges were clearly very angry with the president's manipulation of the judicial system. The Department of Justice's effort to transfer Padilla "gave the appearance that the government was trying to manipulate the court system to prevent the Supreme Court from reviewing the case." To agree with the Bush administration's request, said the appeals court judges, would compound what was "at least an appearance that the government may be attempting to avoid consideration of our decision by the Supreme Court, and also because we believe that this case presents an issue of such especial national importance as to warrant final consideration by that Court, even if only by denial of further review, we deny both the motion and suggestion."[33]

The Bush administration expressed disappointment at the appeals court's surprise ruling. It immediately appealed that judgment to the U.S. Supreme Court. On December 28, 2005, the Solicitor General's Office filed a brief attacking the circuit court's "unwarranted attack" on "Executive discretion" in wartime. Solicitor General Paul Clement's brief said that the fourth circuit court's decision "defie[d] both law and logic," that the federal appeals court had no authority to "disregard a presidential directive," and that the decision was "based on a mischaracterization of events and [was] an unwarranted attack on the exercise of Executive discretion, and, if given effect, would raise profound separation-of-powers concerns."[34]

Newman, expressing her own perplexity at the unfolding events, said, "Nothing in this case surprises me anymore. This [government brief] is an unusual turn of events for the Justice Department to come out against the Fourth Circuit like this, because anybody who looks at precedent would see the Fourth Circuit is a very pro-government circuit that generally finds in favor of the government."[35]

Two days later, on Friday, December 30, 2005, Padilla's lawyers filed their brief with the Supreme Court. They supported the fourth circuit court's order denying the government's request to transfer Padilla into the custody of the Department of Justice. "The government," the brief maintained, "had the power to transfer Padilla from physical military custody for more than three years, yet only now does it deem swift transfer imperative."[36]

The Supreme Court, while still on its Christmas recess, on January 4, 2006, granted the Bush administration's request to transfer Padilla from military to Department of Justice custody. The one-paragraph order granted the government's transfer request. It concluded that "the Court will consider the pending petition for certiorari in due course."[37]

With Padilla now in federal civilian custody in Florida, the justices had to determine their response to Padilla's certiorari petition. For almost three months, during their secret Friday conference sessions of January 13 and 20, February 17 and 24, and March 3, 17, 24, and 31, 2006, the justices wrestled with the Padilla petition for certiorari. At the end of the March 31 conference session, the justices finally decided the fate of the Padilla petition: certiorari denied.

In the end, a very divided Court issued the order denying certiorari on April 3. However, it was a most unusual denial of the petition. Three justices, Justices Breyer, Ginsburg, and Souter, dissented from the denial of certiorari, a very rare occurrence. Denial of a certiorari petition by the justices is the general rule. Ninety-nine percent of such petitions are routinely denied, generally because fewer than four justices vote to grant. In controversial cases, such as death penalty litigation and the detainee rights cases, if the minority are intensely committed to their views, they will issue a dissent from the denial of certiorari. Such a dissent puts their views on paper and gives the legal community additional information and possible guidance regarding future litigation. Only Justice Ginsburg, however, wrote a *dissent* from the denial of certiorari. Her brief, two-page dissent twice quoted Justice Stevens's dissenting opinion in the first Padilla case. It was her response to Stevens's vote not to grant certiorari in *Padilla II*. (His vote to grant, if he had voted that way, would have led the justices to hear *Padilla II* on the merits.)

> This case, here for the second time, raises a question "of profound importance to the Nation" [quoting Stevens]: Does the President have authority to imprison indefinitely a United States citizen arrested on United States soil distant from a zone of combat, based on an Executive declaration that the citizen was, at the time of his arrest, an "enemy combatant"? It is a question the Court heard, and should have decided, two years ago. [Citing the Stevens opinion again:] Nothing the Government has yet done purports to retract the assertion of Executive power Padilla protests. . . . Nothing prevents the Executive from returning to the road it earlier constructed and defended.[38]

Another trio, Chief Justice Roberts and Justices Kennedy and Stevens, joined in a brief opinion that *concurred* in the denial of certiorari. While they approved the administration's transfer of Padilla's case to the federal criminal justice system, they were aware of Padilla's nearly four years of incarceration and would be receptive to further petitions for certiorari filed with the Court regarding his future treatment. (In its brief filed with the Court, Clement wrote that the government "reserved the right" to redesignate Padilla an enemy combatant and send him back to military custody.)

There were, Kennedy continued, "strong prudential considerations disfavoring the exercise of the Court's discretionary power. Even if the Court were to rule in Padilla's favor, his present custody status would be unaffected." However, he wrote, Padilla's case, because it continued to raise "fundamental issues respecting the separation of powers, including consideration of the role and function of the courts, also counsels against addressing those claims when the course of legal proceedings has made them, *at least for now, hypothetical*" (my emphasis).[39] Padilla was entitled, he wrote, to a criminal defendant's full range of protections, including the Sixth Amendment right to a speedy and public trial. Padilla's concerns that may arise in the future "can be addressed if the necessity arises."

"Most significant," observed Linda Greenhouse, was the fact that six justices, a majority of the Court, "warned the administration that federal courts, including the U.S. Supreme Court, stood ready to intervene 'were the government to seek to change the status or conditions of Padilla's custody.'"[40]

What astonished many observers of Padilla's case was that Justice Stevens, *the author of the four-person dissent in Padilla I,* broke ranks with his three dissenting colleagues in *Padilla II.* And it was probably just as surprising for Justices Ginsburg, Breyer, and Souter. Their concurring opinion was seen by many as "[a] strong signal that the Court would be ready to step in quickly if the government returned Mr. Padilla to military custody, or his basic rights were denied in his civilian trial. We trust Justice Kennedy and his colleagues to stay true to that pledge."[41]

The Padilla odyssey had come to rest, for the time being, in the federal district courthouse in Miami, Florida. Padilla and two other codefendants were awaiting the federal criminal trial set to begin in April 2007; they pled not guilty to the conspiracy charges. In early 2007, there was another development in the *Padilla* criminal trial in Miami, Florida: His lawyers asked the federal judge, Marcia Cooke, to delay the start of the trial because of Padilla's incompetence to assist them in his defense. The competency hearing was held in the federal courthouse on February 21, 2007. Two mental health experts hired by the defense testified that Padilla "suffers from post-traumatic stress disorder as a result of his isolation and scores of interrogation sessions (on 87 video tapes) during three years and 8 months in a military brig in South Carolina. 'He's unfit to stand trial,' said Patricia A. Zapf, the psychologist, describing Mr.

Padilla as so 'immobilized by his anxiety' and so distrustful that he is incapable of assisting his own lawyers." A Federal Bureau of Prisons evaluation, however, concluded that Padilla was competent to stand trial. The judge ordered four brig officials and four officials from the Miami Federal Detention Center to testify in the hearing. Judge Cooke ruled on February 28 that Padilla was competent to stand trial and that the conspiracy trial in the federal district court would begin in mid-April 2007"[42] (it began in early May 2007). The Supreme Court's denial of certiorari in April 2006 "averted a potential showdown between the Supreme Court and the Bush Administration over the president's war powers."[43] As will be seen in the discussion of the *Hamdan v. Rumsfeld* litigation in the Supreme Court during 2006, however, the "showdown" between the executive and the judiciary was averted for just a few months.

THE DETAINEE TREATMENT ACT OF 2005

The Abu Ghraib prison scandal of March 2004 and the ensuing firestorm of outrage had an impact on the somnambulant Congress. In the legislative chambers, for the first time since September 11, 2001, congresspersons began to talk about the Bush policy regarding the treatment of enemy combatants.

During the summer of 2005, Senator John McCain (R–AZ), himself a former prisoner of war during the Vietnam War who was repeatedly tortured by his captors, proposed an amendment to the defense appropriation bill of 2006 that would, using the language of international law, ban all "cruel, inhumane, and degrading" treatment of detainees held by U.S. military and intelligence-gathering personnel. His proposal included setting this language in the *U.S. Army Field Manual* and using it as a standard for *all* interrogations—by the military and also by the CIA.

President Bush's response was quick and insistent over the next six months: He would veto any legislation that contained the McCain amendment. As summer turned to fall, the Bush White House saw the growth of irresistible support for the McCain amendment. Bush administration leaders tried to encourage the Republican-controlled Senate to introduce changes in the proposed amendment that would weaken the language. Vice President Cheney "pressed McCain to exempt the CIA from his ban. The Senator refused. [However], to placate the White House, McCain eventually softened his prohibition by adding a legal defense for accused CIA and military interrogators that mimes the extreme exculpatory logic of the Justice Department's August 2002 Bybee memo."[44]

In the end, the Senate passed McCain's torture prohibition by a vote of 90–9. Bush, Cheney, and Rumsfeld, however, were not done with their secretive efforts to emasculate the McCain amendment. If torture was banned, what about the possibility of the Congress *withdrawing* the jurisdiction of the federal courts to hear pending and future habeas actions brought into the federal judicial system by lawyers for the detainees? (Article III, Section 2, the judiciary article in the U.S. Constitution, gives Congress the power to set and to take away the appellate jurisdiction of the Supreme Court and all other courts created by Congress.)

And although the president and Senator McCain met on December 15, 2005, in the White House for a very dramatic handshake signaling surrender on the part of the White House,[45] the administration was still plotting to destroy the impact of the senator's amendment to the 2006 Defense Authorization legislation. Immediately after the December 30, 2005, signing of the 2006 Defense Authorization Bill, President Bush issued his signing statement effectively nullifying the practical importance of the McCain torture ban.

The Bush White House's efforts also led to the passage, on December 21, 2005, of Section 1005 of the Detainee Treatment Act (DTA), Public Law 109-148, 119 Stat. 2739. This new and very controversial section of the McCain amendment was authored by an ally of the White House in the war on terror, Senator Lindsey Graham (R–SC). Section 1005 is a critical segment of the new statute. In its final version, it states, in part, that, *except* for the U.S. Court of Appeals for the District of Columbia,

> no court, justice, or judge shall have jurisdiction to hear or consider—(1) an application for a writ of habeas corpus filed by or on behalf of an alien detained by the Department of Defense at Guantanamo Bay, Cuba; or (2) any other action against the United States or its agents relating to any aspect of the detention by the Department of Defense of an alien at Guantanamo Bay, Cuba, who—(A) currently in military custody; or (B) has been determined by the United States Court of Appeals for the District of Columbia Circuit in accordance with the procedures set forth in section 1005(e) of the Detainee Treatment Act of 2005 to have been properly detained as an enemy combatant. [My emphasis]

Furthermore, the statute underscored the limited jurisdiction of the federal courts by reiterating that "the United States Court of Appeals for the District of Columbia Circuit *shall have exclusive jurisdiction to determine the validity of any final decision of a Combatant Status Review Tribunal that an alien is properly detained as an enemy combatant"* (my emphasis).

In addition, the amendment dramatically narrowed the scope of that one federal appeals court's jurisdiction when hearing enemy combatants petitions:

> The jurisdiction of the United States Court of Appeals for the District of Columbia Circuit on any claims with respect to an alien under this paragraph *shall be limited* to the consideration of—(i) whether the status determination of the Combatant Status Review Tribunal (CSRT) with regard to such alien was consistent with the standards and procedures specified by the Secretary of Defense for Combatant Status Review Tribunals (including the requirement that the conclusion of the Tribunal be supported by *a preponderance of the evidence and allowing a rebuttable presumption in favor of the Government's evidence*); and (ii) to the extent the Constitution and laws of the United States are applicable, whether the use of such standards and procedures to make the determination is consistent with the Constitution and laws of the United States. [My emphasis]

Because the 2005 legislation removed jurisdiction from the U.S. District Courts—who typically review the facts in the habeas petition and then make their decision based on the reading of these facts—and limited the U.S. Court of Appeals for the D.C. circuit to the above-mentioned review issues, very little fact review will occur in these cases.

At the time the legislation was signed into law by the president, there were over 180 habeas actions (for over 300 Guantánamo detainees) pending in the U.S. District Court for the District of Columbia alone. All these actions were asking federal judges "to tell the government to either charge someone in their custody with a crime or let that person go. A habeas action seeks to stop a government from holding someone indefinitely without explanation"— which was precisely the factual situation in all 180 pending actions.[46]

The jurisdictional restrictions placed on the federal courts made the as-passed Graham-introduced amendment to the DTA controversial. For a few days, detainees' counsel in the pending actions thought the statute limited *future* habeas actions. Within days, they—and the nation—were told by President Bush that the DTA precluded any further action on the *pending* habeas appeals as well.

How did this Bush legislative triumph happen? Conspiracy theorists had an easy time showing a White House linkage to the creation of this amendment. On November 7, 2005, Senator Graham, a member of the Senate Armed Services Committee, announced that he planned to add language to the 2006

Defense Authorization Bill "that would eliminate habeas rights for detainees captured during the terrorism fight to halt the 'never-ending litigation that is coming from Guantanamo.'"[47]

Three days later, on the morning of November 10—one day before a national holiday, Veterans Day—the Justice Department asked federal district court judges who had habeas actions pending before them to stay them until some procedural issues were resolved.[48] Later that same day, near the close of a Senate session and before that chamber broke for the holiday, Graham introduced the proposed amendment to the DTA. There were no committee hearings on Graham's amendment; the vote took place that evening.

The remarks of Senator Jeff Bingaman (D–NM) in opposition to the Graham amendment went to one aspect of the problem: "There have been no hearings on this issue in the Judiciary Committee. . . . There have been no hearings in the Armed Services Committee. . . . It is an extraordinary step for this Congress to be taking as an amendment to the Defense bill. . . . It is a very important issue, and we should not be dealing with it here on a late evening on Thursday." Although there were a few complaints raised by Senator Leahy and Senator Carl Levin (D–MI), the vote on the amendment took place that evening. It passed on a mostly party line vote: 49–42. The Senate then adjourned for the holiday.

During the short holiday break, a mini-firestorm of opposition to the Graham amendment occurred. The nonprofit Center for Constitutional Rights immediately issued a statement on its Web site condemning the Graham amendment's passage: "Habeas corpus is a fundamental right that our entire legal foundation is founded on. Unfettered Executive power jeopardizes our free and democratic society. Creating 'no law zones' of unreviewable Executive power at Guantanamo undermines the moral standing of the United States in the eyes of the world and endangers the lives of U.S. soldiers abroad."

On November 14, 2005, a number of senators received a further protest against the Graham amendment. The president of the National Institute of Military Justice, Eugene Fidell, wrote a letter to the chairmen of the Senate Judiciary and Armed Services committees, Senators Arlen Specter and John W. Warner (R–VA), respectively. Fidell called for committee hearings on Senator Graham's amendment, making several essential points:

> Review of CSRT's should lie in a trial court. . . . There is nothing to fear from
> district court review; it is already highly deferential. . . . The McCain Amendment

is unenforceable without habeas. As President Reagan observed in another context, "Trust, but verify." . . . Permitting [such habeas] actions will help avoid detainees falling into a "black hole." . . . We disable ourselves from objecting to flagrant lawlessness elsewhere when we shut the doors to our courts, which are the jewel in the crown of our democracy.[49]

On the Monday following the break, November 14, 2005, Senator Bingaman introduced an amendment that clearly allowed all pending and future habeas actions to continue in the federal courts. His amendment was defeated. Graham then introduced an amendment to replace his amendment that had passed. It was endorsed by Senator Levin. The substitute amendment removed the language that called for the dismissal of all pending habeas actions. It passed, with a vote of 84–14, and was sent to the House of Representatives for approval.

In the House, the Graham-Levin amendment was modified; changes were made regarding judicial review of determinations of the CSRTs. The final vote on the bill was scheduled for December 21, 2005. Senator Richard Durbin (D–IL), just before the final Senate vote, addressed his colleagues. He reminded them of the alterations to the original Graham amendment passed on November 10, 2005:

A critical feature of this amendment is that it is forward looking. . . . *The amendment's jurisdiction-stripping provisions clearly do not apply to pending cases, including the Hamdan v. Rumsfeld case, which is currently pending before the Supreme Court. . . . This amendment does not apply retroactively to revoke the jurisdiction of the courts to consider pending claims invoking the Great Writ of Habeas Corpus* challenging past enemy combatant determinations reached without the safeguards this amendment requires for future determinations. *This amendment alters the original language introduced by Senator Graham so that those pending cases are not affected by this provision.* [My emphasis][50]

No senator rose to disagree with Durbin's understanding of the changes in the DTA. Graham and others who supported his original amendment remained silent after Durbin's comments.

The 2006 Defense Authorization Bill, after the DTA was amended to allow pending habeas actions to proceed, passed overwhelmingly in both houses of Congress. President Bush signed the bill into law on December 30, 2005 (issuing his famous signing statement immediately afterward).

On Tuesday, January 4, 2006, the first day of business after the New Year's holiday break, the Department of Justice, citing the new law, announced that on January 5, 2006, it was going to notify the U.S. district court in the District of Columbia that it intended to move to dismiss all pending habeas actions based on the language of the DTA.

Senator Graham agreed with the White House position, saying that the DTA was intended to shut down pending habeas actions before all federal courts, including the Supreme Court. Indeed, Senator Graham, joined by another Republican senator, Jon Kyl (R–AZ), went so far as to write and file an amicus curiae brief for the Court to consider as it examined the *Hamdan v. Rumsfeld* litigation. Furthermore, the Graham-Levin amendment's section on the definition of "United States" reads as follows: "United States Defined—For purposes of this section, the term 'United States', when used in a geographic sense, is as defined in section 101(a)(38) of the Immigration and Nationality Act *and, in particular, does not include the United States Naval Station, Guantanamo Bay, Cuba*" (my emphasis). If that provision was allowed to stand, unchallenged in the courts, then the Supreme Court's *Rasul* opinion would become a nullity—effectively overturned by the modified Graham-Levin amendment.

On January 12, 2006, Solicitor General Clement, in a twenty-three-page brief, asked the justices to drop all proceedings in the *Hamdan v. Rumsfeld* (05-184) case on the grounds that the DTA "removes the Court's jurisdiction to hear this action." The statute, he maintained, had to be given "immediate effect" by the Supreme Court and all other federal courts: "Congress made it clear that the federal courts no longer have jurisdiction over actions filed on behalf of Guantanamo detainees."[51]

Senator Levin, who had cosponsored the substitute amendment to Graham's November 10 amendment, was outraged. He said, in a statement released to the press: "The Justice Department is in error. Far from deciding that the relevant statutory language applies to pending cases, Congress specifically considered and rejected language that would have stripped the courts of jurisdiction in cases that they had before them."[52]

The *New York Times,* in March 2006, summed up the constitutional crisis that had emerged after the DTA, as amended by Graham and cosponsored by Levin, a Democratic senator, was implemented by the White House: "Since the Republican majority has decided to allow President Bush to usurp Congress's role in matters of national security, the battle to save the constitutional balance of powers moves to the judiciary, . . . when the Supreme Court hears arguments in a case [*Hamdan v. Rumsfeld*] that has become the focus of Mr. Bush's imperial vision of the presidency."[53]

The Bush administration, with the assistance of Senator Graham (and possibly in an amendment process orchestrated by the political wizards in the White House), had evidentially found another way to deny the hundreds of Guantánamo detainees their right to seek habeas corpus relief in federal courts. However, the U.S. Supreme Court did address these bold actions of the White House, as well as other administrative efforts to evade its 2004 *Rasul* decision, in March 2006, when it heard oral arguments in the case of *Hamdan v. Rumsfeld.*

HAMDAN V. RUMSFELD, 2005–2006

Between 1996 and 2001, Salim Ahmed Hamdan was Osama bin Laden's chauffeur and bodyguard. In November 2001 he was captured by Afghani militia and handed over to the U.S. military. He was then shipped to Guantánamo. On July 3, 2003, President Bush issued a military order stating that "there is reason to believe that [Hamdan] was a member of al Qaeda or was otherwise involved in terrorism directed against the United States, and is subject to [Bush's] Military Order of November 13, 2001." Within the month, Hamdan was moved into solitary confinement at Guantánamo. At that point, Hamdan was assigned counsel because he found out that he was to be the first enemy combatant to be tried before a military commission.

The United States issued a document containing the formal charges against Hamdan that would be heard by a military commission. In *United States v. Salim Ahmed Hamdan,* a charging document issued on July 13, 2004, he was charged with conspiracy: "[Hamdan] willfully and knowingly joined an enterprise of persons who shared a common criminal purpose and conspired . . . to commit the following offenses triable by military commission: attacking civilians; attacking civilian objects; murder by an unprivileged belligerent; destruction of property by an unprivileged belligerent; and terrorism." He was further informed that the "charged conduct is triable by a military commission."[54]

Before his trial began, Hamdan had a hearing before a CSRT, which found that Hamdan was either a member of or affiliated with al Qaeda. He was kept in solitary confinement awaiting his trial before the three-person military commission. On August 24, 2004, Hamdan's trial began. Pretrial motions began immediately in a small courtroom located on Guantánamo that had formerly been a dental clinic. Hamdan had a military lawyer for his defense, Navy Lt. Cdr. Charles Swift.

Hamdan's trial was one of four separate military commission trials set to begin that week. All four defendants had been charged with conspiracy to commit terrorist acts. Representatives from a number of civil rights and humanitarian NGOs were present to observe the proceedings. Among them were representatives from the ACLU, the ABA, Human Rights Watch, and Amnesty International.[55]

However, soon after the trial began, on November 8, 2004, it was halted by Judge James Robertson of the U.S. District Court for the District of Columbia.[56] "Because Hamdan has not been determined by a competent tribunal to be an offender triable under the law of war, and because in any event the procedures established [creating the military commissions] by the President's order are 'contrary to or inconsistent' with those applicable to courts-martial, Hamdan's petition [for a writ of habeas corpus] will be granted in part. The government's motion will be denied."[57] Robertson ruled that the government had not properly determined whether or not Hamdan was even an offender who was triable by a special military commission under the law of war.

Robertson also found another problem for the administration: its assertion that "the President has untrammeled power to establish military tribunals [and] that his authority emanates from Article II of the Constitution and is inherent in his role as commander-in-chief." Citing the *Quirin* opinion of the Supreme Court, Robertson rejected that argument and instead ruled that

> [Not under the inherent power of the president but according to the Articles of War], Congress provided for the trial by courts-martial of members of the armed forces and specific classes of persons associated with or serving in the army, [and that] the Articles of War also recognize the "military commission" appointed by military command [Articles 38 and 46 of the Articles of War] as an appropriate tribunal for the trial and punishment of offenses *against the law of war* not ordinarily tried by court-martial. [My emphasis][58]

In his forty-five-page ruling, he concluded that President Bush had not only overstepped his constitutional bounds in establishing the military commissions, but had also improperly rejected the Geneva Conventions as a standard of treatment for enemy detainees as well as a standard for trying unlawful enemy combatants.

Furthermore, "the President is not a panel," Robertson wrote. "The law of war includes the Third Geneva Convention, which requires trial by court-martial as long as Hamdan's POW status is in doubt."[59] But Hamdan, and all the other Guantánamo detainees, never had Article 5 hearings to determine their status; the military constantly claimed such hearings were unnecessary.[60]

Regarding the constitutionality of the military commissions as constructed by the Pentagon, Robertson concluded that the commissions were "remarkably different from a court-martial in two important respects. The first has to do with the structure of the reviewing authority after trial; the second, with the power of the appointing authority or the presiding officer to exclude the accused from hearings and deny him access to evidence presented against him." Although the first distinction was not at all problematic, the second difference was "far more troubling." Not allowing a detainee to confront his accusers in court—or to even be in the courtroom at all—was a "dramatic deviation from the confrontation clause [in the U.S. Constitution's Sixth Amendment; such a deviation] could not be countenanced in any American court. . . . It is also apparent that the right to trial 'in one's presence' is established as a matter of international humanitarian and human rights law."[61]

The White House went ballistic after Robertson's opinion was announced. "We vigorously disagree. . . . The Judge has put terrorism on the same legal footing as legitimate methods of waging war," said Department of Justice spokesperson Mark Corallo.[62] On November 16, Department of Defense lawyers appealed his ruling to the federal appeals court in the District of Columbia along with a motion for an expedited appeal. The solicitor general's brief argued that the Robertson ruling represented "an unprecedented judicial intrusion into the prerogatives of the president; [such an interference has] potentially very broad and dangerous ramifications."[63]

The following day, the U.S. Circuit Court for the District of Columbia agreed to an expedited review of the Department of Justice's appeal of Robertson's ruling. On November 22 Hamdan's lawyers asked the Supreme Court to issue an expedited certiorari petition in order to bypass the appellate court review. The justices, however, denied the petition for expedited consideration on January 18, 2005.

Almost eight months later, in July 2005, Robertson's ruling was overturned by a three-judge panel of the U.S. Court of Appeals for the District of Columbia Circuit. (One of the members of the panel was Judge John Roberts, who within a few months, would be confirmed as the new chief justice of the United States.) On July 15, the federal appellate court panel unanimously overturned the trial judge's ruling.[64]

The three-judge appeals panel held that the 2001 AUMF Resolution gave the president all the authority he needed to detain enemy combatants at Guantánamo and, at the president's discretion, to use military commissions to try certain detainees.[65] Two of the judges, Raymond Randolph and Roberts, believed that, contrary to the district court judge's view of the applicability of the Geneva conventions, while these international laws of war protected detainees, "responsibility for observance and enforcement of these rights is upon political and military authorities"—not on federal courts. These international laws of war were not "judicially enforceable."[66] The third judge, Christopher R. Williams, concurred "in all aspects of the court's opinion except for the conclusion that Common Article 3 does not apply to the United States's conduct toward al Qaeda personnel captured in the conflict in Afghanistan. Because I agree that the Geneva Convention is not enforceable in courts of the United States, . . . I fully agree with the court's judgment."[67]

Neal K. Katyal, a Georgetown University law professor and one of the two lawyers representing Hamdan, said he would file an appeal to the Supreme Court because "[the] ruling places absolute trust in the President, unchecked by the Constitution, statutes of Congress and longstanding treaties ratified by the Senate of the United States."[68] On August 8, 2005, Hamdan's lawyers filed for a writ of certiorari in the Supreme Court. Two questions were presented for the justices to consider: (1) Was the military commission process created by the president "duly authorized under Congress's Authorization for the Use of Military Force (AUMF); the Uniform Code of Military Justice (UCMJ); or the inherent powers of the President?" (2) Can Hamdan "obtain judicial enforcement from an Article III court of rights protected under the 1949 Geneva Convention in an action for a writ of habeas corpus challenging the legality of [his] detention by the Executive branch?"[69]

Briefs

In their brief filed with the Court, Hamdan's lawyers presented the Court with one fundamental reason for granting certiorari:

The court of appeals decision fully resolved several issues [authority of both the AUMF and the UCMJ to establish the military commissions; inability of federal courts to enforce the Geneva Conventions], each of which is appropriate for certiorari, and its resolution is inconsistent with decisions of this court and other circuits. . . . [The appeals court decision], by rejecting longstanding constitutional, international-law, and statutory constraints on military commissions, has given the President that power in tribunals that impose life imprisonment and death. Its decision vests the President with the ability to circumvent the federal courts and time-tested limits on the Executive. No decision, by any court, in the wake of the September 11, 2001 attacks has gone this far.[70]

The response in opposition to the granting of certiorari was filed by the solicitor general on September 7, 2005. As in the government's arguments before the Supreme Court in April 2004, the solicitor general again made a separation-of-powers argument, urging the Court not to intrude into the prerogatives of the president by granting certiorari.

Reading the questions they asked the Court to consider and then to refuse certiorari, one sees, once again, the Bush administration's categorical position on separation of powers:

1. Should courts "abstain from interfering with ongoing military commission proceedings"?
2. Does "the President [have] the authority to establish military commissions"?
3. Does the Third Geneva Convention create "judicially enforceable rights"?
4. Should courts "disregard the President's determination as Commander in Chief that al Qaeda combatants are not covered by the Geneva Convention"?
5. Does Hamdan have an "[actionable] claim of prisoner-of-war status under the Geneva Convention"?
6. Must "the federal regulations governing military commissions . . . conform to the provisions in the Uniform Code of Military Justice that apply only to courts-martial"?[71]

"Further review at this time is unwarranted," was the government's opening argument in its brief. The court of appeals interlocutory[72] order "makes plenary review premature."[73] Let the military commission carry on, the government argued. Hamdan may be acquitted; he may be found guilty. If found guilty, *then* he would have the opportunity to appeal to higher military authorities. The legal treatment of enemy detainees is for the military to manage, and civilian federal judges do not have the right to interpose the federal judiciary into what is clearly constitutionally a presidential matter. Any judicial interference with the president's ability to successfully conduct the ongoing war against terrorism violates the constitutional separation-of-powers principle.

For more than a month the justices wrestled with the *Hamdan* petition for certiorari at their secret Friday conference sessions. It was listed—and relisted—for the conferences of September 26, October 7, 14, and 28th, and November 4. Eight justices participated in the lengthy discussions regarding its fate. Chief Justice Roberts, as one of the three judges in the D.C. circuit court who had ruled against Hamdan in July 2005, did not participate in any of them because he recused himself from participating in any way with the discussion and decision. Evidently Justice O'Connor participated in the discussions, as her replacement—Samuel Alito—had not yet been confirmed by the Senate. And perhaps her presence—and her future absence if the petition was granted—kept the justices from quickly deciding to grant or to deny certiorari in *Hamdan.*

In those conference sessions, the justices faced a really "unappealing" question every week: "What to do about a lower-court decision that gives the president unfettered authority to chuck the Constitution, military law, and the Geneva conventions in trying foreign detainees being held at Guantánamo Bay?"[74] At the November 3 conference session, there were finally four votes to grant certiorari in *Hamdan.* On November 7, 2005, the Supreme Court's orders announced the decision. It would examine Hamdan's challenges to his detention and to being tried before a military commission.

On November 15, 2005, a few weeks later, another federal district court judge in the District of Columbia, Judge Colleen Kollar-Kotelly, issued an order staying the proceedings of another military commission set to try David Hicks, an Australian citizen charged with fighting for the Taliban and held at Guantánamo since 2002. The judge cited the fact that the Supreme Court, a week earlier, had granted certiorari in the *Hamdan* case. The Hicks trial was postponed until after the Supreme Court announced its decision in *Hamdan.*

The briefs on the merits were filed by Hamdan's lawyers, Neal Katyal and Lt. Cdr. Charles Swift, on January 6, 2006. On January 12 the government filed a motion to dismiss the writ of certiorari. The ground cited for dismissal was the recently enacted DTA. (The Court shortly thereafter issued an order deferring any action on the government's motion to dismiss "pending argument on the merits.") On February 23, 2006, Solicitor General Clement, for the respondent, Donald Rumsfeld, filed his brief on the merits.

Hamdan's lawyers' brief emphasized and argued the constitutional issues they raised in their certiorari petition. Separation of powers was the root of the litigation. The case "involves a critical question regarding the [separation and] allocation of power among Congress, the President, and the federal courts in the ongoing 'war on terror.'"

Katyal and Swift asked whether the president had "unilateral authority to try suspected terrorists wholly outside the traditional civilian and military judicial systems, for crimes defined by the President alone, under procedures lacking basic protections, before 'judges' who are his closest subordinates," and whether the president had the power to "disregard treaty obligations that Congress has ratified and the federal courts repeatedly have enforced, obligations that protect not only Hamdan but American service members." They said the court of appeals decision was a "limitless approval of this unprecedented arrogation of power [by President Bush and] must be reversed."

They argued, first, that President Bush's creation, the military commissions, were not authorized by Congress. Furthermore, when he created the commissions, he ignored both statutory and common law constraints on the processes found in—or absent from—these special military tribunals. He has not revived "but invented" a new form of military jurisdiction, and his creation "transgresses *both* boundaries [statutory and common law]." To construe the AUMF's phrase "necessary and appropriate force" as authorizing the military commissions, they argued,

> would provide to the President an almost *limitless authority* that Congress could not have intended and that threatens our divided government. If in the interest of "national security," this Court concludes that the President has such authority, it will be hard pressed to limit, in any principled manner, the President's assertion of similarly unprecedented powers in other areas of civil society, so long as they purport to serve that same objective. [My emphasis]

Even if the military commission had been authorized by Congress, and withstood the preceding arguments, it would fail constitutional muster for three fatal reasons: (1) "The commission fails to provide procedural protections required by statute, long deemed essential to the legitimacy of military tribunals enforcing the law of war." (2) Hamdan "is not an offender subject to commission trial under the law of war." (3) "Moreover, the law of war does not, in fact, extend to the offense with which Hamdan has been charged. Hamdan's single count of conspiracy has never constituted an offense against the law of war."

Finally, they argued that the court of appeals must be reversed because Hamdan is entitled to the protections of the 1949 Third Geneva Convention. Under Common Article 3, until a "'competent tribunal' determines that Hamdan is not a POW, he is entitled to its protections." The court of appeals was mistaken when it ruled that Common Article 3 did not apply to Hamdan— and, even if it did, it "could not be judicially enforced."

Concluding, the brief reemphasized the importance of the case:

> This is the rare case where invalidating the government's action preserves the status quo, a carefully crafted equilibrium in place for many decades. Our fundamental principles of separation of powers have survived many dire threats to this nation's security—from capture of the nation's capital by enemy forces, to Civil War, to the threat of nuclear annihilation during the Cold War—and those principles must not be abandoned now.[75]

The brief for the respondents, Donald Rumsfeld and others, introduced for the justices' consideration the controversial Section 1005 of the DTA, which, the Bush people argued, withdrew the jurisdiction of all federal courts except the U.S. Court of Appeals for the District of Columbia Circuit to hear any habeas actions from Guantánamo detainees. In light of the DTA, Clement's brief suggested *Hamdan* should be dismissed for "lack of jurisdiction. In the alternative, the judgment of the court of appeals should be affirmed." Specifically, the government brief raised and discussed a number of questions that the justices had to ponder and then answer in order to render their decision—hopefully one that respected the government's understanding of the separation-of-powers principle:

1. Did the DTA divest "this Court of jurisdiction over this case"?
2. Should federal courts "abstain from interfering with ongoing military commission proceedings"?
3. Does the president have statutory and constitutional authority to establish these commissions?

4. Do the Geneva Conventions create "judicially enforceable rights"?
5. Was the president correct when he "determined that the Geneva Convention does not cover, or afford prisoner-of-war status to, al Qaeda combatants"?
6. Must "the federal regulations governing military commissions . . . conform to provisions in the Uniform Code of Military Justice that apply by their terms only to courts-martial"?

The initial argument of the solicitor general's brief was that the Supreme Court lacked jurisdiction to hear the case. Hamdan's petition "is jurisdictionally foreclosed by the DTA of 2005 and fatally premature." The controversial legislation instantly became an integral part of the legal debate surrounding President Bush's action creating the military commissions. The legislation, continued the brief, "establishes a statutory rule of abstention that eliminates all jurisdiction over petitioner's pre-trial complaints about his military commission."

The president "had ample authority to convene the military commissions against petitioner." Indeed, the government argued that "even if Congress's support for the President's Military Order were not so clear, the President has the *inherent authority* to convene military commissions to try and punish captured enemy combatants in wartime—*even in the absence of any statutory authorization*" (my emphasis).[76]

An important Supreme Court opinion is relevant here. In the 1952 steel seizure case that addressed the question of whether President Truman acted constitutionally when he seized the steel mills during the Korean War, Justice Robert H. Jackson wrote a concurring opinion that joined a court majority in declaring Truman's actions unconstitutional.

1. When the President acts *pursuant to an express or implied authorization of Congress,* his authority is at its *maximum,* for it includes all that he possesses in his own right plus all that Congress can delegate. In these circumstances, and in these only, may he be said (for what it may be worth) to personify the federal sovereignty. . . .
2. When the President acts in *absence of either a congressional grant or denial of authority,* he can only rely upon his own independent powers, but there is a zone of twilight in which he and Congress may have concurrent authority, or in which its distribution is uncertain. Therefore, congressional inertia, indifference or quiescence may sometimes, at least as a practical matter,

enable, if not invite, measures on independent presidential responsibility. In this area, any actual test of power is likely to depend on the imperatives of events and contemporary imponderables rather than on abstract theories of law. . . .

3. When the President takes *measures incompatible* with the expressed or implied will of Congress, his power is at its *lowest ebb,* for then he can rely only upon his own constitutional powers minus any constitutional powers of Congress over the matter. [My emphasis][77]

Counsel on both sides of the litigation brought Jackson's observations about presidential power to bear on arguments made regarding the constitutionality of the military commissions.

Regarding another issue, that of the Geneva Conventions, the brief for the respondents ended with the argument that "no provisions of domestic law, including the habeas statute, transform the Geneva Convention into a judicially enforceable international instrument."[78]

Dozens of amicus briefs were filed with the Court between January and February 2006. Supporting the plaintiff Hamdan were thirty-nine amicus briefs; there were six supporting the respondents, including one from Republican senators Graham and Kyl—the legislators largely responsible for the solicitor general's argument that the Supreme Court lacked jurisdiction to hear the case.

The amicus curiae brief filed by Graham and Kyl deserves special attention because these "distinguished senators" were caught in a bald-faced lie at the very heart of their brief. Their brief, understandably, rested on the DTA of 2005 and its alleged withdrawal of federal jurisdiction to hear pending as well as future habeas actions from Guantánamo detainees from all but one federal court. They argued in the brief that the "legislative history" of the DTA clearly makes that very controversial point of law. To show evidence of the legislative history of the DTA, the two senators quoted extensively from the daily journal of both houses of Congress, the *Congressional Record.* They cite an "extensive colloquy" between the two of them on December 21, 2005, the day the Defense Authorization Bill was passed—with the DTA included. (Not surprisingly, the Clement brief for the government also cited this live "colloquy" between Graham and Kyl.) However, as Emily Bazelon pointed out,

> The problem is that Kyl and Graham's colloquy *didn't actually happen* on December 21st. It was inserted into the *Congressional Record* just before the law

passed, which means that the "colloquy" did not alert other members of Congress to the views it contains. . . . What is utterly nonstandard [about the insertion] is implying to the Supreme Court that testimony was live when it wasn't. . . . The colloquy is even scripted to sound live. "Mr. President, I see that we are nearing the end of our allotted time," Kyl "says" at one point. At another [another senator] appears to interject a question, "If I might interrupt," he begins. [My emphasis][79]

The Graham-Kyl duplicity is mentioned in the petitioner's reply brief's rejoinder to the government's claims of lack of federal court jurisdiction:

> "The Act concerned only the federal courts [it did not, as the government argued, "expressly recognize and ratify" Hamdan's military commission]. . . . Not a single word of its [the DTA's] text, or even the *post hoc* colloquy and briefing by Senators Graham and Kyl, suggest otherwise. [In a footnote (6) at this point, the brief added that] "Senator Graham and Kyl's *amicus* brief suggests that their December 21, 2005 colloquy took place on the Senate floor. A C-Span recording of the Senate debate on the Conference Report, however, shows that the colloquy was inserted in the Record after the fact, . . . and counsel has verified it with individuals present in the chamber at the time.[80]

Oral Argument

Oral argument was heard in the Supreme Court's courtroom on March 28, 2006. Given the significance of the litigation and the large number of amicus curiae briefs filed, the Court allotted ninety minutes for oral argument. The Court also permitted a live audio broadcast of the oral argument. Since the chief justice recused himself, the senior associate justice, John Paul Stevens, presided.

Looming over the courtroom was a major question that had not been foreseen when the Court granted certiorari in *Hamdan* in early November 2005: the impact of the DTA of 2005 on the actions of the Supreme Court. "The court must decide," wrote one observer, "whether it retains the right to proceed with this case at all." Not since the 1868 post–Civil War case of *Ex Parte McCardle* has the Supreme Court "permitted Congress to divest it of jurisdiction over a case it has already agreed to decide."[81]

Neal Katyal appeared on behalf of the petitioner and addressed the justices first. He immediately turned to the jurisdictional matter. "The DTA, while certainly not a model of clarity, does not divest this Court of jurisdiction."[82] He argued that "there was a strong desire by the Congress not to interfere with this Court's traditionally exercised jurisdiction."

Scalia: "You say [the DTA] could be read to preclude cases in the lower courts, but not here."

Katyal: "That's right. . . . One claim is that the jurisdiction-stripping provision applies to pending cases. That, we reject."

Alito: "Why can't the petitioner raise these claims after the military commission issued its decision. I mean, criminal litigation review after the final decision is the general rule."

Katyal: "If this were like a criminal proceeding, we wouldn't be here. We're challenging the lawfulness of the tribunal itself. This isn't a challenge to some decision that a court makes. This is a challenge to the court itself. . . . This is a military commission that is literally unbounded by laws, the Constitution, or treaties. And, Justice Alito, if you adopt the government's position here, it effectively replicates the blank check that this court rejected in *Hamdi*."

Katyal turned the discussion to the merits, the charge of conspiracy against Hamdan. Is the charge, Katyal asked the jurists, one "that violates the laws of war? We believe it doesn't, for two essential reasons." First, the conspiracy charge had, for centuries, been rejected as a violation of the international laws of war. The second reason was that "the commission is operating in totally uncharted waters, because it's charging a violation in a stateless, territoryless conflict, something as to which the full laws of war have never applied." Katyal further noted: "This case is a challenge to the lawfulness of the underlying tribunal and the charge that's against [Hamdan]. Even if the [military commission] is authorized, allowing this charge of conspiracy would open the floodgates to the president to charge whatever he wants."

Alito: "Can't the conspiracy charge be amended?"

Katyal: "Conspiracy is a stand-alone offense. One can charge, as a war crime, attacking civilians and the like, as a pure crime, but what you can't do is charge conspiracy. . . . It has been rejected by international law, because it's too vague."

Kennedy: "[Why] can't the tribunal figure it out [the conspiracy charge controversy], in the first instance, assuming the tribunal is properly authorized?"

Katyal: "It is the role of this court to confine the tribunal to its lawful jurisdiction. That's what we think you should do here. The tribunal itself can't be the judge of its own jurisdiction."

Kennedy: "Well, suppose we remand the case to the D.C. circuit for it to go into all these arguments?"

Katyal: "The public interest is best served by this Court—to set some limits."

Katyal was then able to shift the discussion to another argument: The military commission created by the Bush administration "defies the UCMJ. It, in Article 36, sets minimal ground rules for military justice. And it says that the President can't act in ways that are contrary to, or inconsistent with, this chapter. . . . And the government's position is that they don't have to abide by the UCMJ. . . . We're asking this Court to apply the minimal baseline rules of the UCMJ to the military commissions that operate at GTMO."

Justice Scalia then returned the argument to the DTA: "Might not the act also function as a retroactive approval of what the President has done?"

This question by a skeptical justice gave Katyal an opening to reiterate, in the final minutes of his time, the essential points he had been arguing: "There's nothing in the text of the act itself—there's nothing in the legislative history, or even the post—even the brief filed by Senators Graham and Kyl, which suggests, in any way, that this [the DTA] was ratification [of Bush's military commissions]. But suppose it were, Justice Scalia. Suppose it did ratify some sort of military commission. I don't believe that it authorized this military commission with this charge, conspiracy, in this conflict, a stateless, territoryless conflict, with these procedures, procedures that violate the UCMJ."

Paul Clement, the U.S. solicitor general, then took his turn at the lectern. The Geneva Conventions' applicability came into play a great deal during Clement's forty-five minutes before the justices. As one reporter noted, "Members of the Court seemed attracted to invoking the Geneva Conventions, saying that the Bush position created a double standard because it accuses alleged terrorists of violating the laws of war while denying them the protections of the same laws of war."[83] Clement, however, began his presentation by "turning first" to the jurisdictional issue that arose because of the passage of the DTA of 2005.

Stevens: "What sources of law have the commissions generally enforced over the years, beginning with George Washington? Just Army regulations or American law or foreign law? What are the basic sources of law that they can enforce?"[84]

Clement: "They basically enforce the laws of war. . . . In this context, you have a controlling executive act in the form of the regulations *themselves* that make it clear that the executive views things like conspiracy to violate the laws of war to be actionable under the laws of war" (my emphasis).

Stevens: "And do the laws of war then have any application to the procedures that they have to follow?"

Clement: "I don't think that the law of war is—you know, extensively regulates procedure."

Souter: "If the military commissions are operating under the law of war, you've got to accept that one law of war here is the Geneva Convention right to a presumption of POW status unless there is a determination by a competent tribunal otherwise. Don't you go from the frying pan into the fire, in effect, when you take the position that the laws of war are what the tribunal is applying?"

Clement: "Okay, that [status determination] can be brought to the military commissions, but they could adjudicate it and say that the Geneva Conventions don't apply here."

Souter: "Do you agree that the Geneva Convention applies as part of the laws of war?"

Clement: "Well, I don't think that the Geneva Convention applies in this particular conflict."

Souter: "'I don't see how you can have it both ways!'"

Clement: "We're not trying to have it both ways, Justice Souter. The fact that the Geneva Conventions are part of the law of war doesn't mean that [Hamdan] is entitled to any protection under those conventions."

Kennedy: "If a group is going to try somebody, [must] we wait until that group of people finishes the trial before the Court—before habeas intervenes to determine the authority of the tribunal to hold and to try?"

Clement: "*Well, with respect, Justice Kennedy, this isn't 'a group of people.' This is the president* invoking an authority that he's exercised in virtually every war we've had" (my emphasis).

Kennedy then returned to the function of habeas corpus: "I thought that the historic function of habeas is to test the jurisdiction and the legitimacy of a court."

Clement: "[With the passage of the DTA], Congress has made it clear that, whatever else is true, these military commission proceedings can proceed, and exclusive review can be done after the fact, after completion, in the [federal] D.C. circuit."

Souter: "Exclusive review of what? I don't see that the DTA preserves a right to review of the very issue that they want to raise here."

Clement: "Well, I think I disagree. They can come in and challenge [the commission's procedures] after their conviction, they are perfectly free to do that."

Justice Breyer's question returned the argument to the scope of the DTA and the portent for the federal judiciary if the legislation is constitutional: "If we accepted your interpretation [of the DTA], how could we possibly avoid the most terribly difficult and important question of whether Congress can constitutionally deprive this court of jurisdiction in habeas cases? . . . What is the answer to the claim that it is not constitutional for Congress, without suspending the writ of habeas corpus, to [remove] jurisdiction from the courts?"

Clement: "This case, and most of the cases, doesn't raise a serious Suspension Clause[85] problem, for the simple reason that I think deferring review or channeling it to the [D.C.] court of Appeals does not amount to a suspension."

Ginsburg: "It would be an extraordinary act, I think, to withdraw jurisdiction over a pending case."

Stevens: "[Regarding the DTA], do you say it's a permissible suspension of the Writ or that it's *not* a suspension of the Writ?"

Clement: "It's both."

Stevens: "Well, it can't be both! [But] is it your position that [Congress] did not suspend the writ. You're not arguing that it's a justifiable suspension of the writ."

Clement: "Well, I think the terms of the Suspension Clause would be satisfied here because of the exigencies of 9/11. If the question is, Am I taking the position that Congress *consciously* thought that it was suspending the writ? Then I would say no. . . . And if you think, in order for there to be a valid suspension, Congress has to do it *consciously* [that's not so]. *My view would be that if Congress, sort of, stumbles upon a suspension of the writ, but the preconditions are satisfied, that would still be constitutionally valid*" (my emphasis).

Then came a lengthy exchange that turned the oral argument into high drama. It was a tense set of exchanges between the solicitor general and Justice Souter.

Souter: "Can Congress, in fact, limit jurisdiction without suspending habeas corpus? Did Congress, when it passed the DTA in December 2005, effectively strip the Supreme Court of the right to hear habeas appeals from the GTMO detainees? Can the Congress validly suspend it inadvertently?"

Clement: "My view would be that if Congress sort of stumbles upon a suspension of the Writ, that the preconditions are satisfied, that would still be constitutionally valid. Okay."

Souter (stunned): "You're saying that the writ *was suspended by inadvertence! Isn't there a pretty good argument that the suspension of the writ is the most stupendously significant act that the Congress of the United States can take and therefore we ought to be at least a little slow to accept your argument that it can be done from pure inadvertence?*" (my emphasis).

Clement: "I think at least if you're talking about the extension of the writ to enemy combatants held outside the territory of the United States—"

Souter: "Now wait a minute! The writ is the writ. There are not two writs of habeas corpus, for some cases and for other cases."

The exchange ended, probably because both men were drained, and another justice, Justice Ginsburg, interrupted with her question: "This law [DTA] was proposed and enacted some weeks after this Court granted cert in this very case. It is an extraordinary act, I think, to withdraw jurisdiction from this Court in a pending case."

Clement: "What Congress has done here is that [it] has modified the jurisdiction of all the courts, and that has had the effect of eliminating jurisdiction in this Court over a pending case."

Justice Breyer's question went back to the question of whether the military commissions President Bush created were war crimes tribunals to begin with: "You want to say that these [actions by Hamdan] are war crimes. One, this is not a war, at least not an ordinary war. Two, it's not a war crime, because [conspiracy] doesn't fall under international law. And, three, it's not a war crime tribunal or commission, because no emergency, civil courts are open, there is no military commander asking for it, it's not like past history! And if the president can do this, he can set up a commission and go to Toledo [Ohio] and pick up an alien, and not have any trial at all, except before that special commission."

Clement's response to Breyer's lengthy question was a repetition of the government's arguments in the briefs and during oral argument. The theme was consistent: When the president determines something, for example, "that conspiracy is an actionable violation of the law of war," or that Guantánamo detainees tried by military commissions do not have procedural rights enumerated in the Geneva Conventions and other laws of war, that's the end of the argument. The president has constitutional, statutory, and inherent powers to make these kinds of decisions. Period. "He's made that clear. And so I think that has to be taken into account in [the Court's] analysis."

Breyer: "Is it the President, not the Congress, defining the content of the law, the criminal law, under which a person will be tried? Isn't there a 'separation of powers' problem there?"

Clement: "I sure hope not, Justice Breyer!"

Stevens: "But I don't think [our constitutional history has] approved of [the President's] adding additional crimes under the law of war. I don't think we have ever held that the President can make something a crime which was not already a crime under the law of war."

Clement: "I think that may be true, Justice Stevens."

After a few more minutes, the solicitor general's time expired.

Katyal's rebuttal was quite brief, for he only had three minutes left. He briefly hammered at the solicitor general's view that conspiracy was an actionable offense in international laws of war. Such a view, Katyal said, has been "rejected . . . everywhere"—except, evidently, in the White House and in the Department of Justice:[86]

> The government's argument, in the end, is one that this Court has rejected in [earlier cases], because it depends on the idea that the President has ultimate flexibility with respect to these military commissions. . . . Finally, Justices, we'd just point out that the predicate of abstention is not met here. This is an ad hoc trial in which the procedures are all defined with the President. He says the laws of war do not apply when we're talking about protecting this vulnerable individual at GTMO. But then he says they do apply and permit him to charge Mr. Hamdan with the one offense which is rejected entirely at international law. . . . Just enforce the lawful uses of military commissions and the historic role of this Court.

The case was submitted at 12:31 p.m., and the Court adjourned for the day. Within a few days, the justices would meet in their secret conference session to discuss and vote on this and the other cases heard in oral arguments earlier in the week. The fur begins to fly as the justices discuss the case on Friday, then vote, then write and circulate their thoughts about the case. In the initial conference session after oral argument, for the very first time the justices voice their views on the issue and then tell the others how they come down on the legal questions. In *Hamdan,* as in the other detainee cases, there were dichotomous views freely expressed in the conference—and in the subsequent stages of the Court's decision-making process, the writing and editing of their various opinions. On the very last day of the Court's 2005 term, the justices announced their judgment in *Hamdan v. Rumsfeld.*

The Court's Judgment

On June 29, 2006, the justices announced their judgment in *Hamdan*. They ruled 5–3 against the Bush administration. However, the justices wrote six opinions, taking up a total of 185 pages in the *U.S. Reports.*

Justice Stevens wrote the majority opinion and judgment. It was both an "opinion" of the Court (meaning that five justices agreed with each other on the question and how the Court must answer it) and a "judgment" of the Court (meaning, in *Hamdan,* that some sections of the Stevens opinion could only muster four votes): Parts I through IV, VI through VI-D-iii, VI-D-v, and VII of his opinion were joined by Justices Breyer, Ginsburg, Kennedy, and Souter. Parts V and VI-D-iv of the Stevens opinion were joined by Justices Breyer, Ginsburg, and Souter.

For all eight participating justices, the threshold question was whether the DTA of 2005 withdrew the jurisdiction of the Supreme Court (and almost all other federal courts) to hear the case at this time. If it did, then the Court must end all discussion of the substantive questions raised in *Hamdan.*

Justice Stevens's opinion denied the government's motion to dismiss the case because of Section 1005(e) of the DTA:

> The Government argues that §§1005(e)(1) and 1005(h) had the immediate effect, upon enactment, of repealing federal jurisdiction not just over detainee habeas actions yet to be filed but also over any such actions then pending in any federal court—including this Court. Accordingly, it argues, we lack jurisdiction to review the Court of Appeals' decision below. . . . Ordinary principles of statutory construction suffice to rebut the Government's theory—at least insofar as this case, which was pending at the time the DTA was enacted, is concerned.

In this part (II) of the opinion, Justice Stevens made specific reference to the duplicitous behavior of Republican senators Graham and Kyl and also underscored the point that Congress did not intend to withdraw federal court jurisdiction from *pending* cases:

> While statements attributed to the final bill's two other sponsors, Senators Graham and Kyl, arguably contradict Senator Levin's contention that the final version of the Act preserved jurisdiction over pending habeas cases, see 151 Cong. Rec. S14263–S14264 (Dec. 21, 2005), those statements appear to have been inserted into the Congressional Record *after* the Senate debate. All statements made during the debate itself support Senator Levin's understanding that the final text of the DTA would not render subsection (e)(1) applicable to pending cases. . . . The inapposite November 14, 2005, statement of Senator Graham, which JUSTICE

SCALIA cites as evidence of that Senator's "assumption that pending cases are covered," follows directly after the uncontradicted statement of his co-sponsor, Senator Levin, assuring members of the Senate that "the amendment will not strip the courts of jurisdiction over [pending] cases."[87]

The next question the Stevens opinion addressed, in Part III, was the government's contention that "we should apply the 'judge-made rule that civilian courts should await the final outcome of on-going military proceedings before entertaining an attack on those proceedings.'" The Supreme Court majority rejected this argument by applying *Quirin*, "the most relevant precedent":

> In *Quirin*, the President convened a military commission to try the saboteurs, who then filed habeas corpus petitions in the United States District Court for the District of Columbia challenging their trial by commission. We granted the saboteurs' petition for certiorari to the Court of Appeals before judgment. Far from abstaining pending the conclusion of military proceedings, which were ongoing, we convened a special Term to hear the case and expedited our review. That course of action was warranted, we explained, "[i]n view of the public importance of the questions raised by [the cases] and of the duty which rests on the courts, in time of war as well as in time of peace, to preserve unimpaired the constitutional safeguards of civil liberty, and because in our opinion the public interest required that we consider and decide those questions without any avoidable delay." As the Court of Appeals [in *Hamdan*] recognized, *Quirin* "provides a compelling historical precedent for the power of civilian courts to entertain challenges that seek to interrupt the processes of military commissions."

The Stevens opinion then, in Part IV, addressed the military commission concept itself. "Contrary to the Government's assertion," wrote Stevens, "even *Quirin* did not view the [congressional] authorization as a sweeping mandate for the President to 'invoke military commissions when he deems them necessary.'" Additionally, congressional authorization was given "with the express condition that the President and those under his command comply with the law of war. . . . The Government would have us dispense with the inquiry that the *Quirin* Court undertook and find in either the AUMF or the DTA specific, overriding authorization for the very commission that has been convened to try Hamdan. Neither of these congressional Acts, however, expands the President's authority to convene military commissions."

Neither the 2001 AUMF Resolution nor the DTA of 2005 can be read to provide "specific and overriding authorization" for the creation by the president, of the military commission, to try Hamdan:

First, . . . there is nothing in the text or legislative history of the AUMF even hinting that Congress intended to expand or alter the authorization in Article 21 of the UCMJ.[88] Likewise, the DTA cannot be read to authorize this commission. Although the DTA, unlike either Article 21 or the AUMF, was enacted after the President had convened Hamdan's commission, it contains no language authorizing that tribunal or any other at Guantanamo Bay. The statute pointedly reserves judgment on whether "the Constitution and laws of the United States are applicable" in reviewing such decisions and whether, if they are, the "standards and procedures" used to try Hamdan and other detainees actually violate the "Constitution and laws."

Together, the UCMJ, the AUMF, and the DTA at most acknowledge a general presidential authority to convene military commissions in circumstances where justified under the "Constitution and laws," including the law of war.

Stevens then, in Part V of the opinion, turned to the question that relentlessly followed: whether "Hamdan's military commission [was] justified. It is to that inquiry we now turn." Military commissions, throughout American history, Stevens wrote, have served three purposes: (1) "They have substituted for civilian courts at times and in places where martial law has been declared." (2) "Commissions have been established to try civilians as part of a temporary military government over occupied enemy territory or territory regained from an enemy where civilian government cannot and does not function." (3) "When the commission was convened as an 'incident to the conduct of war'" when there is a need "to seize and subject to disciplinary measures those enemies who in their attempt to thwart or impede our military effort have violated the law of war." Given these three historic reasons for creating military commissions, was there a "military necessity" for the military commission to exist? The majority emphatically concluded that there was no reason for its existence.

Furthermore, wrote Stevens, "the offense [the government] alleges is not triable by [a] law-of-war military commission":

There is no suggestion that Congress has, in exercise of its constitutional authority to "define and punish . . . Offences against the Law of Nations,"[89] positively identified "conspiracy" as a war crime. . . . At a minimum, the Government must make a substantial showing that the crime for which it seeks to try a defendant by military commission is acknowledged to be an offense against the law of war. That burden is far from satisfied here. The crime of "conspiracy" . . . does not appear in either the Geneva Conventions or the Hague Conventions— the major treaties on the law of war.

In Part VI the majority concluded that the military commission *lacked the power to proceed* because its structure and procedures violated both the UCMJ and the four 1949 Geneva Conventions: "The UCMJ conditions the President's use of military commissions on compliance not only with the American common law of war, but also with the rest of the UCMJ itself, insofar as applicable, and with the 'rules and precepts of the law of nations.'"

The commission's procedures provided Hamdan with the barest of due process protections. The Commission Order 1 enumerated the protections. However, Stevens wrote,

> these rights are subject to one glaring condition: The accused and his civilian counsel may be excluded from, and precluded from ever learning what evidence was presented during, any part of the proceeding that either the Appointing Authority or the presiding officer decides to "close." Grounds for such closure "include the protection of information classified or classifiable . . . ; information protected by law or rule from unauthorized disclosure; the physical safety of participants in Commission proceedings, including prospective witnesses; intelligence and law enforcement sources, methods, or activities; and other national security interests." Appointed military defense counsel must be privy to these closed sessions, but may, at the presiding officer's discretion, be forbidden to reveal to his or her client what took place therein.

Finally, the presiding officer could deny Hamdan and Katyal access to classified and "protected information," so long as the presiding officer concludes that the withheld evidence is "probative" and that its admission without Hamdan's knowledge would not result in the denial of a full and fair trial.

The majority agreed with the petitioner's argument. They concluded that the commission's procedures were not in accord with either the UCMJ or the Geneva Conventions.[90]

> Article 36[91] places two restrictions on the President's power to promulgate rules of procedure for courts-martial and military commissions alike. First, no procedural rule he adopts may be "contrary to or inconsistent with" the UCMJ—however practical it may seem. Second, the rules adopted must be "uniform insofar as practicable." That is, the rules applied to military commissions must be the same as those applied to courts-martial unless such uniformity proves impracticable. . . . Under the circumstances, then, the rules applicable in courts-martial must apply. Since it is undisputed that Commission Order No. 1 deviates in many significant respects from those rules, it necessarily violates Article 36(b).

After more than seventy pages, Stevens's opinion concluded with the following assessment:

> We have assumed, as we must, that the allegations made in the Government's charge against Hamdan are true. We have assumed, moreover, the truth of the message implicit in that charge—viz., that Hamdan is a dangerous individual whose beliefs, if acted upon, would cause great harm and even death to innocent civilians, and who would act upon those beliefs if given the opportunity. It bears emphasizing that Hamdan does not challenge, and we do not today address, the Government's power to detain him for the duration of active hostilities in order to prevent such harm. But in undertaking to try Hamdan and subject him to criminal punishment, the Executive is bound to comply with the Rule of Law that prevails in this jurisdiction. The judgment of the Court of Appeals is reversed, and the case is remanded for further proceedings.

Justice Breyer wrote a short separate opinion, joined by Justices Souter and Ginsburg. Reacting to a few of the dissenters' criticism of the majority opinion, he wrote:

> The dissenters say that today's decision would "sorely hamper the President's ability to confront and defeat a new and deadly enemy." They suggest that it undermines our Nation's ability to "preven[t] future attacks" of the grievous sort that we have already suffered. That claim leads me to state briefly what I believe the majority sets forth both explicitly and implicitly at greater length. The Court's conclusion ultimately rests upon a single ground: Congress has not issued the Executive a "blank check." Cf. *Hamdi v. Rumsfeld*. Indeed, Congress has denied the President the legislative authority to create military commissions of the kind at issue here. Nothing prevents the President from returning to Congress to seek the authority he believes necessary. Where, as here, no emergency prevents consultation with Congress, judicial insistence upon that consultation does not weaken our Nation's ability to deal with danger. To the contrary, that insistence strengthens the Nation's ability to determine—through democratic means—how best to do so. The Constitution places its faith in those democratic means. Our Court today simply does the same.[92]

Justice Kennedy filed an opinion concurring in part, joined by Breyer, Ginsburg, and Souter. He explained why he could not join the entire Stevens opinion for the majority:

> I would not decide whether Common Article 3's standard necessarily requires that the accused have the right to be present at all stages of a criminal trial. I would rely on other deficiencies noted here and in the opinion by the Court— deficiencies that relate to the structure and procedure of the commission and that

inevitably will affect the proceedings—as the basis for finding the military commissions lack authorization under 10 U.S.C. §836 and fail to be regularly constituted under Common Article 3 and §821. I likewise see no need to address the validity of the conspiracy charge against Hamdan. . . . In light of the conclusion that the military commissions at issue are unauthorized Congress may choose to provide further guidance in this area. Congress, not the Court, is the branch in the better position to undertake the sensitive task of establishing a principle not inconsistent with the national interest or international justice. Finally, for the same reason, I express no view on the merits of other limitations on military commissions described as elements of the common law of war in Part V of Justice Stevens' opinion. With these observations I join the Court's opinion with the exception of Parts V and VI-D-iv.[93]

Justice Scalia filed a twenty-four-page dissenting opinion, joined by Justices Alito and Thomas. His dissent focused on the question of Court jurisdiction. For Scalia, unlike the majority, the DTA "*unambiguously* provides that no court, *justice,* or judge shall have jurisdiction to consider the habeas application of a GTMO detainee" (my emphasis). The majority's conclusion that the Court "has jurisdiction to hear, consider, and render judgment . . . is patently erroneous. And even if it were not, the jurisdiction supposedly retained should, in an exercise of sound equitable discretion, not be exercised."[94]

Scalia ridiculed the majority's reliance on the legislative history of the DTA "to buttress its implausible reading of Section 1005 (e)." Stevens's observations, including the floor debate printed in the Congressional Record, are irrelevant "unless one indulges the fantasy that Senate floor speeches are attended (like the Philippics of Demosthenes) by throngs of eager listeners, instead of being delivered (like Demosthenes' practice sessions on the beach) alone into a vast emptiness." The DTA unambiguously withdrew jurisdiction from the U.S. Supreme Court in cases pending before the Court. However, "opportunistically," the majority "ignores" the 2005 statute's message, much to the chagrin of the dissenter.

Justice Thomas filed a lengthy dissenting opinion, joined by Justice Scalia and, in part, Justice Alito:

> For the reasons set forth in Justice Scalia's dissent, it is clear that this Court lacks jurisdiction to entertain petitioner's claims. The Court having concluded otherwise, it is appropriate to respond to [its] resolution of the merits of petitioner's claims because its opinion openly flouts our well-established duty to respect the Executive's judgment in matters of military operations and foreign

affairs. The Court's evident belief that it is qualified to pass on the "[m]ilitary necessity" of the Commander in Chief's decision to employ a particular form of force against our enemies is so antithetical to our constitutional structure that it simply cannot go unanswered. I respectfully dissent.[95]

As he had argued in his *Hamdi* dissent, Thomas again wrote about the "structural advantages attendant to the Executive Branch—namely, the decisiveness, 'activity, secrecy, and dispatch' that flow from the Executive's 'unity.'" Quoting the AUMF, he noted that in our federal system, with its separation of powers, the president is owed deference by the Court and the Congress:

> Under this framework, the President's decision to try Hamdan before a military commission for his involvement with al Qaeda is entitled to a heavy measure of deference. In the present conflict, Congress has authorized the President "to use all necessary and appropriate force against those nations, organizations, or persons *he determines* planned, authorized, committed, or aided the terrorist attacks that occurred on September 11, 2001 . . . in order to prevent any future acts of international terrorism against the United States by such nations, organizations or persons."

Thomas disagreed with *every* substantive point made by the majority, from the DTA's clear message, to the power of the military commission to proceed without constraint,[96] to the meaning of conspiracy: "Today a plurality of this Court would hold that conspiracy to massacre innocent civilians does not violate the laws of war [a position that is] unsustainable." For Thomas, the majority's "willingness to second-guess the determination of the political branches that these conspirators must be brought to justice is both unprecedented and dangerous."

He also categorically rejected the plurality's argument that the military commission was unlawful because it violated Common Article 3 of the Geneva Conventions as well as various provisions of the Third Geneva Convention: "These contentions," he argued, "are meritless and untenable."

Concluding his dissent, Thomas argued that President Bush's decisions "about the nature of the present conflict with respect to members of al Qaeda operating in Afghanistan represents a core exercise of his commander-in-chief authority that this Court is bound to respect"—but has not.

Justice Alito filed a dissenting opinion, joined in part by Justices Scalia and Thomas, as to parts I–III. His ten-page dissent was the shortest of the three dissents. For the newest justice, only the 110th jurist to sit on the High Bench since 1789, the Court lacked jurisdiction to hear the case.

He focused on the majority's reasoning that Common Article 3 of the Geneva Conventions called for a *"regularly constituted court* affording all the judicial guarantees which are recognized as indispensable by civilized peoples." The Court majority relied on this segment of the article in concluding that the military commission did not meet the minimal requirements for a "regularly constituted court." Because there were no reasons presented why the commission deviated from conventional court-martial standards, and the procedures established for the commission's proceedings "impermissibly differ[ed] from those provided under the Uniform Code of Military Justice," the military commission was unlawful.

Alito, however, disagreed with the majority's conclusion. For him, the phrase meant "a court that has been appointed, set up, or established in accordance with the domestic law of the appointing country."[97] Given his definition of "regularly constituted court," he had to dissent. For Alito, "there is no reason why a court that differs in structure or composition from an ordinary military court must be viewed as having been improperly constituted." Although courts from a municipal court to an international court such as the International Tribunal for the Former Yugoslavia "are 'differently constructed' and differ substantially in many other respects, they are all 'regularly constituted.'"

Toward the end of his short dissent, Alito returned to his opening comments about the three elements of Common Article 3 of the Geneva Conventions: "First, the commissions qualify as courts. Second, the commissions were appointed, set up, and established pursuant to an order of the President, just like the commission in *Ex parte Quirin*. . . . Finally, the commission procedures, taken as a whole, and including the availability of review by a United States Court of Appeals and by this Court, do not provide a basis for deeming the commissions to be illegitimate."

Alito concluded his dissent by quoting analyses of Common Article 3 maintaining that its major goal was to prevent summary justice: "*It is only 'summary justice' which it is intended to prohibit*" and pointing out that "whatever else may be said about the system that was erected by Military Commission Order No. 1, and augmented by the DTA, this system . . . does not dispense 'summary justice.'"

Reactions to the Decision

"The Supreme Court did the nation a favor yesterday," wrote a commentator in the online journal *TomPaine.commonsense*. "It confirmed a basic—but contested—cornerstone of the Republic that we have a government of laws, not of the president or the vice president's whims."[98]

One immediate response to the *Hamdan* decision was the filing of hundreds of supplemental motions emphasizing "the Supreme Court's holding that individuals may invoke the Geneva Conventions protections against mistreatment." Bill Goodman, the legal director of one of the filing groups, the Center for Constitutional Rights, applauded the decision. "We think the Supreme Court's statements about the Geneva Conventions revitalizes those petitions. It should give them more traction."[99]

By the fall of 2006, there were more than 500 petitions in the federal courts awaiting action. Furthermore, some lawyers thought that *Hamdan* could apply to detainees held in Afghanistan and Iraq—and even to those held by the CIA in secret locations around the globe. "What's truly striking about the ruling is that *all* detainees, even al Qaeda members, are entitled to the protections of Geneva," said Kenneth Roth, the executive director of Human Rights Watch, another advocacy group.[100]

For Harold Koh, the dean of the Yale Law School, *Hamdan* was "a stunning rejection of the government's approach going back to just after September 11th that it did not have to respond within the framework of international and constitutional law."[101]

Katyal, Hamdan's civilian attorney, saw the Supreme Court's decision as "dramatically changing the way the administration conducts detention and interrogation operations. If you're a CIA officer, an interrogator, you have to worry about your liability. This administration may not prosecute, but it also cannot inoculate you from the decisions of some future administration. I think individuals are not going to risk that kind of liability."[102]

All observers felt the Supreme Court had "delivered a stunning rebuke to the Bush administration over its plan to try Guantanamo detainees before military commissions."[103] The Court's opinion, "repudiating the Bush administration's plan to put GTMO detainees on trial before military commissions," was seen as a "sweeping and categorical defeat" for Bush. It "left human rights lawyers . . . almost speechless with surprise and delight, using words like 'fantastic,' 'amazing,' and 'remarkable.'"[104]

The Common Article 3 holding by the majority was very significant with regard to its implications for detainee treatment by the U.S. military and the CIA. Because Common Article 3 bars all "humiliating and degrading" treatment, the behavior of the military toward the detainees—horrifically depicted in the Abu Ghraib photos—implied that U.S. military had violated domestic criminal law.

Equally clear for all who have followed the Court's actions in these enemy combatant cases was the unavoidable question, How would the Bush administration respond to this dramatic 5–3 decision? The Bush administration's lawyers and top political leaders—including Bush and Cheney—were stunned and angered by the *Hamdan* decision. Its sweep was totally unexpected, and it sent a clear message restricting the unilateral use of presidential power. The very day the decision was announced, the president responded to reporters' queries about *Hamdan* by saying, "I want to find a way forward." He said that his senior staff would meet with legislators to plan some sort of legislative response to the Court's ruling.

THE ADMINISTRATION'S INITIAL RESPONSE

An immediate consequence of the Court decision was the historic memo that Deputy Secretary of Defense Gordon England sent on July 7, 2006, to *every* command and office in the Department of Defense. Its title was "Application of Common Article 3 of the Geneva Conventions to the Treatment of Detainees in the Department of Defense." Gordon wrote:

> The Supreme Court has determined that Common Article 3 to the Geneva Conventions of 1949 *applies as a matter of law to the conflict with Al Qaeda.* The Court found that the military commissions as constituted by the Department of Defense are not consistent with Common Article 3.
>
> It is my understanding that, aside from the military commission procedures, existing DoD orders, policies, directives, execute orders, and doctrine comply with the standards of Common Article 3 and, therefore, actions by DoD personnel that comply with such issuances would comply with the standards of Common Article 3. . . . In addition, you will recall the President's prior directive that "the United States Armed Forces shall continue to treat detainees humanely," humane treatment being the overarching requirement of Common Article 3.
>
> You will ensure that all DoD personnel adhere to these standards. In this regard, I request that you promptly review all relevant directives, regulations, policies, practices, and procedures under your purview to ensure that they comply with the standards of Common Article 3.
>
> Your reply confirming completion of this review should be submitted . . . no later than three weeks from the date of this memorandum. [My emphasis][105]

"For the first time, the Bush administration has conceded that enemy combatants are entitled to minimal protections under the Geneva Conventions," wrote the *Economist,* regarding the England memo.[106] The Gordon memo explicitly made it clear that even the most fiendish al Qaeda detainee's interrogation must be constrained by the Geneva Conventions. And if that fiend is charged with an offense against the laws of war, the Geneva Conventions apply. But with the presidency of George W. Bush, one needed to ask, How long would this cave-in to the rule of law last? Not too long, as Chapter 6 illustrates.

Lieutenant Commander Swift, the appointed military lawyer for Hamdan, also felt the consequences of the case. The Bush administration's response to his success on behalf of his client was bitter. Despite, or because of, his success in his three-year defense of Hamdan,[107] and despite being named one of the nation's 100 most influential lawyers in the nation by the *National Law Journal,* he was passed over for promotion in late 2005. "I may be one of the most influential lawyers in America," he said to a reporter, "but I won't be in the military much longer. That irony did strike me."[108] (He did not endear himself to the White House when, in one of his briefs, he compared his boss, President Bush, to King George III.)

The major response of the Bush administration was the seemingly *now*-heartfelt need to enter into negotiations with Congress, an action Bush, Cheney, Rumsfeld, and Addington had "previously spurned."[109] *Hamdan* forced this political turnabout. Stevens's opinion had given the president two choices: (1) Use the UCMJ court-martial procedures to try detainees, or (2) work with Congress to draw up a new set of rules and procedures for the military commissions. The president, ruled the Court majority, does not unilaterally set detainee rules—whether they are rules for military commissions or regulations for the interrogation of al Qaeda detainees.

In early July 2006 Tony Snow, the president's spokesperson, told reporters, "The White House is now working with Congress to try to come up with a means of providing justice for detainees at GTMO in a manner that's consistent with the Supreme Court's ruling."[110] White House and Department of Defense lawyers, as well as the attorney general and Lieutenant Commander Swift, among others, appeared before a number of congressional committees, including the House and the Senate Armed Services committees, to discuss the next steps for Congress and the administration regarding the treatment of the enemy detainees.

Some administration lawyers felt Congress should do "minor tweaking" on the president's military commissions—the very institutions struck down by the Supreme Court in *Hamdan*—and then ratify these tweaks by passing legislation. However, legislators, including key Republican senators, seriously disagreed with that essentially noncompliant strategy. Instead, they argued for use of the court-martial device as a constitutional response to *Hamdan*. Senator Warner, Republican chairman of the Senate Armed Services Committee, insisted that "it's got to be dealt with so that we do not face a future court challenge, and also so that the international community recognizes our credibility in dealing with these things."[111]

The days of testimony in Congress clearly revealed yet another division within the Bush administration. Whereas the hard-liners, including Attorney General Gonzales and others in the Department of Justice, wanted Congress to simply tweak and then validate the president's military commission format, other administration spokespersons, especially the DOD's lawyers and the military lawyers in JAG, believed there must be a clearly defined process that would be in accord with the *Hamdan* order of the Supreme Court.

The JAG lawyers, in particular, saw the Supreme Court decision as validation of their long-held view—rejected by the Bush ideologues in 2003 and early 2004—that America's detainee policy violated the international laws of war. "I do agree with the [Court's] reinforcement of the message that Common Article 3 is a baseline standard," said Maj. Gen. Scott C. Black, the Army JAG. "And I would say that, at least in the U.S. Army—and I'm confident in the other services—we've been training to that standard and living to that standard since the beginning of our Army, and we continue to do so."[112]

The general's testimony directly conflicted with that of Stephen Bradbury, the acting chief of the Department of Justice's Office of Legal Counsel. In testimony before a Senate committee, he said, "The United States has never before applied Common Article 3 in the context of an armed conflict with international terrorists. [Application of that article] will create a degree of uncertainty for those who fight to defend us from terrorist attack."[113] His testimony was clearly misleading because the U.S. military, up to 2001, applied more restrictive guidelines—found in the Rules of Engagement and in the UCMJ—than those suggested in Common Article 3.

What the nearly one week of public testimony in July 2006 revealed was the continued presence in the White House, the Vice President's Office, and the Department of Justice of a strong "backlash" against the Court's *Hamdan* decision.[114] Based on their past noncompliant behavior, the expectation was that the Bush administration would develop new tactics to avoid the clear message in *Hamdan*. The critics were not wrong. As chapter 6 will explore, the president and his surrogates in the administration, manipulating a still-acquiescent Republican Congress, acted in a way that clearly skirted the essence of the Supreme Court's *Hamdan* decision and, more ominously, withdrew both the right of detainees to petition for a writ of habeas corpus in federal courts and the federal courts' power of judicial review in this controversial legal venue.

6. Bush Trumps the U.S. Supreme Court: The 2006 Military Commissions Act

The question is, and has always been, whether the exercise of [presidential power] to imprison people seized in connection with the war on terror, would be restrained by the rule of law.

JOSEPH MARGULIES, 2006[1]

Democrats are concerned about such quaint and obsolete concepts as the rule of law. None of that for Republicans, they are tough and realistic.

ATTRIBUTED TO KARL ROVE, 2006[2]

As demonstrated in this book—and so many others[3]—President Bush's policies in his war on terror "amount to a radical assertion of executive authority."[4] They reflect his and his mentor Dick Cheney's belief that the presidency is the only institution in our federal system that can act decisively—without any interference from the coordinate branches of government. Justice Thomas's *Hamdan* dissent, to some extent, reflects the White House position: There are "structural advantages attendant to the Executive Branch—namely, the decisiveness, activity, secrecy, and dispatch that flow from the Executive's 'unity,'" that give the president all the authority he needs to react to the war against the United States. (It should be noted that in the enemy combatants cases, Thomas's words were more restrained than those that emanated from the White House.)

The Bush "sweeping assertions of unilateral executive power"[5]—rejecting the restraints in the Constitution—are antithetical to the idea of representative government. Until 2004 and 2006, when the Supreme Court heard and ruled in *Rasul, Hamdi,* and *Hamdan,* there were no brakes applied to the presidential runaway train. Although there were, in the United States, some bloggers, other media commentators, and NGOs who shouted loudly and regularly about the actions of the executive branch, there was very little criticism from the opposition party—the Democrats—and none by the Republican majorities in Congress.[6]

Finally, in 2004, the justices began to try to rein in the Bush administration's radical use of presidential war powers. While hearing arguments in *Rasul* and *Hamdi,* the justices were reading their newspapers. And in April 2004 *all* the papers, news weeklies, and television talking heads were discussing the Abu Ghraib atrocities and the content of the until-then top-secret 2002 memos sent to and from the White House regarding treatment of detainees, the irrelevancy of the Geneva Conventions, and official approval of interrogation techniques that amounted, in the eyes of many, to torture.

Indeed, on April 28, 2004, during the oral argument in *Hamdi,* Justice Ginsburg asked the government's lawyer, Deputy Solicitor General Clement, whether the government was torturing the detainees. Clement answered, quickly and briefly, "We don't do that." That very night, all the television networks led their newscasts with the first photographs of U.S. military personnel mistreating enemy detainees in Abu Ghraib prison. Even an administration stalwart, Justice Scalia, was appalled with the Bush administration's behavior. At one point in the *Hamdi* oral argument, he exclaimed to Clement, "You're asking for more power than George Washington had!"

The 2006 *Hamdan* opinion, however, was, many thought, a "historic event, a defining moment in the ever-shifting balance of power."[7] That opinion, even more than the earlier 2004 opinions of the Court, called attention to the Constitution's essential principles of checks and balances, the separation of powers, habeas corpus protection, and judicial review. However, this opinion of the Court, as well as the 2004 opinions, also called attention to Alexander Hamilton's view of the inherent weakness of the Supreme Court: It can decide controversial cases like *Hamdan,* but it does not have any mechanism to compel President Bush or Congress to respect constitutional principles when they do not want to. The justices only have the power of their words, and if Bush or Congress does not want to hear them, then the Court is powerless to immediately respond.

Hamdan answered some of the questions that had been in view since 2001 but had gone unanswered by Congress and the media: Habeas corpus is a near-absolute guarantee of due process and can only be suspended—and then only by Congress—in response to invasion or insurrection. Congress cannot accidentally stumble into unconsciously suspending the writ.[8] Vague, misleading statutes, such as the DTA of 2005, cannot take away the jurisdiction of federal courts to respond on the merits to habeas actions. There are due process protections—found in the U.S. Constitution, U.S. statutes, U.S. treaties, and the international law of war—that cannot be unilaterally rejected by the president. Even, perhaps especially, in a critical period such as wartime, the nation must adhere to these vitally important principles. Finally, the Constitution does not give the president the green light to act in contradiction to the fundamental rules of law found in the Constitution.

The response of the Bush administration's lawyers and policy makers to the 5–3 decision of the Court was to find a way to comply and yet not comply with *Hamdan*. They succeeded when the Republican-controlled Congress, once again, bowed to the immense pressures placed on the members by the Bush administration.

Initially, however, it looked as if the Bush administration was ready to comply with *Hamdan*. Only one week after the decision came down, Deputy Secretary of Defense England issued his July 7, 2006, memo to all the leaders in the Department of Defense, explicitly acknowledging that the Supreme Court had affirmed the applicability of Common Article 3 to the conflict with al Qaeda and seeming to reflect a change in the White House policy on the treatment of its enemy detainees. It was a change brought about by a coordinate branch—the Supreme Court—because the president's actions clearly warranted such a constitutional check. However, the England memo was illusory. Within weeks, the Bush lawyers had drafted legislation, the Military Commissions Act, that was 180 degrees removed from England's view of Geneva and habeas corpus.

Hamdan suggested that the Bush surrogates deal substantively with the other coordinate branch of the national government: the dormant and thoroughly bullied U.S. Congress. Some legislators, after *Hamdan*, had the temerity to criticize the president. Senator Graham, the sponsor of the controversial Section 1005 amendment to the DTA, "challenging the White House lawyers, . . . bounced in his chair, rolled his eyes, shook his head, and raised his voice, warning at one point that if they pushed the president's approach, 'It's going to be a long hot summer.'"[9] The White House would have to *really* work with the Congress to respond to the Court's *Hamdan* ruling, he suggested. This, of course, was pure Graham rhetoric. In the end, he, too, caved in to White House pressure to pass legislation the president wanted.

The Bush administration, including, at one point late in the drafting process, the president himself, really worked Congress to get a bill that would enable the president to continue down the path he had taken after September 11. The legislation introduced during the summer of 2006, the Military Commissions Act, became law in mid-October 2006.

The *Hamdan* decision was a fairly clear rebuke to the governing philosophy of President Bush, Vice President Cheney, and their ideologically driven staffs. Again, Senator Graham: "There is a strain of legal reasoning in this administration that believes in a time of war the other two branches have a diminished role or no role. It's sincere, it's heartfelt, but after today [after *Hamdan*], it's wrong."[10] As Bruce Fein, a conservative legal scholar and an official in the Reagan administration, said after *Hamdan* came down, "This idea of a coronated president instead of an inaugurated president has been dealt a sharp rebuke."[11] However, by the time the post-*Hamdan* posturing and the debates surrounding the Military Commissions Act ended in late September 2006, Bush still had his crown perched on his head.

THE MILITARY COMMISSIONS ACT OF 2006

Unfortunately, the classic, centuries-old protection afforded by the habeas corpus petition was turned upside down and sideways by the Military Commissions Act (MCA) of 2006. This controversial legislation contained language[12] that withdrew federal court jurisdiction to hear or even consider hearing habeas corpus petitions filed by any alien detained by the government as an enemy combatant—or under investigation for being an enemy combatant. (Implicit in the MCA is the view that citizens labeled enemy combatants are also barred from asking a court for habeas corpus.)

By the end of July 2006 the White House hard-liners had won the internal battle between them and the JAG lawyers. Attorney General Gonzales told Senators Warner, McCain, and Graham that the president would shortly submit to Congress a proposed bill that would contain a military tribunal structure with only minor changes from the military commissions that had been ruled unconstitutional by the Court in late June 2006. This time around, however, the White House paid lip service to the Supreme Court message by seeking the cooperation of Congress. And according to one Senate Republican staffer, initial congressional feeling after *Hamdan* came down was that "clearly, [the administration] believes that we have to take more from the UCMJ than the administration, at this time, wants."[13]

One week later, someone in the Department of Defense leaked to the *New York Times* and the *Washington Post* a thirty-two-page draft of proposed legislation developed by the Department of Justice and the Vice President's Office titled "A Bill to Facilitate Bringing Enemy Combatants to Justice through Full and Fair Trial by Military Commissions, and for Other Purposes" (short title: "Enemy Combatant Military Commissions Act of 2006").[14] As published in the newspaper, the draft legislation plainly laid out the Bush administration's initial effort to avoid following the Supreme Court's order. Some of the most controversial provisions of the proposed bill:

- An individual labeled an enemy combatant could be detained indefinitely without trial and without the right to seek habeas corpus review in federal courts.
- Hearsay evidence, unless it was deemed "unreliable," would be allowable.
- The military commission format would be preserved.
- A military judge must preside over the trial.
- There is no provision for a speedy trial; detainees "may be tried and punished at any time without limitations."
- No matter how gathered, evidence would be admissible "if the military judge determines it has probative value."
- "Statements obtained by the use of torture" would be barred.
- Evidence obtained during interrogations where "coercion" was employed would be admissible unless the military judge found it "unreliable."
- Exclusion of detainees from the trial would be "no broader than necessary."
- Habeas corpus petitions filed by detainees would be barred.
- The Geneva Conventions would not be "a source of judicially enforceable individual rights."[15]

Clearly, the early draft legislation, written by Stephen Bradbury, the acting chief of the Department of Justice's OLC, was a transparent effort to continue the Bush administration's hard work to outflank the Supreme Court. In what was probably the understatement of the summer, John Yoo, one of the drafters of the USA Patriot Act in 2001 and the president's 2001 Military Commission Order, presently a law professor at Berkeley, said, "This draft shows that the executive branch doesn't think the Supreme Court got the questions on the Geneva Conventions right in Hamdan."[16] The Bush administration hard-liners prevailed, and the MCA as finally passed in late September and signed into law in mid-October 2006 is essentially what the president's lawyers argued for during the summer.

The proposed legislation was formally presented by the Bush administration to the Senate Judiciary Committee on August 2, 2006. During that first week in August, White House and Department of Justice lawyers, including Attorney General Gonzales, testified on behalf of the proposed MCA. Not surprisingly, senior JAG generals also appeared before the committee to criticize the proposed bill. Their fundamental concern was the issue of "reciprocity": Would captured American military be treated according to Geneva Conventions, or would they be treated the way enemy combatants held by the U.S. military were?[17] Neal Katyal, who represented Hamdan before the Supreme Court, commented simply, "Basically, this [proposal] is trying to overrule *Hamdan*."

As put forward by the Bush lawyers, the proposed MCA, by amending the War Crimes Act of 1996,[18] immunized any past criminal behavior, going back to 1996, by the detainees' interrogators. The retroactive immunization extended to all CIA operatives, military interrogators, military personnel, and political appointees (who gave the orders or approved of specific "torture lite" techniques). A delegation of the ICRC visited both the Department of Defense and the State Department to voice their concerns about immunizing these possible criminal actions. Their effort was wasted, as later events were to show.[19] (The immunization appeared in the final version of the MCA.)

By early September 2006, sharp differences between the Bush administration and three senior Republican senators, Warner, McCain, and Graham, surfaced in the media. The three men, all military veterans, believed that the Bush proposal, as it stood, made mincemeat of the protections found in Common Article 3 of the Geneva Conventions. They sided with the JAG generals and quickly drafted an alternative legislative proposal that challenged the Bush document's essential principles regarding the treatment of enemy detainees. Although this action by the three Republican rebels temporarily halted the progress of the Bush proposal in the Senate, the House of Representatives had no difficulty with the MCA and passed the Bush version by a large margin.

At the same time, the Department of Defense issued a directive that repudiated some of the "torture lite" techniques that had been used to coerce enemy detainees to reveal information. Included in the list of now-banned techniques were forced nudity, water-boarding, and the use of military dogs, stress positions, hooding, and sleep and food deprivation. In addition to abandoning these "aggressive" techniques, the directive (and the accompanying revised *Army Field Manual*) created a uniform standard of treatment for both POWs and enemy combatants.[20]

The irony, of course, was that the new Department of Defense directive was at great odds with the Bush administration's proposed MCA. Legal experts who reviewed the changes in the Department of Defense directive and the proposed MCA said that the legislation would allow military and CIA operatives "to use many of the very techniques disavowed by the Pentagon. 'It is a Jekyll and Hyde routine,' Martin S. Lederman, who teaches constitutional law at Georgetown University, said of the administration's dual approaches."[21] In short, the emergent dual-track protocol would enable CIA operatives to act more harshly, to "operate with a freer hand," in their interrogations of high-level detainees than the military interrogators could under the new Department of Defense directive.

By mid-September the three Republican rebels began to focus on a small number of issues in their conversations with the Bush lawyers. They disputed the provision that allowed evidence to be used that was not seen by the alleged enemy combatant, and the Bush definition of torture. The trio wanted the Common Article 3 definition used in the legislation, while the Department of Justice lawyers insisted on using the "shock the conscience" standard once used in Supreme Court opinions written by the conservative and brilliant Justice Felix Frankfurter.[22] They also insisted that a clear, definitive redline be included in the legislation regarding the scope of CIA interrogations of alleged enemy combatants.

On September 14, 2006, in another temporary rebuff to the president, the Senate Judiciary Committee, chaired by Warner, passed the Warner-McCain-Graham version of the MCA by a vote of 15–9. (All Democratic senators joined the trio to pass the alternative MCA.)[23] The day before this vote, former secretary of state Colin Powell wrote to Senator McCain. The letter supported the alternative version and was critical of the Bush's bill:

> I just returned to town and learned about the debate taking place in Congress to redefine Common Article 3 of the Geneva Convention. I do not support such a step and believe it would be inconsistent with the McCain Amendment on torture which I supported last year. . . . The world is beginning to doubt the moral basis

of our fight against terrorism. To redefine Common Article 3 would add to those doubts. Furthermore, it would put our own troops at risk.[24]

(The following day Tony Snow, the president's press secretary, told the White House reporters that Colin Powell failed to "understand what we're trying to do here.")[25]

By mid-September 2006 the heavy artillery was being brought into the fray. Vice President Cheney and the new White House chief of staff, Joshua Bolton, visited the trio to lobby and negotiate with them. The Republican leadership, led by Senate Majority Leader Bill Frist (R–TN), categorically rejected the alternative version of the MCA passed out of the Warner committee and publicly supported the Bush plan. And on September 15, 2006, President Bush himself visited the Senate and afterward held a press conference in the White House Rose Garden.

Bush "blasted"[26] the three errant Republicans, focusing primarily on McCain, for potentially putting the nation at risk. Bush passionately defended his version of the MCA's proposed rules for the treatment, interrogation, and prosecution of terrorist suspects held by the American military and by the CIA: "If our professionals (CIA operatives) do not have clear standards in the law [the "shock the conscience" standard], the [interrogation] program is not going to go forward."[27] Bush then asked the gathering, perhaps rhetorically, "What does the (Common Article 3 phrase) 'outrages on personal dignity' mean?" It was too vague a standard for the interrogators to correctly interpret, Bush maintained.

By September 18, 2006, the embarrassing impasse had not ended. Bush lawyers sent the rebel trio some new ideas focusing on the treatment of detainees held at Guantánamo and other prisons and dropping the Bush language that redefined the obligations of the United States under Common Article 3. Three days later, the trio accepted the proposed changes in the Bush version of the MCA. By the end of September, literally hours before Congress adjourned for the election recess, both houses agreed on the new language. The chief participants in the final negotiations were the three Republican rebel senators; the vice president; the president's counsel, Dan Bartlett; Stephen J. Hadley, the president's national security adviser; and other senior staff of the vice president. The meeting, an all-day affair, was held in the vice president's office in the Senate building.

Essentially the agreement was based on President Bush's promise "to drop his insistence on allowing prosecutors of suspected terrorists to introduce classified evidence kept secret from the defendant."[28] In mid-October President Bush signed the MCA of 2006 into law.

At no time did the Republican rebel trio criticize the MCA proposal's treatment of habeas corpus. Just before the final vote in the Senate, Senator Leahy spoke to the absence of any debate on the "more sweeping issue" of the death of habeas rights for the more than 500 prisoners held at Guantánamo—plus others who would be detained as alleged enemy combatants in the future. In Leahy's view, the Bush MCA rejected basic hallmarks of due process. He maintained that the bill

> departs even more radically from our most fundamental values. It would permit the President to detain indefinitely—even for life—any alien, whether in the United States or abroad, whether a foreign resident or a lawful permanent resident, without any meaningful opportunity for the alien to challenge his detention. . . . [He would be] detained indefinitely, and unaccountably, until proven innocent. . . . The Constitution prohibits the suspension of the writ of *habeas corpus* "unless when in Cases of Rebellion or Invasion the public Safety may require it." I have no doubt that this bill, which would permanently eliminate the writ of habeas for all aliens within and outside the United States whenever the government says they might be enemy combatants, violates that prohibition. And I have no doubt that the Supreme Court would ultimately conclude that this attempt by the Bush-Cheney administration to abolish basic liberties and evade essential judicial review and unaccountability is unconstitutional.[29]

On September 26 Leahy and two Republican senators, Specter and Gordon Smith (R–OR), introduced an amendment to overturn the Bush bill's habeas restrictions by allowing foreign nationals in military or CIA custody to use the habeas route to challenge the legality of their detentions after one year. The Bush response arguing against habeas rights for detainees was simple: Terrorists were not entitled to the rights U.S. citizens have, including the right to file for habeas corpus. As Attorney General Gonzales said, incorrectly, "The Constitution doesn't say every individual in the United States or every citizen is granted or assured the right to habeas. [It] doesn't say that."[30] The Leahy-Specter-Smith amendment was defeated in the Senate.

During these chaotic final days before the vote, a letter signed by thirty-one former U.S. ambassadors was sent to Congress. The letter said that "to eliminate habeas corpus relief for the citizens of other countries who have fallen into our hands cannot but make a mockery" of the Bush administration's efforts to promote democracy.[31] This plea, however, went unacknowledged.

The MCA of 2006 as signed by President Bush in mid-October 2006 is very close to the original proposal presented by the president to the Senate in early August. Among the major, and controversial, aspects of the new legislation are the following sections:[32]

- The "enemy combatants" phrase was broadened in the legislation to include those who "purposefully and materially supported hostilities against the United States." A legal resident in America could be so labeled for making out a check to a supposed Islamic charity. Once identified as an enemy combatant, a person was subject to summary arrest and indefinite detention without the habeas appeal route.[33]
- Habeas corpus was barred for all detainees in U.S. military prisons.[34]
- The UCMJ's provisions for a speedy trial and for protection against coerced self-incrimination are *specifically* declared inapplicable.[35]
- No provision exists for judicial review of any aspect of the new protocols, except the review of verdicts by the new military commissions. No appeals are allowed in the MCA that invoke the Geneva Conventions or other international humanitarian laws "as sources of rights and protections."[36]
- Coerced evidence would be permissible if the military judge thought it was reliable.[37]
- The president was given the power to "interpret the meaning and the application of the Geneva Conventions."[38]
- Offenses enumerated in the final version of the MCA were narrowly drawn; for example, the notion that the rape of a detainee is a form of torture was rejected.[39]

All assessments of the MCA of 2006, whether critical or supportive of the bill, must conclude that President Bush "achieved a signal victory, shoring up with legislation his determined conduct of the campaign against terrorism in the face of challenges from critics and the courts."[40] As in 2001 and 2002, the Republican Congress once again gave the president what he asked for in August 2006. Unless the Supreme Court hears petitions from the adversely affected detainees at Guantánamo, the Republican legislation "allows the president to identify enemies, imprison them indefinitely and interrogate them—albeit with a ban on the harshest treatment—beyond the reach of the full court reviews traditionally afforded criminal defendants and ordinary defendants."[41]

The MCA of 2006 is the government's response to the Court's *Hamdan* decision. However, lawsuits will inevitably come to the federal courts and ultimately to the U.S. Supreme Court. In part, these lawsuits will challenge those segments of the MCA that removed federal court jurisdiction from hearing such appeals in the first place. And it is equally clear that these new petitions to the Supreme Court will elevate the conflict between the president and the judiciary to new heights of contentiousness and importance. *Hamdan* will seem like a walk in the park if the Court accepts petitions dealing with the MCA's treatment of habeas corpus and of judicial review, to name just two controversial litigation possibilities.

Whether the justices of the U.S. Supreme Court will want to go a third round in the political ring with the president will be answered in part by the result of the 2006 midterm elections. The Court, as an old political sage once wrote, generally follows the election returns.

The year 2006 was an election year. Both houses of Congress were controlled by Republicans; there was, however, a growing sense in Washington, D.C., and around the nation of Republican Party vulnerability. The Bush administration, too, is in the sunset of its tumultuous and contentious reign of command and control of America's foreign and war policies. What may make the difference in President Bush's thus-far successful end runs around past Supreme Court rulings is that, at a minimum, he has been forced into some kind of relationship with Congress, an institution that has responded with molecular speed to his assertions of presidential power at home and on the battlefields. The paradox is obvious: The *Hamdan* decision forced Bush to ask Congress to legislate. The Republican majorities legislated. And President Bush received, in the MCA of 2006, just what he sought.

Given that the Department of Justice lawyers, immediately after President Bush signed the MCA into law on October 15, 2006, asked federal district court judges to dismiss the hundreds of pending habeas petitions from Guantánamo detainees, the constitutionality of the MCA was immediately challenged in the federal courts. Furthermore, as columnist Andrew Cohen wrote in the *Washington Post* a few days after the MCA of 2006 was passed, it's now the Supreme Court's ball.[42]

I do agree, however, with Cohen's concluding words: "Soon we will know, too, whether the latest White House plan to try the Guantánamo Bay detainees passes the baseline legal tests that it needs to. A great constitutional showdown is at hand and if anyone tells you they know how it will turn out they are lying."[43] And the showdown clock began after the votes were tallied on November 7, 2006.

Epilogue:
The 2006 Midterm Elections and a
Return to the U.S. Supreme Court

*Belated as it is, Rumsfeld's departure does have
encouraging aspects. Above all, it suggests that the most
imperial presidency of modern times can still be held
accountable by the voters.*

BOSTON GLOBE, NOVEMBER 9, 2006[1]

*The separation of powers is an essential mechanism for
correcting the errors to which each branch of government
would be prone in the absence of a competitive
environment.*

RICHARD A. POSNER, 2006[2]

On Tuesday, November 7, 2006, election day in America, the sovereign people spoke and President Bush and his party were, to use the president's phrase, "thumped" at the polls. Congress, both the Senate and the House of Representatives, were taken by the Democrats. The essential message of the voters: Change the direction of the Iraqi war *now*. It was a historic vote: "For the first time in American history, Americans have gone to the polls in wartime and rejected that war."[3]

In a comprehensive series of exit polls reported in the *Washington Post*, 59 percent of all voters expressed "dissatisfaction or anger" with the Bush administration. Of that figure, 56 percent of the voters said they "support withdrawing some or all U.S. troops from Iraq." (Another statistic from these exit interviews indicated that 41 percent "rated corruption 'extremely important' to their decision.")[4]

On November 7–8, 2006, Greenberg Quinlin Rosner Research surveyed exit responses of over 1,100 voters in 132 swing-GOP districts and recorded the following exit responses: Fifty-nine percent of respondents felt the United States is moving in the wrong direction. The Iraq war was rated the most important issue by 41 percent of respondents, followed by the economy (26 percent), moral values and corruption (23 percent each), and terrorism (22 percent). Forty-six percent of respondents strongly disapproved of President Bush's handling of the job—twice as many as strongly approved (23 percent). For 67 percent of respondents, the issue of which party controls Congress was a factor in voting; 32 percent said it was not.[5]

It is abundantly clear that the American voters, even though they had a very low opinion of congressional behavior since 2001,[6] wanted change and rejected the Iraq war policy preferences of the president and the Cheney/Rumsfeld faction.

THE ELECTION'S IMMEDIATE AFTERMATH

Within the day, President Bush made the decision to replace his controversial secretary of defense, Donald Rumsfeld. The announcement was made at a White House press conference on Wednesday, November 8, 2006. Rumsfeld's "strategic errors of epic proportions"[7] as well as his acerbic personality, made him a lightening rod in the Bush administration. While the announcement, however belated, pleased Democrats and other critics of Bush's overall policy on Iraq, terrorism, and enemy combatants, it infuriated Republicans, especially congressional Republicans who lost their seats in the election:[8]

> "The president correctly decided that this decision does not belong in the political realm. And a decision as important as your secretary of defense should not be made based on some partisan political advantage. It would send a terrible signal to our troops, to our allies, even to our enemies," [Bush Chief of Staff Josh] Bolten said.
>
> [However,] former House Speaker Newt Gingrich has suggested that if Bush replaced Rumsfeld two weeks before the election, voters would not have been as angry about the unpopular Iraq war. Republicans would have gained the boost they needed, according to Gingrich, to retain their majority in the Senate and hold on to 10 to 15 more House seats.
>
> Sen. Arlen Specter, R–Pa., the outgoing chairman of the Senate Judiciary Committee, agreed with that assessment.
>
> Bush should have removed Rumsfeld "as soon as he had made up his mind. And that's a hard thing to calculate. But it's highly doubtful that he made up his mind between the time the election returns came in on Tuesday and Wednesday when Rumsfeld was out. And if Rumsfeld had been out, you bet it would have made a difference," Specter said. "I'd still be chairman of the Judiciary Committee."[9]

At the November 8 press conference, Bush announced Rumsfeld's replacement: Robert M. Gates. The defense secretary was formerly the president of Texas A&M University and the director of the CIA (1991–1993). By all accounts, Gates is a very different, more pragmatic personality than his predecessor. For example, in the past Gates has said that the United States should enter discussions with Iraq's neighbors, Iran and Syria. He has condemned the National Security Council, the CIA, and the DIA for misleading the president on whether Iraq had weapons of mass destruction. He has been critical of the president's 2003 national security policy for the nation. On that issue, Gates has consistently maintained that America must never launch another preemptive strike without "unambiguous" intelligence.[10]

Barely a week after the election, Department of Justice lawyers filed a six-page document in the U.S. Court of Appeals for the Fourth Circuit, in Richmond, Virginia, in which the Bush administration argued that the MCA of 2006 applied to foreigners captured and held *in* the United States as well as enemy combatants captured abroad and held at Guantánamo.[11] The government's brief asked the federal appeals court to dismiss the case "for lack of jurisdiction" because of the MCA of 2006. (Conceivably, if the government argument was accepted by federal judges, all aliens residing in the United States would be in jeopardy of detention under the MCA of 2006. In the brief the Bush administration maintained that the MCA "made clear that the provision eliminating habeas jurisdiction applies to all pending habeas actions . . . *regardless* of the location of the detention" [my emphasis].)[12]

The brief was filed in federal court because Ali Saleh Kahlah al-Marri, a citizen of Qatar, was arrested in 2001 while attending university in America and has been held in a military brig in South Carolina since then as an enemy combatant. The Bush administration has maintained since his detention that al-Marri "is a sleeper agent for Al Qaeda." Al-Marri's lawyers maintain that because he was arrested and detained in America, he has the same rights as anyone else in detention in the United States.[13]

On the same day, November 13, 2006, because hundreds of habeas appeals had been filed since *Hamdan* was announced in late June 2006, other Department of Justice attorneys filed briefs in the U.S. Court of Appeals for the District of Columbia Circuit defending the constitutionality of the MCA of 2006. According to the government filings, which asked the federal court to dismiss all the pending cases, the Guantánamo detainees have no constitutional rights. Giving these enemy combatants access to the federal courts was banned by the MCA; granting them access "would severely impair the military's authority to defend this country."[14] And, about the same time, in the U.S. Court of Appeals for the District of Columbia Circuit, lawyers for hundreds of Guantánamo detainees asked the federal appeals court to strike down the provision in the MCA that barred habeas corpus petitions from the jurisdiction of all federal courts. A final incident speaks volumes about the potential impact of the 2006 election results: "Senate Democrats Plan Overhaul of the [MCA] Bill" trumpeted the headline in the November 17, 2006, issue of the *Hill*, the "newspaper for and about the U.S. Congress." The article reported that Senator Chris Dodd (D–CT) had introduced legislation that would amend the quickly passed MCA of 2006. Said Dodd, "[My] bill goes back and undoes what was done [in the MCA]."[15]

THE DEMOCRATIC-CONTROLLED 110TH CONGRESS

The change in congressional committee chairpersons in January 2007 is an immediate consequence of the Democratic Party's victory. With the shift of power in both houses to the Democrats, investigations are the order of the day for the new congressional leaders. Replacing the absolutely ineffective Republican leaders is a host of frustrated, angry, and very focused Democrats who want and will demand answers to questions that have been ignored for six years by the Bush administration.

Senator Leahy is the new Senate Judiciary Committee chair and, in the House of Representatives, John Conyers (D–MI) is the new chair of the House Judiciary Committee. Both were and remain harsh critics of the Bush administration's thus-far successful effort (in the MCA of 2006) to eviscerate habeas corpus due process rights for alleged terrorists held at Guantánamo. Leahy has called the MCA a piece of "un-American" legislation and has vowed to review and remove its harshest segments.[16]

Leahy has already asked the Department of Justice to turn over some documents he believes established standards for the military on how terrorism suspects are detained and interrogated. In addition, he wants the government to turn over all documents "that interpret the scope of interrogation practices permitted and prohibited by the DTA or the MCA." In his November 17, 2006, request to Attorney General Gonzales, Leahy wrote, "The American people deserve to have detailed and accurate information about the role of the Bush

Administration in developing the interrogation policies and practices that have engendered such deep criticism and concern at home and abroad."[17]

On December 5, 2006, Leahy, along with the former chair of the Senate Judiciary Committee, Senator Specter, introduced a bill to restore habeas corpus. The proposed legislation, entitled the Habeas Corpus Restoration Act (HCRA) of 2006 (S. 4081), would reinstate federal court jurisdiction over all Guantánamo detainees as well as others detained elsewhere as suspected enemy combatants.[18] If passed—and if signed by President Bush (an extremely dim proposition)—it would repeal the two provisions of the MCA of 2006 that withdrew federal court jurisdiction to hear habeas appeals from detainees. "This bill would restore the great writ of habeas corpus, a cornerstone of American liberty for hundreds of years that Congress and the President rolled back in an unprecedented and unnecessary way with September's Military Commissions Act," said Leahy when he introduced the bill.[19]

On the House side of Congress, Conyers, as minority leader on the House Judiciary Committee over the past two years (2004–2006), has not been popular with Republicans within or outside the White House. He has "requested investigations of the administration's renditions of suspected terrorists, [Secretary of State] Condoleezza Rice's possible transgression of the Hatch Act prohibitions against campaigning on the job, DOJ attempts to obstruct the hydra-headed Jack Abramoff investigation, and [has introduced] proposals for the possible impeachment of President Bush."[20]

While the Democrats were in the minority, these legislators, along with Senator Levin of Michigan, the new chair of the Senate Armed Services Committee, and others, "bitterly lamented the refusal of the administration to provide Congress with documents vital to understanding the treatment of detainees." However, after the election, they "should have more leverage to obtain these memos."[21] Like his colleague Levin, Representative Ike Skelton (D–MO), the incoming chair of the House Armed Services Committee, has been a constant critic of Bush's war on terror policies.

There is no guarantee that these legislators will receive the requested information from the Bush administration. It came as no surprise that the administration's initial response, on November 18, 2006, to Leahy's documents request was not encouraging. Brian Roehrkasse, the Department of Justice spokesperson, said that "it is vital to protect national security secrets" and that the Department of Justice would "weigh whether the documents being sought fall under the category of confidential deliberations."[22] In mid-December

2006 Leahy again asked for the documents and said, "I expect to get answers. If I don't, then I really think we should subpoena."[23]

On another controversial issue, the NSA's warrantless wiretap program, Senator Leahy, less than one week after the election, said to reporters, "We have been asked to make sweeping and fundamental changes in [FISA] law for reasons we do not know and in order to legalize secret, unlawful actions that the administration has refused to fully disclose. If legislation is needed for judicial review, then we should write that legislation together, in a bipartisan and thoughtful way."[24]

Senator Levin has told the media that his committee will look into the CIA's extraordinary rendition process: "I'm not comfortable with the system. I think that there's been some significant abuses which have not made us more secure, but have made us less secure and have also perhaps cost us some real allies, as well as not producing particularly useful information. So I think the system needs a thorough review, and as the military would say, a thorough scrubbing."[25]

Stanley Brand, a former general counsel to Speaker of the House Tip O'Neill, wrote, "A vigorous examination of the administration's conduct is not only the appropriate action as a matter of constitutional prerogative, it is the politically necessary response to voters' overwhelming rejection of the current Congress's failure to assert itself in this area."[26] And Democratic chairs and leaders of both chambers' Intelligence, Armed Services, and Judiciary committees have promised something that has been missing from the Republican Congress since 2001: *real* congressional investigation and oversight of executive department actions in the wars on terrorism. The critical reality is not how the president will respond to these demands from Congress, but, after six years, the very existence of these *insistent* demands rolling down Capital Hill to the White House.

WHAT WILL THE PRESIDENT DO NOW?

"The power to suspend habeas corpus," wrote Judge Richard Posner, "is essentially the power to suspend constitutional rights—if you cannot get a judge to hear your case, the government can do whatever it wants with you."[27] The 2006 MCA categorically bars all enemy combatants—in the United States and in Guantánamo—from seeking federal judicial review of their detention. As Posner noted, "suspending [or barring persons from seeking] habeas corpus is a terrifying power; it enables the government to imprison people [indefinitely] at will and prevents them from challenging their imprisonment in court."[28]

As already noted, leading congressional Democrats, including Democratic Senators Levin, Leahy, Dodd, and Durbin, the new Senate Democratic Party whip, among the many Democrats who voted against the MCA, have already introduced legislation or have promised to review and amend controversial segments of that and other laws in the 110th Congress. And, on the other side, President Bush and his vice president, Dick Cheney, have equally strong feelings about retention of the MCA as signed in October 2006.

How this clash plays out will be seen in late 2007 and 2008. Will the president seek some sort of compromise with congressional Democrats, or will he veto any legislation that attempts to overturn the MCA's bar against habeas corpus for all alleged enemy combatants? Will his commitment to the defense of national security at all costs, even if it means denial of due process to alleged enemy detainees, lead to some sort of constitutional crisis?

Since 9/11, President Bush has consistently—and defiantly—invoked his "radical theory of unilateral executive authority" in defending his actions and policies on the terrorist wars.[29] Although in the days after his party's "thumping," Bush sounded conciliatory, his view of a largely unimpeded presidency fighting the terrorist wars is a fundamental axiom for him. And consequently Bush may refuse to cooperate with Conyers's and Leahy's committee requests for documents and other information. And Bush most assuredly would veto the proposed Leahy-Specter-Dodd legislation should it be passed in both houses of Congress. As a result, a major constitutional controversy could quickly unfold, possibly paralyzing government.[30]

Certainly, the Justice Department briefs filed in federal courts (in the U.S. Court of Appeals for the Fourth Circuit and the U.S. Court of Appeals for the District of Columbia Circuit) defending and even extending the scope of the MCA suggest conflict ahead rather than compromise. These latest categorical arguments are not unusual in the war on terror. Since 2001 government lawyers have argued for and defended the most strident actions of the executive branch.

In the six-page brief, the Department of Justice and the Bush administration lawyers, after the election returns were in, took what one legal critic called "the most extreme step yet taken by [the administration] to suspend constitutional rights that, since the nation's founding, have protected all people detained within the United States. . . . [It signals the] Administration's determination to push ahead with the government's most extreme and ambitious attempt to extend its power."[31]

On February 20, 2007, a divided panel of federal appeals judges in the Court of Appeals, Fourth Circuit, upheld the controversial MCA. By a 2–1 vote in the combined cases of *Al Odah v. USA* (06-1195) and *Boumediene v. Bush* (06-1196), the panel ruled that Guantánamo detainees did not have the right to challenge their imprisonment in federal courts. Judge A. Raymond Randolph wrote that to declare the MCA unconstitutional would "defy the will of Congress." For the two judges, "federal courts have no jurisdiction in these cases. Our only recourse is to vacate . . . and dismiss the cases for lack of jurisdiction." The dissenting judge, Judith W. Rogers, wrote that since Congress has not suspended the writ, its actions (in the MCA) "exceed its powers."[32]

One final observation: Although Rumsfeld is gone, Cheney, the éminence grise of the Bush administration, will remain in office until January 20, 2009. On ABC-TV news during the weekend after the midterm elections, he said that "it doesn't matter" what voters think because the Bush administration has "got the basic strategy right": "It may not be popular with the public—it doesn't matter in the sense that we have to continue the mission and do what we think is right. And that's exactly what we are doing. We're not running for office. We're doing what we think is right."[33] The important unanswered question is whether President Bush, encouraged by his vice president's steel will, will continue to adhere to his strongly held beliefs (and those of Cheney) in the face of public and Democratic party opposition.

BACK TO THE U.S. SUPREME COURT IN 2008? YOU BET!

The political reality after the 2006 elections is, if anything, more complex than before. The president still has some options, albeit fewer, in his war on terror, and both he and the vice president are still strongly committed to battling the terrorist wars until *victory* is achieved, even at the cost of some basic civil rights. In addition, the posture of the Justice Department and White House lawyers regarding the detention of suspected enemy combatants is even more unyielding than in earlier briefs filed in federal courts. Furthermore, compromise is almost certainly impossible on habeas corpus, NSA wiretapping, and other controversies.

Any one of these issues would once again bring the Supreme Court into the constitutional storm. For example, the administration might refuse to allow Bush deputies to appear before congressional committees, might fail to obey subpoenas served on executive officers, or might refuse to turn over documents requested by chairs of congressional committees. However, it is certain that the habeas litigation controversy will reach the Supreme Court for a third time. Lawyers representing the Guantánamo detainees said, after the recent federal appeals court ruling validated the MCA, that they would "quickly petition"[34] the U.S. Supreme Court to hear the case. And, in all probability, there will be at least four votes cast, in a conference session, that will enable the Court to revisit the contentious issue of the scope of due process rights for detainees held in prison in Bush's war on terrorism.

But not right away. The Supreme Court procrastinated when, on April 2, 2007, it denied certiorari on an *expedited* basis to review two petitions from Guantánamo detainees who challenged the constitutionality of the MCA. Although there were three votes (Breyer, Ginsberg, and Souter) to grant certiorari in both cases (thereby bypassing the U.S. Court of Appeals review of the cases—*Al Odah v. Bush* and *Boumediene v. Bush*), the crucial fourth vote to grant the petitions was withheld by Justices John Paul Stevens and Anthony Kennedy.[36] This means that it will not be until the 2008 term of the Court that the question of the constitutionality of MCA, especially the sections that prohibit detainees from petitioning for a writ of habeas corpus in any federal court, will be addressed by the justices.

Congress, too, has procrastinated. Even though the Democrats are in the majority in both houses for the first time in a dozen years, and even though Senators Chris Dodd (D-CT) and Patrick Leahy (D-VT), among others as already noted, introduced legislation in the Senate in December—even *before* they assumed power in January 2007—that would in effect overturn the MCA, nothing has happened. Any one of the proposed anti-MCA bills would have invalidated the draconian MCA, either in its entirety or with regard to its harshest, unconstitutional segments regarding habeas corpus.

However, there have been no hearings scheduled for discussion of the proposed legislation in the spring 2007 term of Congress. In the meantime, lower federal judges, the trial court judges in the Fourth Circuit and in the District of Columbia, have validated the MCA and have rejected petitions filed by lawyers for the detainees seeking habeas relief in the federal courts.

Both the justices and the legislators are well aware of the capacity of the Bush operatives in the White House and Office of Legal Counsel to turn this serious issue of constitutional law into a question of the appropriate treatment of the detainees, who can readily be vilified by the Bush administration. We can only speculate as to the reasons for such procrastination by the two coordinate branches of the federal government in the face of what seem to be clearly unconstitutional actions.

OUR VULNERABLE REPUBLIC SHOULDERS ON

On election day 2006 American voters ended an era of imperial presidential actions. With the loss of his rubber-stamp Republican Congress, the president can no longer confidently act in the ways he has acted since September 11, 2001. A prodding, investigating opposition party is now in control of the "first branch" of the national government; Democratic Party leaders in the new Congress will act very differently—for example, with regard to reviewing past legislation such as the MCA of 2006 and with regard to the president's warrantless NSA-operated terrorist surveillance program.

"The separation of powers is an essential mechanism for correcting the errors to which each branch of government would be prone in the absence of a competitive environment," observed Judge Posner in 2006. The midterm election results put the federal political system back into some sort of equilibrium. The dominant hope is that the many errors committed by an imperial presidency will be corrected. We will soon see just how fruitful the 2006 electoral "thumping" will prove to be.

In the end, there is the fundamental question raised in the book's introduction: Can national security demands and the U.S. Constitution's constraints coexist? *They must.* The nation has seen that question repeated throughout its history: during and after the Civil War, World War I, and World War II. Ultimately, the principles at the heart of representative government endured—although after *all* of these battles there was pain and death and tragedy and injustice. For over forty years, for example, Japanese Americans lived with the physical and mental scars of being labeled subversive enemies of their country during World War II. They were incarcerated and spent years in relocation centers. They lost all their property. They lost their dignity. However, in 1987 Congress, on behalf of the nation, formally apologized for the cruel mistreatment of almost 100,000 citizens and provided $20,000 for every person incarcerated during the war (or to their survivors).[35]

The lesson taken from the tragedy of the Japanese Americans, applied to the treatment of enemy combatants, is not a good one. It was more than forty years before Congress took any action to remediate the tragedy of more than 120,000 innocent persons, over 70,000 of them citizens of the United States. For the many unfortunate detainees at Guantánamo, there may never be any action taken to enable them to challenge their detention by the U.S. military—especially if the provisions of the MCA of 2006 are held to be valid.

Is America vulnerable? Sure it is. Every society is vulnerable to change, especially potentially disastrous authoritarian changes that rob citizens of the fundamental values common to that society. In the past, the nation has experienced "dithering" Congresses, kangaroo courts, and "slapstick justice."[36] And in the past, the values associated with representative government have surfaced, bloodied but nevertheless still functioning.

President Bush's arrogant behavior has cost the society a great deal. At home, his feckless actions in Iraq and with regard to the treatment of enemy detainees lost him the unity and respect he possessed after September 11. In early 2002 his popularity rating was at its peak. More than 90 percent of Americans—Republican and Democrat—supported his leadership. Abroad, after September 11 the nations of the world supported President Bush's initial responses to the attacks. They joined him when the Taliban's regime was attacked in October 2001. This support evaporated rapidly, because of the Iraq war, because of the arrogance of the president's assertions about the uses of power, and because there was a seemingly uninterested American public and a cipher called Congress.

In the end, it was the "least dangerous branch," as Alexander Hamilton called the Supreme Court, that began to bring the society back to some sort of constitutional check-and-balance equilibrium. It was the justices, not Congress, who told the president that he can't do whatever he wants to do in his battles against terrorists. There is something called the Constitution, they reminded the president. There are the statutes. There are the treaties. There is the rule of law. And in America, the law is king. To date, no person wears a crown for very long in American government.

Underscoring this principle, the U.S. Supreme Court, on the last day of its

2006 term, surprised everyone when it granted rehearing petitions in the two detainee cases, *Boumediene v. Bush* and *Al Odah v. United States,* that had been denied certiorari on April 2, 2007. In a brief "certiorari granted" note published on June 29, 2007, the earlier denials were vacated and the petitions for writs of certiorari granted. No one recalled the last time a petition for rehearing had been granted. A vote of five justices is required, including at least one who voted to deny certiorari when the petitions were first heard. Evidently the three dissenters, Justices Souter, Ginsburg, and Bryer, were joined by Justices Stevens and Kennedy, who had concurred with the denial of certiorari but issued a cautionary concurrence. The Supreme Court has taken a most unusual step in deciding during its 2007 term whether the MCA of 2006, denying detainees habeas corpus rights, is or is not constitutional.

Appendix 1

Authorization for Use of Military Force (AUMF) Resolution

September 18, 2001
Public Law 107-40 [S.J. Res. 23]
107th Congress

Joint Resolution

To authorize the use of United States Armed Forces against those responsible for the recent attacks launched against the United States.

Whereas, on September 11, 2001, acts of treacherous violence were committed against the United States and its citizens; and

Whereas, such acts render it both necessary and appropriate that the United States exercise its rights to self-defense and to protect United States citizens both at home and abroad; and

Whereas, in light of the threat to the national security and foreign policy of the United States posed by these grave acts of violence; and

Whereas, such acts continue to pose an unusual and extraordinary threat to the national security and foreign policy of the United States; and

Whereas, the President has authority under the Constitution to take action to deter and prevent acts of international terrorism against the United States: Now, therefore, be it

Resolved by the Senate and House of Representatives of the United States of America in Congress assembled,

SECTION 1. SHORT TITLE.

This joint resolution may be cited as the "Authorization for Use of Military Force."

SEC. 2. AUTHORIZATION FOR USE OF UNITED STATES ARMED FORCES.

(a) That the President is authorized to use all necessary and appropriate force against those nations, organizations, or persons he determines planned, authorized, committed, or aided the terrorist attacks that occurred on September 11, 2001, or harbored such organizations or persons, in order to prevent any future acts of international terrorism against the United States by such nations, organizations or persons.

Document available at http://news.findlaw.com/wp/docs/terrorism/sjres23.es.html.

(b) War Powers Resolution Requirements.—
   (1) Specific statutory authorization.—Consistent with section 8(a)(1) of the War Powers Resolution, the Congress declares that this section is intended to constitute specific statutory authorization within the meaning of section 5(b) of the War Powers Resolution.
   (2) Applicability of other requirements.—Nothing in this resolution supercedes any requirement of the War Powers Resolution.

Approved September 18, 2001.

Appendix 2

Presidential Military Order 1

November 13, 2001

Detention, Treatment, and Trial of Certain Non-Citizens in the War against Terrorism

By the authority vested in me as President and as Commander in Chief of the Armed Forces of the United States by the Constitution and the laws of the United States of America, including the Authorization for Use of Military Force Joint Resolution (Public Law 107-40, 115 Stat. 224) and sections 821 and 836 of title 10, United States Code, it is hereby ordered as follows:

SECTION 1. FINDINGS.

(a) International terrorists, including members of al Qaida, have carried out attacks on United States diplomatic and military personnel and facilities abroad and on citizens and property within the United States on a scale that has created a state of armed conflict that requires the use of the United States Armed Forces.

(b) In light of grave acts of terrorism and threats of terrorism, including the terrorist attacks on September 11, 2001, on the headquarters of the United States Department of Defense in the national capital region, on the World Trade Center in New York, and on civilian aircraft such as in Pennsylvania, I proclaimed a national emergency on September 14, 2001 (Proc. 7463, Declaration of National Emergency by Reason of Certain Terrorist Attacks).

(c) Individuals acting alone and in concert involved in international terrorism possess both the capability and the intention to undertake further terrorist attacks against the United States that, if not detected and prevented, will cause mass deaths, mass injuries, and massive destruction of property, and may place at risk the continuity of the operations of the United States Government.

(d) The ability of the United States to protect the United States and its citizens, and to help its allies and other cooperating nations protect their nations and their citizens, from such further terrorist attacks depends in significant part upon using the United States Armed Forces to identify terrorists and those who support them, to disrupt their activities, and to eliminate their ability to conduct or support such attacks.

(e) To protect the United States and its citizens, and for the effective conduct of military operations and prevention of terrorist attacks, it is necessary for individuals

Available at http://www.state.gov/coalition/cr/prs/6077.htm.

subject to this order pursuant to section 2 hereof to be detained, and, when tried, to be tried for violations of the laws of war and other applicable laws by military tribunals.

(f) Given the danger to the safety of the United States and the nature of international terrorism, and to the extent provided by and under this order, I find consistent with section 836 of title 10, United States Code, that it is not practicable to apply in military commissions under this order the principles of law and the rules of evidence generally recognized in the trial of criminal cases in the United States district courts.

(g) Having fully considered the magnitude of the potential deaths, injuries, and property destruction that would result from potential acts of terrorism against the United States, and the probability that such acts will occur, I have determined that an extraordinary emergency exists for national defense purposes, that this emergency constitutes an urgent and compelling government interest, and that issuance of this order is necessary to meet the emergency.

SEC. 2. DEFINITION AND POLICY.

(a) The term "individual subject to this order" shall mean any individual who is not a United States citizen with respect to whom I determine from time to time in writing that:

(1) there is reason to believe that such individual, at the relevant times,

(i)　is or was a member of the organization known as al Qaida;

(ii)　has engaged in, aided or abetted, or conspired to commit, acts of international terrorism, or acts in preparation therefor, that have caused, threaten to cause, or have as their aim to cause, injury to or adverse effects on the United States, its citizens, national security, foreign policy, or economy; or

(iii)　has knowingly harbored one or more individuals described in subparagraphs (i) or (ii) of subsection 2(a)(1) of this order; and

(2) it is in the interest of the United States that such individual be subject to this order.

(b) It is the policy of the United States that the Secretary of Defense shall take all necessary measures to ensure that any individual subject to this order is detained in accordance with section 3, and, if the individual is to be tried, that such individual is tried only in accordance with section 4.

(c) It is further the policy of the United States that any individual subject to this order who is not already under the control of the Secretary of Defense but who is under the control of any other officer or agent of the United States or any State shall, upon delivery of a copy of such written determination to such officer or agent, forthwith be placed under the control of the Secretary of Defense.

SEC. 3. DETENTION AUTHORITY OF THE SECRETARY OF DEFENSE.
ANY INDIVIDUAL SUBJECT TO THIS ORDER SHALL BE—

(a) detained at an appropriate location designated by the Secretary of Defense outside or within the United States;

(b) treated humanely, without any adverse distinction based on race, color, religion, gender, birth, wealth, or any similar criteria;

(c) afforded adequate food, drinking water, shelter, clothing, and medical treatment;

(d) allowed the free exercise of religion consistent with the requirements of such detention; and

(e) detained in accordance with such other conditions as the Secretary of Defense may prescribe.

SEC. 4. AUTHORITY OF THE SECRETARY OF DEFENSE REGARDING TRIALS OF INDIVIDUALS SUBJECT TO THIS ORDER.

(a) Any individual subject to this order shall, when tried, be tried by military commission for any and all offenses triable by military commission that such individual is alleged to have committed, and may be punished in accordance with the penalties provided under applicable law, including life imprisonment or death.

(b) As a military function and in light of the findings in section 1, including subsection (f) thereof, the Secretary of Defense shall issue such orders and regulations, including orders for the appointment of one or more military commissions, as may be necessary to carry out subsection (a) of this section.

(c) Orders and regulations issued under subsection (b) of this section shall include, but not be limited to, rules for the conduct of the proceedings of military commissions, including pretrial, trial, and post-trial procedures, modes of proof, issuance of process, and qualifications of attorneys, which shall at a minimum provide for—

(1) military commissions to sit at any time and any place, consistent with such guidance regarding time and place as the Secretary of Defense may provide;

(2) a full and fair trial, with the military commission sitting as the triers of both fact and law;

(3) admission of such evidence as would, in the opinion of the presiding officer of the military commission (or instead, if any other member of the commission so requests at the time the presiding officer renders that opinion, the opinion of the commission rendered at that time by a majority of the commission), have probative value to a reasonable person;

(4) in a manner consistent with the protection of information classified or classifiable under Executive Order 12958 of April 17, 1995, as amended, or any successor Executive Order, protected by statute or rule from unauthorized disclosure, or otherwise protected by law, (A) the handling of, admission into evidence of, and access to materials and information, and (B) the conduct, closure of, and access to proceedings;

(5) conduct of the prosecution by one or more attorneys designated by the Secretary of Defense and conduct of the defense by attorneys for the individual subject to this order;

(6) conviction only upon the concurrence of two-thirds of the members of the commission present at the time of the vote, a majority being present;

(7) sentencing only upon the concurrence of two-thirds of the members of the commission present at the time of the vote, a majority being present;

. . .

SEC. 7. RELATIONSHIP TO OTHER LAW AND FORUMS.

(a) Nothing in this order shall be construed to—

(1) authorize the disclosure of state secrets to any person not otherwise authorized to have access to them;

(2) limit the authority of the President as Commander in Chief of the Armed Forces or the power of the President to grant reprieves and pardons; or

(3) limit the lawful authority of the Secretary of Defense, any military commander, or any other officer or agent of the United States or of any State to detain or try any person who is not an individual subject to this order.

(b) With respect to any individual subject to this order—

(1) military tribunals shall have exclusive jurisdiction with respect to offenses by the individual; and

(2) the individual shall not be privileged to seek any remedy or maintain any proceeding, directly or indirectly, or to have any such remedy or proceeding sought on the individual's behalf, in (i) any court of the United States, or any State thereof, (ii) any court of any foreign nation, or (iii) any international tribunal.

. . .

[7](e) I reserve the authority to direct the Secretary of Defense, at any time hereafter, to transfer to a governmental authority control of any individual subject to this order. Nothing in this order shall be construed to limit the authority of any such governmental authority to prosecute any individual for whom control is transferred.

. . .

GEORGE W. BUSH
THE WHITE HOUSE,
November 13, 2001.

Appendix 3

Third Geneva Convention of 1949:
Relative to the Treatment of Prisoners of War.
Geneva, August 12, 1949 (Preamble, Parts I and II, Articles 1–24)

PREAMBLE

The undersigned Plenipotentiaries of the Governments represented at the Diplomatic Conference held at Geneva from April 21 to August 12, 1949, for the purpose of revising the Convention concluded at Geneva on July 27, 1929, relative to the Treatment of Prisoners of War, have agreed as follows:

PART I. GENERAL PROVISIONS

Art 1. The High Contracting Parties undertake to respect and to ensure respect for the present Convention in all circumstances.

Art 2. In addition to the provisions which shall be implemented in peace time, the present Convention shall apply to all cases of declared war or of any other armed conflict which may arise between two or more of the High Contracting Parties, even if the state of war is not recognized by one of them.

The Convention shall also apply to all cases of partial or total occupation of the territory of a High Contracting Party, even if the said occupation meets with no armed resistance.

Although one of the Powers in conflict may not be a party to the present Convention, the Powers who are parties thereto shall remain bound by it in their mutual relations. They shall furthermore be bound by the Convention in relation to the said Power, if the latter accepts and applies the provisions thereof.

Art 3. In the case of armed conflict not of an international character occurring in the territory of one of the High Contracting Parties, each Party to the conflict shall be bound to apply, as a minimum, the following provisions:

(1) Persons taking no active part in the hostilities, including members of armed forces who have laid down their arms and those placed hors de combat by sickness, wounds, detention, or any other cause, shall in all circumstances be treated humanely, without any adverse distinction founded on race, colour, religion or faith, sex, birth or wealth, or any other similar criteria. To this end the following acts are

and shall remain prohibited at any time and in any place whatsoever with respect to the above-mentioned persons:
(a) violence to life and person, in particular murder of all kinds, mutilation, cruel treatment and torture;
(b) taking of hostages;
(c) outrages upon personal dignity, in particular, humiliating and degrading treatment;
(d) the passing of sentences and the carrying out of executions without previous judgment pronounced by a regularly constituted court affording all the judicial guarantees which are recognized as indispensable by civilized peoples.
(2) The wounded and sick shall be collected and cared for.

An impartial humanitarian body, such as the International Committee of the Red Cross, may offer its services to the Parties to the conflict.

The Parties to the conflict should further endeavour to bring into force, by means of special agreements, all or part of the other provisions of the present Convention.

The application of the preceding provisions shall not affect the legal status of the Parties to the conflict.

Art 4.

A. Prisoners of war, in the sense of the present Convention, are persons belonging to one of the following categories, who have fallen into the power of the enemy:
(1) Members of the armed forces of a Party to the conflict, as well as members of militias or volunteer corps forming part of such armed forces.
(2) Members of other militias and members of other volunteer corps, including those of organized resistance movements, belonging to a Party to the conflict and operating in or outside their own territory, even if this territory is occupied, provided that such militias or volunteer corps, including such organized resistance movements, fulfil the following conditions:
    (a) that of being commanded by a person responsible for his subordinates;
    (b) that of having a fixed distinctive sign recognizable at a distance;
    (c) that of carrying arms openly;
    (d) that of conducting their operations in accordance with the laws and customs of war.
(3) Members of regular armed forces who profess allegiance to a government or an authority not recognized by the Detaining Power.
(4) Persons who accompany the armed forces without actually being members thereof, such as civilian members of military aircraft crews, war correspondents, supply contractors, members of labour units or of services responsible for the welfare of the armed forces, provided that they have received authorization, from the armed forces which they accompany, who shall provide them for that purpose with an identity card similar to the annexed model.
(5) Members of crews, including masters, pilots and apprentices, of the merchant

marine and the crews of civil aircraft of the Parties to the conflict, who do not benefit by more favourable treatment under any other provisions of international law.

(6) Inhabitants of a non-occupied territory, who on the approach of the enemy spontaneously take up arms to resist the invading forces, without having had time to form themselves into regular armed units, provided they carry arms openly and respect the laws and customs of war.

B. The following shall likewise be treated as prisoners of war under the present Convention:

(1) Persons belonging, or having belonged, to the armed forces of the occupied country, if the occupying Power considers it necessary by reason of such allegiance to intern them, even though it has originally liberated them while hostilities were going on outside the territory it occupies, in particular where such persons have made an unsuccessful attempt to rejoin the armed forces to which they belong and which are engaged in combat, or where they fail to comply with a summons made to them with a view to internment.

(2) The persons belonging to one of the categories enumerated in the present Article, who have been received by neutral or non-belligerent Powers on their territory and whom these Powers are required to intern under international law, without prejudice to any more favourable treatment which these Powers may choose to give and with the exception of Articles 8, 10, 15, 30, fifth paragraph, 58-67, 92, 126 and, where diplomatic relations exist between the Parties to the conflict and the neutral or non-belligerent Power concerned, those Articles concerning the Protecting Power. Where such diplomatic relations exist, the Parties to a conflict on whom these persons depend shall be allowed to perform towards them the functions of a Protecting Power as provided in the present Convention, without prejudice to the functions which these Parties normally exercise in conformity with diplomatic and consular usage and treaties.

C. This Article shall in no way affect the status of medical personnel and chaplains as provided for in Article 33 of the present Convention.

Art 5. The present Convention shall apply to the persons referred to in Article 4 from the time they fall into the power of the enemy and until their final release and repatriation.

Should any doubt arise as to whether persons, having committed a belligerent act and having fallen into the hands of the enemy, belong to any of the categories enumerated in Article 4, such persons shall enjoy the protection of the present Convention until such time as their status has been determined by a competent tribunal.

Art 6. In addition to the agreements expressly provided for in Articles 10, 23, 28, 33, 60, 65, 66, 67, 72, 73, 75, 109, 110, 118, 119, 122 and 132, the High Contracting Parties may conclude other special agreements for all matters concerning which they may deem it suitable to make separate provision. No special agreement shall adversely affect the situation of prisoners of war, as defined by the present Convention, nor restrict the rights which it confers upon them.

Prisoners of war shall continue to have the benefit of such agreements as long as the Convention is applicable to them, except where express provisions to the contrary are contained in the aforesaid or in subsequent agreements, or where more favourable measures have been taken with regard to them by one or other of the Parties to the conflict.

Art 7. Prisoners of war may in no circumstances renounce in part or in entirety the rights secured to them by the present Convention, and by the special agreements referred to in the foregoing Article, if such there be.

Art 8. The present Convention shall be applied with the cooperation and under the scrutiny of the Protecting Powers whose duty it is to safeguard the interests of the Parties to the conflict. For this purpose, the Protecting Powers may appoint, apart from their diplomatic or consular staff, delegates from amongst their own nationals or the nationals of other neutral Powers. The said delegates shall be subject to the approval of the Power with which they are to carry out their duties.

The Parties to the conflict shall facilitate to the greatest extent possible the task of the representatives or delegates of the Protecting Powers.

The representatives or delegates of the Protecting Powers shall not in any case exceed their mission under the present Convention. They shall, in particular, take account of the imperative necessities of security of the State wherein they carry out their duties.

Art 9. The provisions of the present Convention constitute no obstacle to the humanitarian activities which the International Committee of the Red Cross or any other impartial humanitarian organization may, subject to the consent of the Parties to the conflict concerned, undertake for the protection of prisoners of war and for their relief.

Art 10. The High Contracting Parties may at any time agree to entrust to an organization which offers all guarantees of impartiality and efficacy the duties incumbent on the Protecting Powers by virtue of the present Convention.

When prisoners of war do not benefit or cease to benefit, no matter for what reason, by the activities of a Protecting Power or of an organization provided for in the first paragraph above, the Detaining Power shall request a neutral State, or such an organization, to undertake the functions performed under the present Convention by a Protecting Power designated by the Parties to a conflict.

If protection cannot be arranged accordingly, the Detaining Power shall request or shall accept, subject to the provisions of this Article, the offer of the services of a humanitarian organization, such as the International Committee of the Red Cross, to assume the humanitarian functions performed by Protecting Powers under the present Convention.

Any neutral Power or any organization invited by the Power concerned or offering itself for these purposes, shall be required to act with a sense of responsibility towards the Party to the conflict on which persons protected by the present Convention depend, and shall be required to furnish sufficient assurances that it is in a position to undertake the appropriate functions and to discharge them impartially.

No derogation from the preceding provisions shall be made by special agreements between Powers one of which is restricted, even temporarily, in its freedom to negotiate with the other Power or its allies by reason of military events, more particularly where the whole, or a substantial part, of the territory of the said Power is occupied.

Whenever in the present Convention mention is made of a Protecting Power, such mention applies to substitute organizations in the sense of the present Article.

Art 11. In cases where they deem it advisable in the interest of protected persons, particularly in cases of disagreement between the Parties to the conflict as to the application or interpretation of the provisions of the present Convention, the Protecting Powers shall lend their good offices with a view to settling the disagreement.

For this purpose, each of the Protecting Powers may, either at the invitation of one Party or on its own initiative, propose to the Parties to the conflict a meeting of their representatives, and in particular of the authorities responsible for prisoners of war, possibly on neutral territory suitably chosen. The Parties to the conflict shall be bound to give effect to the proposals made to them for this purpose. The Protecting Powers may, if necessary, propose for approval by the Parties to the conflict a person belonging to a neutral Power, or delegated by the International Committee of the Red Cross, who shall be invited to take part in such a meeting.

PART II. GENERAL PROTECTION OF PRISONERS OF WAR

Art 12. Prisoners of war are in the hands of the enemy Power, but not of the individuals or military units who have captured them. Irrespective of the individual responsibilities that may exist, the Detaining Power is responsible for the treatment given them.

Prisoners of war may only be transferred by the Detaining Power to a Power which is a party to the Convention and after the Detaining Power has satisfied itself of the willingness and ability of such transferee Power to apply the Convention. When prisoners of war are transferred under such circumstances, responsibility for the application of the Convention rests on the Power accepting them while they are in its custody.

Nevertheless, if that Power fails to carry out the provisions of the Convention in any important respect, the Power by whom the prisoners of war were transferred shall, upon being notified by the Protecting Power, take effective measures to correct the situation or shall request the return of the prisoners of war. Such requests must be complied with.

Art 13. Prisoners of war must at all times be humanely treated. Any unlawful act or omission by the Detaining Power causing death or seriously endangering the health of a prisoner of war in its custody is prohibited, and will be regarded as a serious breach of the present Convention. In particular, no prisoner of war may be subjected to physical mutilation or to medical or scientific experiments of any kind which are not justified by the medical, dental or hospital treatment of the prisoner concerned and carried out in his interest.

Likewise, prisoners of war must at all times be protected, particularly against acts of violence or intimidation and against insults and public curiosity.

Measures of reprisal against prisoners of war are prohibited.

Art 14. Prisoners of war are entitled in all circumstances to respect for their persons and their honour.

Women shall be treated with all the regard due to their sex and shall in all cases benefit by treatment as favourable as that granted to men.

Prisoners of war shall retain the full civil capacity which they enjoyed at the time of their capture. The Detaining Power may not restrict the exercise, either within or without its own territory, of the rights such capacity confers except in so far as the captivity requires.

Art 15. The Power detaining prisoners of war shall be bound to provide free of charge for their maintenance and for the medical attention required by their state of health.

Art 16. Taking into consideration the provisions of the present Convention relating to rank and sex, and subject to any privileged treatment which may be accorded to them by reason of their state of health, age or professional qualifications, all prisoners of war shall be treated alike by the Detaining Power, without any adverse distinction based on race, nationality, religious belief or political opinions, or any other distinction founded on similar criteria.

PART III. CAPTIVITY

Art 17. Every prisoner of war, when questioned on the subject, is bound to give only his surname, first names and rank, date of birth, and army, regimental, personal or serial number, or failing this, equivalent information.

If he wilfully infringes this rule, he may render himself liable to a restriction of the privileges accorded to his rank or status.

Each Party to a conflict is required to furnish the persons under its jurisdiction who are liable to become prisoners of war, with an identity card showing the owner's surname, first names, rank, army, regimental, personal or serial number or equivalent information, and date of birth. The identity card may, furthermore, bear the signature or the fingerprints, or both, of the owner, and may bear, as well, any other information the Party to the conflict may wish to add concerning persons belonging to its armed forces. As far as possible the card shall measure 6.5 x 10 cm. and shall be issued in duplicate. The identity card shall be shown by the prisoner of war upon demand, but may in no case be taken away from him.

No physical or mental torture, nor any other form of coercion, may be inflicted on prisoners of war to secure from them information of any kind whatever. Prisoners of war who refuse to answer may not be threatened, insulted, or exposed to unpleasant or disadvantageous treatment of any kind.

Prisoners of war who, owing to their physical or mental condition, are unable to state their identity, shall be handed over to the medical service. The identity of such prisoners shall be established by all possible means, subject to the provisions of the preceding paragraph.

The questioning of prisoners of war shall be carried out in a language which they understand.

Art 18. All effects and articles of personal use, except arms, horses, military equipment and military documents, shall remain in the possession of prisoners of war, likewise their metal helmets and gas masks and like articles issued for personal protection. Effects and articles used for their clothing or feeding shall likewise remain in their possession, even if such effects and articles belong to their regulation military equipment.

At no time should prisoners of war be without identity documents. The Detaining Power shall supply such documents to prisoners of war who possess none.

Badges of rank and nationality, decorations and articles having above all a personal or sentimental value may not be taken from prisoners of war.

Sums of money carried by prisoners of war may not be taken away from them except by order of an officer, and after the amount and particulars of the owner have been recorded in a special register and an itemized receipt has been given, legibly inscribed with the name, rank and unit of the person issuing the said receipt. Sums in the currency of the Detaining Power, or which are changed into such currency at the prisoner's request, shall be placed to the credit of the prisoner's account as provided in Article 64.

The Detaining Power may withdraw articles of value from prisoners of war only for reasons of security; when such articles are withdrawn, the procedure laid down for sums of money impounded shall apply.

Such objects, likewise sums taken away in any currency other than that of the Detaining Power and the conversion of which has not been asked for by the owners, shall be kept in the custody of the Detaining Power and shall be returned in their initial shape to prisoners of war at the end of their captivity.

Art 19. Prisoners of war shall be evacuated, as soon as possible after their capture, to camps situated in an area far enough from the combat zone for them to be out of danger.

Only those prisoners of war who, owing to wounds or sickness, would run greater risks by being evacuated than by remaining where they are, may be temporarily kept back in a danger zone.

Prisoners of war shall not be unnecessarily exposed to danger while awaiting evacuation from a fighting zone.

Art 20. The evacuation of prisoners of war shall always be effected humanely and in conditions similar to those for the forces of the Detaining Power in their changes of station.

The Detaining Power shall supply prisoners of war who are being evacuated with sufficient food and potable water, and with the necessary clothing and medical attention. The Detaining Power shall take all suitable precautions to ensure their safety during evacuation, and shall establish as soon as possible a list of the prisoners of war who are evacuated.

If prisoners of war must, during evacuation, pass through transit camps, their stay in such camps shall be as brief as possible.

Art 21. It may impose on them the obligation of not leaving, beyond certain limits, the camp where they are interned, or if the said camp is fenced in, of not going outside its perimeter. Subject to the provisions of the present Convention relative to penal and disciplinary sanctions, prisoners of war may not be held in close confinement except where necessary to safeguard their health and then only during the continuation of the circumstances which make such confinement necessary.

Prisoners of war may be partially or wholly released on parole or promise, in so far as is allowed by the laws of the Power on which they depend. Such measures shall be taken particularly in cases where this may contribute to the improvement of their state of health. No prisoner of war shall be compelled to accept liberty on parole or promise.

Upon the outbreak of hostilities, each Party to the conflict shall notify the adverse Party of the laws and regulations allowing or forbidding its own nationals to accept liberty on parole or promise. Prisoners of war who are paroled or who have given their promise in conformity with the laws and regulations so notified, are bound on their personal honour scrupulously to fulfil, both towards the Power on which they depend and towards the Power which has captured them, the engagements of their paroles or promises. In such cases, the Power on which they depend is bound neither to require nor to accept from them any service incompatible with the parole or promise given.

Art 22. Prisoners of war may be interned only in premises located on land and affording every guarantee of hygiene and healthfulness. Except in particular cases which are justified by the interest of the prisoners themselves, they shall not be interned in penitentiaries.

Prisoners of war interned in unhealthy areas, or where the climate is injurious for them, shall be removed as soon as possible to a more favourable climate.

The Detaining Power shall assemble prisoners of war in camps or camp compounds according to their nationality, language and customs, provided that such prisoners shall not be separated from prisoners of war belonging to the armed forces with which they were serving at the time of their capture, except with their consent.

Art 23. No prisoner of war may at any time be sent to, or detained in areas where he may be exposed to the fire of the combat zone, nor may his presence be used to render certain points or areas immune from military operations.

Prisoners of war shall have shelters against air bombardment and other hazards of war, to the same extent as the local civilian population. With the exception of those engaged in the protection of their quarters against the aforesaid hazards, they may enter such shelters as soon as possible after the giving of the alarm. Any other protective measure taken in favour of the population shall also apply to them.

Detaining Powers shall give the Powers concerned, through the intermediary of the Protecting Powers, all useful information regarding the geographical location of prisoner of war camps.

Whenever military considerations permit, prisoner of war camps shall be indicated in the day-time by the letters PW or PG, placed so as to be clearly visible from the air. The Powers concerned may, however, agree upon any other system of marking. Only prisoner of war camps shall be marked as such.

Art 24. Transit or screening camps of a permanent kind shall be fitted out under conditions similar to those described in the present Section, and the prisoners therein shall have the same treatment as in other camps.

Appendix 4

Convention against Torture and Other Cruel, Inhuman,
or Degrading Treatment or Punishment,
Entered into Force June 26, 1987 (Preamble, Part I)

The States Parties to this Convention,

Considering that, in accordance with the principles proclaimed in the Charter of the United Nations, recognition of the equal and inalienable rights of all members of the human family is the foundation of freedom, justice and peace in the world,

Recognizing that those rights derive from the inherent dignity of the human person,

Considering the obligation of States under the Charter, in particular Article 55, to promote universal respect for, and observance of, human rights and fundamental freedoms,

Having regard to article 5 of the Universal Declaration of Human Rights and article 7 of the International Covenant on Civil and Political Rights, both of which provide that no one shall be subjected to torture or to cruel, inhuman or degrading treatment or punishment,

Having regard also to the Declaration on the Protection of All Persons from Being Subjected to Torture and Other Cruel, Inhuman or Degrading Treatment or Punishment, adopted by the General Assembly on 9 December 1975,

Desiring to make more effective the struggle against torture and other cruel, inhuman or degrading treatment or punishment throughout the world,

Have agreed as follows:

PART I

Article I

1. For the purposes of this Convention, the term "torture" means any act by which severe pain or suffering, whether physical or mental, is intentionally inflicted on a person for such purposes as obtaining from him or a third person information or a confession, punishing him for an act he or a third person has committed or is suspected of having committed, or intimidating or coercing him or a third person, or for any reason based on discrimination of any kind, when such pain or suffering is inflicted by or at the instigation of or with the consent or acquiescence of a public official or other person acting in an official capacity. It does not include pain or suffering arising only from, inherent in or incidental to lawful sanctions.

Available at http://www.unhchr.ch/html/menu3/b/h_cat39.htm.

2. This article is without prejudice to any international instrument or national legislation which does or may contain provisions of wider application.

Article 2

1. Each State Party shall take effective legislative, administrative, judicial or other measures to prevent acts of torture in any territory under its jurisdiction.

2. No exceptional circumstances whatsoever, whether a state of war or a threat of war, internal political instability or any other public emergency, may be invoked as a justification of torture.

3. An order from a superior officer or a public authority may not be invoked as a justification of torture.

Article 3

1. No State Party shall expel, return ("refouler") or extradite a person to another State where there are substantial grounds for believing that he would be in danger of being subjected to torture.

2. For the purpose of determining whether there are such grounds, the competent authorities shall take into account all relevant considerations including, where applicable, the existence in the State concerned of a consistent pattern of gross, flagrant or mass violations of human rights.

Article 4

1. Each State Party shall ensure that all acts of torture are offences under its criminal law. The same shall apply to an attempt to commit torture and to an act by any person which constitutes complicity or participation in torture.

2. Each State Party shall make these offences punishable by appropriate penalties which take into account their grave nature.

Article 5

1. Each State Party shall take such measures as may be necessary to establish its jurisdiction over the offences referred to in article 4 in the following cases:
   (a) When the offences are committed in any territory under its jurisdiction or on board a ship or aircraft registered in that State;
   (b) When the alleged offender is a national of that State;
   (c) When the victim is a national of that State if that State considers it appropriate.

2. Each State Party shall likewise take such measures as may be necessary to establish its jurisdiction over such offences in cases where the alleged offender is present in any territory under its jurisdiction and it does not extradite him pursuant to article 8 to any of the States mentioned in paragraph 1 of this article.

3. This Convention does not exclude any criminal jurisdiction exercised in accordance with internal law.

Article 6

1. Upon being satisfied, after an examination of information available to it, that the circumstances so warrant, any State Party in whose territory a person alleged to have committed any offence referred to in article 4 is present shall take him into custody or take other legal measures to ensure his presence. The custody and other legal measures shall be as provided in the law of that State but may be continued only for such time as is necessary to enable any criminal or extradition proceedings to be instituted.

2. Such State shall immediately make a preliminary inquiry into the facts.

3. Any person in custody pursuant to paragraph 1 of this article shall be assisted in communicating immediately with the nearest appropriate representative of the State of which he is a national, or, if he is a stateless person, with the representative of the State where he usually resides.

4. When a State, pursuant to this article, has taken a person into custody, it shall immediately notify the States referred to in article 5, paragraph 1, of the fact that such person is in custody and of the circumstances which warrant his detention. The State which makes the preliminary inquiry contemplated in paragraph 2 of this article shall promptly report its findings to the said States and shall indicate whether it intends to exercise jurisdiction.

Article 7

1. The State Party in the territory under whose jurisdiction a person alleged to have committed any offence referred to in article 4 is found shall in the cases contemplated in article 5, if it does not extradite him, submit the case to its competent authorities for the purpose of prosecution.

2. These authorities shall take their decision in the same manner as in the case of any ordinary offence of a serious nature under the law of that State. In the cases referred to in article 5, paragraph 2, the standards of evidence required for prosecution and conviction shall in no way be less stringent than those which apply in the cases referred to in article 5, paragraph 1.

3. Any person regarding whom proceedings are brought in connection with any of the offences referred to in article 4 shall be guaranteed fair treatment at all stages of the proceedings.

Article 8

1. The offences referred to in article 4 shall be deemed to be included as extraditable offences in any extradition treaty existing between States Parties. States Parties undertake to include such offences as extraditable offences in every extradition treaty to be concluded between them.

2. If a State Party which makes extradition conditional on the existence of a treaty receives a request for extradition from another State Party with which it has no extradition treaty, it may consider this Convention as the legal basis for extradition in

respect of such offences. Extradition shall be subject to the other conditions provided by the law of the requested State.

3. States Parties which do not make extradition conditional on the existence of a treaty shall recognize such offences as extraditable offences between themselves subject to the conditions provided by the law of the requested State.

4. Such offences shall be treated, for the purpose of extradition between States Parties, as if they had been committed not only in the place in which they occurred but also in the territories of the States required to establish their jurisdiction in accordance with article 5, paragraph 1.

Article 9

1. States Parties shall afford one another the greatest measure of assistance in connection with criminal proceedings brought in respect of any of the offences referred to in article 4, including the supply of all evidence at their disposal necessary for the proceedings.

2. States Parties shall carry out their obligations under paragraph 1 of this article in conformity with any treaties on mutual judicial assistance that may exist between them.

Article 10

1. Each State Party shall ensure that education and information regarding the prohibition against torture are fully included in the training of law enforcement personnel, civil or military, medical personnel, public officials and other persons who may be involved in the custody, interrogation or treatment of any individual subjected to any form of arrest, detention or imprisonment.

2. Each State Party shall include this prohibition in the rules or instructions issued in regard to the duties and functions of any such person.

Article 11

Each State Party shall keep under systematic review interrogation rules, instructions, methods and practices as well as arrangements for the custody and treatment of persons subjected to any form of arrest, detention or imprisonment in any territory under its jurisdiction, with a view to preventing any cases of torture.

Article 12

Each State Party shall ensure that its competent authorities proceed to a prompt and impartial investigation, wherever there is reasonable ground to believe that an act of torture has been committed in any territory under its jurisdiction.

Article 13

Each State Party shall ensure that any individual who alleges he has been subjected to torture in any territory under its jurisdiction has the right to complain to, and to have his case promptly and impartially examined by, its competent authorities. Steps shall be taken to ensure that the complainant and witnesses are protected against all ill-treatment or intimidation as a consequence of his complaint or any evidence given.

Article 14

1. Each State Party shall ensure in its legal system that the victim of an act of torture obtains redress and has an enforceable right to fair and adequate compensation, including the means for as full rehabilitation as possible. In the event of the death of the victim as a result of an act of torture, his dependants shall be entitled to compensation.

2. Nothing in this article shall affect any right of the victim or other persons to compensation which may exist under national law.

Article 15

Each State Party shall ensure that any statement which is established to have been made as a result of torture shall not be invoked as evidence in any proceedings, except against a person accused of torture as evidence that the statement was made.

Article 16

1. Each State Party shall undertake to prevent in any territory under its jurisdiction other acts of cruel, inhuman or degrading treatment or punishment which do not amount to torture as defined in article 1, when such acts are committed by or at the instigation of or with the consent or acquiescence of a public official or other person acting in an official capacity. In particular, the obligations contained in articles 10, 11, 12 and 13 shall apply with the substitution for references to torture of references to other forms of cruel, inhuman or degrading treatment or punishment.

2. The provisions of this Convention are without prejudice to the provisions of any other international instrument or national law which prohibits cruel, inhuman or degrading treatment or punishment or which relates to extradition or expulsion.

Appendix 5

Detainee Treatment Act of 2005
(Title X—Matters Relating to Detainees)

SEC. 1001. SHORT TITLE.

This title may be cited as the "Detainee Treatment Act of 2005."

SEC. 1002. UNIFORM STANDARDS FOR THE INTERROGATION OF PERSONS UNDER THE DETENTION OF THE DEPARTMENT OF DEFENSE.

(a) In General–No person in the custody or under the effective control of the Department of Defense or under detention in a Department of Defense facility shall be subject to any treatment or technique of interrogation not authorized by and listed in the United States Army Field Manual on Intelligence Interrogation.

(b) Applicability–Subsection (a) shall not apply with respect to any person in the custody or under the effective control of the Department of Defense pursuant to a criminal law or immigration law of the United States.

(c) Construction–Nothing in this section shall be construed to affect the rights under the United States Constitution of any person in the custody or under the physical jurisdiction of the United States.

SEC. 1003. PROHIBITION ON CRUEL, INHUMAN, OR DEGRADING TREATMENT OR PUNISHMENT OF PERSONS UNDER CUSTODY OR CONTROL OF THE UNITED STATES GOVERNMENT.

(a) In General–No individual in the custody or under the physical control of the United States Government, regardless of nationality or physical location, shall be subject to cruel, inhuman, or degrading treatment or punishment.

(b) Construction–Nothing in this section shall be construed to impose any geographical limitation on the applicability of the prohibition against cruel, inhuman, or degrading treatment or punishment under this section.

(c) Limitation on Supersedure–The provisions of this section shall not be superseded, except by a provision of law enacted after the date of the enactment of this Act which specifically repeals, modifies, or supersedes the provisions of this section.

(d) Cruel, Inhuman, or Degrading Treatment or Punishment Defined–In this section, the term "cruel, inhuman, or degrading treatment or punishment" means the cruel, unusual, and inhumane treatment or punishment prohibited by the Fifth, Eighth, and Fourteenth Amendments to the Constitution of the United States, as defined in the United States Reservations, Declarations and Understandings to the United Nations Convention against Torture and Other Forms of Cruel, Inhuman or Degrading Treatment or Punishment done at New York, December 10, 1984.

SEC. 1004. PROTECTION OF UNITED STATES GOVERNMENT PERSONNEL ENGAGED IN AUTHORIZED INTERROGATIONS.

(a) Protection of United States Government Personnel–In any civil action or criminal prosecution against an officer, employee, member of the Armed Forces, or other agent of the United States Government who is a United States person, arising out of the officer, employee, member of the Armed Forces, or other agent's engaging in specific operational practices, that involve detention and interrogation of aliens who the President or his designees have determined are believed to be engaged in or associated with international terrorist activity that poses a serious, continuing threat to the United States, its interests, or its allies, and that were officially authorized and determined to be lawful at the time that they were conducted, it shall be a defense that such officer, employee, member of the Armed Forces, or other agent did not know that the practices were unlawful and a person of ordinary sense and understanding would not know the practices were unlawful. Good faith reliance on advice of counsel should be an important factor, among others, to consider in assessing whether a person of ordinary sense and understanding would have known the practices to be unlawful. Nothing in this section shall be construed to limit or extinguish any defense or protection otherwise available to any person or entity from suit, civil or criminal liability, or damages, or to provide immunity from prosecution for any criminal offense by the proper authorities.

(b) Counsel–The United States Government may provide or employ counsel, and pay counsel fees, court costs, bail, and other expenses incident to the representation of an officer, employee, member of the Armed Forces, or other agent described in subsection (a), with respect to any civil action or criminal prosecution arising out of practices described in that subsection, under the same conditions, and to the same extent, to which such services and payments are authorized under section 1037 of title 10, United States Code.

SEC. 1005. PROCEDURES FOR STATUS REVIEW OF DETAINEES OUTSIDE THE UNITED STATES.

(a) Submittal of Procedures for Status Review of Detainees at Guantanamo Bay, Cuba, and in Afghanistan and Iraq–

(1) IN GENERAL–Not later than 180 days after the date of the enactment of this Act, the Secretary of Defense shall submit to the Committee on Armed Services and the Committee on the Judiciary of the Senate and the Committee on

Armed Services and the Committee on the Judiciary of the House of Representatives a report setting forth–

(A) the procedures of the Combatant Status Review Tribunals and the Administrative Review Boards established by direction of the Secretary of Defense that are in operation at Guantanamo Bay, Cuba, for determining the status of the detainees held at Guantanamo Bay or to provide an annual review to determine the need to continue to detain an alien who is a detainee; and

(B) the procedures in operation in Afghanistan and Iraq for a determination of the status of aliens detained in the custody or under the physical control of the Department of Defense in those countries.

(2) DESIGNATED CIVILIAN OFFICIAL–The procedures submitted to Congress pursuant to paragraph (1)(A) shall ensure that the official of the Department of Defense who is designated by the President or Secretary of Defense to be the final review authority within the Department of Defense with respect to decisions of any such tribunal or board (referred to as the "Designated Civilian Official") shall be a civilian officer of the Department of Defense holding an office to which appointments are required by law to be made by the President, by and with the advice and consent of the Senate.

(3) CONSIDERATION OF NEW EVIDENCE–The procedures submitted under paragraph (1)(A) shall provide for periodic review of any new evidence that may become available relating to the enemy combatant status of a detainee.

(b) Consideration of Statements Derived with Coercion–

(1) ASSESSMENT–The procedures submitted to Congress pursuant to subsection (a)(1)(A) shall ensure that a Combatant Status Review Tribunal or Administrative Review Board, or any similar or successor administrative tribunal or board, in making a determination of status or disposition of any detainee under such procedures, shall, to the extent practicable, assess–

(A) whether any statement derived from or relating to such detainee was obtained as a result of coercion; and

(B) the probative value (if any) of any such statement.

(2) APPLICABILITY–Paragraph (1) applies with respect to any proceeding beginning on or after the date of the enactment of this Act.

(c) Report on Modification of Procedures–The Secretary of Defense shall submit to the committees specified in subsection (a)(1) a report on any modification of the procedures submitted under subsection (a). Any such report shall be submitted not later than 60 days before the date on which such modification goes into effect.

(d) Annual Report–

(1) REPORT REQUIRED–The Secretary of Defense shall submit to Congress an annual report on the annual review process for aliens in the custody of the Department of Defense outside the United States. Each such report shall be submitted in unclassified form, with a classified annex, if necessary. The report shall be submitted not later than December 31 each year.

(2) ELEMENTS OF REPORT–Each such report shall include the following with respect to the year covered by the report:

(A) The number of detainees whose status was reviewed.

(B) The procedures used at each location.

(e) Judicial Review of Detention of Enemy Combatants–

(1) IN GENERAL–Section 2241 of title 28, United States Code, is amended by adding at the end the following:

(A) Except as provided in section 1005 of the Detainee Treatment Act of 2005, no court, justice, or judge shall have jurisdiction to hear or consider–

(B) an application for a writ of habeas corpus filed by or on behalf of an alien detained by the Department of Defense at Guantanamo Bay, Cuba; or

(C) any other action against the United States or its agents relating to any aspect of the detention by the Department of Defense of an alien at Guantanamo Bay, Cuba, who–

(i) is currently in military custody; or

(ii) has been determined by the United States Court of Appeals for the District of Columbia Circuit in accordance with the procedures set forth in section 1005(e) of the Detainee Treatment Act of 2005 to have been properly detained as an enemy combatant.

(2) REVIEW OF DECISIONS OF COMBATANT STATUS REVIEW TRIBUNALS OF PROPRIETY OF DETENTION–

(A) IN GENERAL–Subject to subparagraphs (B), (C), and (D), the United States Court of Appeals for the District of Columbia Circuit shall have exclusive jurisdiction to determine the validity of any final decision of a Combatant Status Review Tribunal that an alien is properly detained as an enemy combatant.

(B) LIMITATION ON CLAIMS–The jurisdiction of the United States Court of Appeals for the District of Columbia Circuit under this paragraph shall be limited to claims brought by or on behalf of an alien–

(i) who is, at the time a request for review by such court is filed, detained by the Department of Defense at Guantanamo Bay, Cuba; and

(ii) for whom a Combatant Status Review Tribunal has been conducted, pursuant to applicable procedures specified by the Secretary of Defense.

(C) SCOPE OF REVIEW–The jurisdiction of the United States Court of Appeals for the District of Columbia Circuit on any claims with respect to an alien under this paragraph shall be limited to the consideration of–

(i) whether the status determination of the Combatant Status Review Tribunal with regard to such alien was consistent with the standards and procedures specified by the Secretary of Defense for Combatant Status Review Tribunals (including the requirement that the conclusion of the Tribunal be supported by a preponderance of the evidence and allowing a rebuttable presumption in favor of the Government's evidence); and

(ii) to the extent the Constitution and laws of the United States are applicable, whether the use of such standards and procedures to make the determination is consistent with the Constitution and laws of the United States.

(D) TERMINATION ON RELEASE FROM CUSTODY–The jurisdiction of the United States Court of Appeals for the District of Columbia Circuit with respect to the claims of an alien under this paragraph shall cease upon the release of such alien from the custody of the Department of Defense.

(3) REVIEW OF FINAL DECISIONS OF MILITARY COMMISSIONS–

(A) IN GENERAL–Subject to subparagraphs (B), (C), and (D), the United States Court of Appeals for the District of Columbia Circuit shall have exclusive jurisdiction to determine the validity of any final decision rendered pursuant to Military Commission Order No. 1, dated August 31, 2005 (or any successor military order).

(B) GRANT OF REVIEW–Review under this paragraph–

(i) with respect to a capital case or a case in which the alien was sentenced to a term of imprisonment of 10 years or more, shall be as of right; or

(ii) with respect to any other case, shall be at the discretion of the United States Court of Appeals for the District of Columbia Circuit.

(C) LIMITATION ON APPEALS–The jurisdiction of the United States Court of Appeals for the District of Columbia Circuit under this paragraph shall be limited to an appeal brought by or on behalf of an alien–

(i) who was, at the time of the proceedings pursuant to the military order referred to in subparagraph (A), detained by the Department of Defense at Guantanamo Bay, Cuba; and

(ii) for whom a final decision has been rendered pursuant to such military order.

(D) SCOPE OF REVIEW–The jurisdiction of the United States Court of Appeals for the District of Columbia Circuit on an appeal of a final decision with respect to an alien under this paragraph shall be limited to the consideration of–

(i) whether the final decision was consistent with the standards and procedures specified in the military order referred to in subparagraph (A); and

(ii) to the extent the Constitution and laws of the United States are applicable, whether the use of such standards and procedures to reach the final decision is consistent with the Constitution and laws of the United States.

(4) RESPONDENT–The Secretary of Defense shall be the named respondent in any appeal to the United States Court of Appeals for the District of Columbia Circuit under this subsection.

(f) Construction–Nothing in this section shall be construed to confer any constitutional right on an alien detained as an enemy combatant outside the United States.

(g) United States Defined–For purposes of this section, the term "United States," when used in a geographic sense, is as defined in section 101(a)(38) of the Immigration and Nationality Act and, in particular, does not include the United States Naval Station, Guantanamo Bay, Cuba.

(h) Effective Date–

   (1) IN GENERAL–This section shall take effect on the date of the enactment of this Act.

   (2) REVIEW OF COMBATANT STATUS TRIBUNAL AND MILITARY COMMISSION DECISIONS–Paragraphs (2) and (3) of subsection (e) shall apply with respect to any claim whose review is governed by one of such paragraphs and that is pending on or after the date of the enactment of this Act.

SEC. 1006. TRAINING OF IRAQI FORCES REGARDING TREATMENT OF DETAINEES.

(a) Required Policies–

   (1) IN GENERAL–The Secretary of Defense shall ensure that policies are prescribed regarding procedures for military and civilian personnel of the Department of Defense and contractor personnel of the Department of Defense in Iraq that are intended to ensure that members of the Armed Forces, and all persons acting on behalf of the Armed Forces or within facilities of the Armed Forces, ensure that all personnel of Iraqi military forces who are trained by Department of Defense personnel and contractor personnel of the Department of Defense receive training regarding the international obligations and laws applicable to the humane detention of detainees, including protections afforded under the Geneva Conventions and the Convention against Torture.

   (2) ACKNOWLEDGMENT OF TRAINING–The Secretary shall ensure that, for all personnel of the Iraqi Security Forces who are provided training referred to in paragraph (1), there is documented acknowledgment of such training having been provided.

   (3) DEADLINE FOR POLICIES TO BE PRESCRIBED–The policies required by paragraph (1) shall be prescribed not later than 180 days after the date of the enactment of this Act.

(b) Army Field Manual–

   (1) TRANSLATION–The Secretary of Defense shall provide for the United States Army Field Manual on Intelligence Interrogation to be translated into Arabic and any other language the Secretary determines appropriate for use by members of the Iraqi military forces.

   (2) DISTRIBUTION–The Secretary of Defense shall provide for such manual, as translated, to be provided to each unit of the Iraqi military forces trained by Department of Defense personnel or contractor personnel of the Department of Defense.

(c) Transmittal of Regulations–Not less than 30 days after the date on which regulations, policies, and orders are first prescribed under subsection (a), the Secretary of Defense shall submit to the Committee on Armed Services of the Senate and the Committee on Armed Services of the House of Representatives copies of such regulations, policies, or orders, together with a report on steps taken to the date of the report to implement this section.

(d) Annual Report–Not less than one year after the date of the enactment of this Act, and annually thereafter, the Secretary of Defense shall submit to the Committee on Armed Services of the Senate and the Committee on Armed Services of the House of Representatives a report on the implementation of this section.

Appendix Six

Military Commissions Act of 2006 (Excerpts)

One Hundred Ninth Congress of the United States of America

AT THE SECOND SESSION

Begun and held at the City of Washington on Tuesday, the third day of January, two thousand and six

An Act

To authorize trial by military commission for violations of the law of war, and for other purposes.

Be it enacted by the Senate and House of Representatives of the United States of America in Congress assembled,

SECTION 1. SHORT TITLE; TABLE OF CONTENTS.

(a) SHORT TITLE.—This Act may be cited as the "Military Commissions Act of 2006"

§ 948a. Definitions.

In this chapter:

(1) UNLAWFUL ENEMY COMBATANT.—(A) The term 'unlawful enemy combatant' means—

    (i) a person who has engaged in hostilities or who has purposefully and materially supported hostilities against the United States or its co-belligerents who is not a lawful enemy combatant (including a person who is part of the Taliban, al Qaeda, or associated forces); or

    (ii) a person who, before, on, or after the date of the enactment of the Military Commissions Act of 2006, has been determined to be an unlawful enemy combatant by a Combatant Status Review Tribunal or another competent tribunal established under the authority of the President or the Secretary of Defense.

§ 948b. Military commissions generally

. . .

[§ 948b](d) INAPPLICABILITY OF CERTAIN PROVISIONS.—(1) The following provisions of this title shall not apply to trial by military commission under this chapter:

    (A) Section 810 (article 10 of the Uniform Code of Military Justice), relating to speedy trial, including any rule of courts-martial relating to speedy trial.

Document available at http://www.loc.gov/rr/frd/Military_Law/pdf/PL-109-366.pdf.

(B) Sections 831(a), (b), and (d) (articles 31(a), (b), and (d) of the Uniform Code of Military Justice), relating to compulsory self-incrimination.

(C) Section 832 (article 32 of the Uniform Code of Military Justice), relating to pretrial investigation.

§ 948c. Persons subject to military commissions

Any alien unlawful enemy combatant is subject to trial by military commission under this chapter.

§ 948r. Compulsory self-incrimination prohibited; treatment of statements obtained by torture and other statements.

. . .

[§ 948r](c) STATEMENTS OBTAINED BEFORE ENACTMENT OF DETAINEE TREATMENT ACT OF 2005.—A statement obtained before December 30, 2005 (the date of the enactment of the Defense Treatment Act of 2005) in which the degree of coercion is disputed may be admitted only if the military judge finds that— (1) the totality of the circumstances renders the statement reliable and possessing sufficient probative value; and (2) the interests of justice would best be served by admission of the statement into evidence.

§ 950g. Review by the United States Court of Appeals for the District of Columbia Circuit and the Supreme Court.

(a) EXCLUSIVE APPELLATE JURISDICTION.—(1)(A) Except as provided in subparagraph (B), the United States Court of Appeals for the District of Columbia Circuit shall have exclusive jurisdiction to determine the validity of a final judgment rendered by a military commission (as approved by the convening authority) under this chapter.

(B) The Court of Appeals may not review the final judgment until all other appeals under this chapter have been waived or exhausted.

. . .

[§ 950g](c) SCOPE OF REVIEW.—The jurisdiction of the Court of Appeals on an appeal under subsection (a) shall be limited to the consideration of—

(1) whether the final decision was consistent with the standards and procedures specified in this chapter; and

(2) to the extent applicable, the Constitution and the laws of the United States.

(d) SUPREME COURT.—The Supreme Court may review by writ of certiorari the final judgment of the Court of Appeals pursuant to section 1257 of title 28.

§ 950j. Finality of proceedings, findings, and sentences.

(a) FINALITY.—The appellate review of records of trial provided by this chapter, and the proceedings, findings, and sentences of military commissions as approved, reviewed, or affirmed as required by this chapter, are final and conclusive. Orders publishing the proceedings of military commissions under this chapter are binding upon all departments, courts, agencies, and officers of the United States, except as otherwise provided by the President.

(b) PROVISIONS OF CHAPTER SOLE BASIS FOR REVIEW OF MILITARY COMMISSION PRO-CEDURES AND ACTIONS.—Except as otherwise provided in this chapter and notwithstanding any other provision of law (including section 2241 of title 28 or any other habeas corpus provision), no court, justice, or judge shall have jurisdiction to hear or consider any claim or cause of action whatsoever, including any action pending on or filed after the date of the enactment of the Military Commissions Act of 2006, relating to the prosecution, trial, or judgment of a military commission under this chapter, including challenges to the lawfulness of procedures of military commissions under this chapter.

SEC. 5. TREATY OBLIGATIONS NOT ESTABLISHING GROUNDS FOR CERTAIN CLAIMS.

(a) IN GENERAL.—No person may invoke the Geneva Conventions or any protocols thereto in any habeas corpus or other civil action or proceeding to which the United States, or a current or former officer, employee, member of the Armed Forces, or other agent of the United States is a party as a source of rights in any court of the United States or its States or territories.

SEC. 6. IMPLEMENTATION OF TREATY OBLIGATIONS.

. . .

(3) INTERPRETATION BY THE PRESIDENT.—
(A) As provided by the Constitution and by this section, the President has the authority for the United States to interpret the meaning and application of the Geneva Conventions and to promulgate higher standards and administrative regulations for violations of treaty obligations which are not grave breaches of the Geneva Conventions.
(B) The President shall issue interpretations described by subparagraph (A) by Executive Order published in the Federal Register.
(C) Any Executive Order published under this paragraph shall be authoritative (except as to grave breaches of common Article 3) as a matter of United States law, in the same manner as other administrative regulations.

SEC. 7. HABEAS CORPUS MATTERS.

(a) IN GENERAL.—Section 2241 of title 28, United States Code, is amended by striking both the subsection (e) added by section 1005(e)(1) of Public Law 109-148 (119 Stat. 2742) and the subsection (e) added by section 1405(e)(1) of Public Law 109-163 (119 Stat. 3477) and inserting the following new subsection (e):
(e)(1) No court, justice, or judge shall have jurisdiction to hear or consider an application for a writ of habeas corpus filed by or on behalf of an alien detained by

the United States who has been determined by the United States to have been properly detained as an enemy combatant or is awaiting such determination.

(2) Except as provided in paragraphs (2) and (3) of section 1005(e) of the Detainee Treatment Act of 2005 (10 U.S.C. 801 note), no court, justice, or judge shall have jurisdiction to hear or consider any other action against the United States or its agents relating to any aspect of the detention, transfer, treatment, trial, or conditions of confinement of an alien who is or was detained by the United States and has been determined by the United States to have been properly detained as an enemy combatant or is awaiting such determination.

(b) EFFECTIVE DATE.—The amendment made by subsection (a) shall take effect on the date of the enactment of this Act, and shall apply to all cases, without exception, pending on or after the date of the enactment of this Act which relate to any aspect of the detention, transfer, treatment, trial, or conditions of detention of an alien detained by the United States since September 11, 2001.

SEC. 8. REVISIONS TO DETAINEE TREATMENT ACT OF 2005 RELATING TO PROTECTION OF CERTAIN UNITED STATES GOVERNMENT PERSONNEL.

. . .

(b) PROTECTION OF PERSONNEL.—Section 1004 of the Detainee Treatment Act of 2005 (42 U.S.C. 2000dd-1) shall apply with respect to any criminal prosecution that—

(1) relates to the detention and interrogation of aliens described in such section;

(2) is grounded in section 2441(c)(3) of title 18, United States Code; and

(3) relates to actions occurring between September 11, 2001, and December 30, 2005.

Notes

1. Quoted by Nina Totenberg, Public Broadcasting System, *All Things Considered,* March 9, 2006.

2. "Enemy combatants" is the term used by President George W. Bush and his surrogates to describe *all* prisoners and alleged terrorists captured and detained since the United States and its allies began military operations in Afghanistan in October 2001 and in Iraq in March 2003. As will be noted later in the book, the term is legally meaningless. Domestic and international law define persons detained in war as either *lawful* or *unlawful* prisoners, or as innocent civilians. Lawful detainees are called prisoners of war (POWs) and have a bevy of legal rights while held captive. Unlawful ones—saboteurs, spies, or others who act in violation of international laws of war—are not protected by international law and can be tried by either a military or a civilian court for their actions or for conspiring to act. The MCA, signed in mid-October 2006, contains the most recent definition of "enemy combatant" in sections 948a (see appendix 6) and 948c. Also see Aziz Huq, "We Are All Enemy Combatants Now," *TomPaine. commonsense.* August 2, 2006, http://www.tompaine.com/articles/2006/08/02/were_all _enemy_combatants_now.php.

3. In the case of *Hamdan v. Rumsfeld,* 126 S. Ct. 2749 (2006), argued before the Court in March 2006, Salim Ahmed Hamdan petitioned for a writ of habeas corpus, challenging the lawfulness of Secretary of Defense Rumsfeld's plan to try him for alleged war crimes before a military commission convened under special orders issued by the president rather than before a court-martial convened under the Uniform Code of Military Justice (UCMJ). On June 29, 2006, in a 5–3 ruling the Supreme Court rejected Congress's attempts to strip the Court of jurisdiction over habeas corpus appeals by detainees at Guantánamo Bay, although Congress had previously passed the Detainee Treatment Act (DTA), which took effect on December 30, 2005.

The treaty between the United States and Cuba establishing the U.S. jurisdiction at Guantánamo Bay was signed on February 23, 1903. Under the provisions of the treaty, the United States was granted "complete jurisdiction and control in perpetuity." "Lease of Lands for Coaling and Naval Stations, U.S.-Cuba," February 23, 1903, *Treaty Ser.* no. 418 (6 Bevans 113).

4. Quoted in Dahlia Lithwick, "Because I Say So," *Slate,* March 28, 2006, www. slate.com/id/2138841. In the oral argument before the Supreme Court in *Hamdan v. Rumsfeld,* the solicitor general argued that the DTA takes away—*absolutely*—the jurisdiction of the federal judges and of the Supreme Court to hear Hamdan's case, as well as all other petitions for habeas review from other Guantánamo detainees. He said that it was not necessary for Congress to have "consciously thought it was suspending

the Writ." Perhaps the legislators just "stumble[d] upon a suspension of the Writ [which would also be fine]," he concluded (see chapter 5).

5. During the Korean War, President Harry S. Truman ordered Secretary of Commerce Charles Sawyer to seize the steel mills in order to continue manufacturing necessary war materials. The steel unions were preparing to strike for higher wages when the president issued the order. Truman argued that in a time of national emergency, the president can act contrary to congressional statutes and is immune from judicial checks on the use of his executive powers. In the steel seizure case (*Youngstown Sheet and Tube Co. v. Sawyer,* 343 U.S. 579 [1952]), the Supreme Court majority rejected this claim of near-absolute presidential power in time of national emergency or war. See Howard Ball and Phillip Cooper, *Of Power and Right* (New York: Oxford University Press, 1986).

6. At the time, 1787–1788, the citizens of the thirteen states were heatedly debating whether to accept the then-very-radical Constitution, with its representative, republican form of government.

7. The executive (the president), the legislative (the two houses of Congress), and the judicial (the U.S. Supreme Court and all inferior federal courts created by Congress) are the three branches of the federal government identified in the first three articles of the 1787 U.S. Constitution.

8. Federalist No. 47, in James Madison, Alexander Hamilton, and John Jay, *The Federalist Papers,* edited by Isaac Kramnick (New York: Penguin Books, 1987), 303.

9. Tony Judt, "New World Order," *New York Review of Books,* July 14, 2005, 18.

CHAPTER ONE. PRESIDENTIAL POWER VERSUS THE CONSTITUTION'S LIMITS ON POWER

1. George W. Bush, "Information Sharing, Patriot Act Vital to Homeland Security: Remarks by the President in a Conversation on the USA Patriot Act," April 20, 2004, www.whitehouse.gov/news/releases/2004/04/20040420-2.html.

2. Attributed to George W. Bush by unnamed sources quoted in Doug Thompson, "Bush on the Constitution: 'Just a Goddamned Piece of Paper,'" The Rant, *Capitol Hill Blue,* December 9, 2005, www.capitolhillblue.com/artman/publish/article_7779.shtml.

3. George W. Bush, Address to a Joint Session of Congress and the American People, September 20, 2001, http://www.whitehouse.gov/news/releases/2001/09/200109 20-8.html.

4. Comment of U.S. Attorney General Alberto Gonzales, talk to the American Bar Association's Committee on Law and National Security, February 24, 2004, p. 2, http://www.abanet.org/natsecurity/.

5. Quoted in "Q&A/Emerging Issues: Facing Terror after London," *New York Times,* July 10, 2005.

6. The definitive account of the Bush administration's plans for a war against Iraq is

found in Michael R. Gordon and General Bernard E. Trainor, *Cobra II: The Inside Story of the Invasion and Occupation of Iraq* (New York: Pantheon, 2006). See also documents published in 2005 in the British press, under the umbrella title "The Downing Street Memo," which revealed that President Bush, National Security Adviser Rice, Vice President Cheney, and Secretary of Defense Rumsfeld were prepared to go to war against Iraq after 9/11 and were pressing Prime Minister Tony Blair for British military support in the upcoming (March 2003) preemptive war against Iraq. The memo contains meeting minutes transcribed during the prime minister's meeting on July 23, 2002, with President Bush. It was first published by the London *Times* on May 1, 2005. See www.downingstreetmemo.com/. In June 2005 the *Los Angeles Times* published additional documents prepared for Prime Minister Blair by his top foreign policy aides. See John Daniszewski, "New Memos Detail Early Plans for Invading Iraq," *Los Angeles Times,* June 15, 2005, www.latimes.com/, and Ron Suskind, *The One Percent Doctrine: Deep Inside America's Pursuit of Its Enemies since 9/11* (New York: Simon and Schuster, 2006), 22–25.

7. Gonzales, talk to the American Bar Association's Committee on Law and National Security, 3.

8. See, for example, the latest Bush administration policy on the fair treatment of enemy combatants, the Military Commissions Act of 2006, passed by Congress at the end of September 2006 (see appendix 6).

9. Bob Herbert, "The Fear Factor," *New York Times,* April 17, 2006.

10. George W. Bush, "Humane Treatment of al Qaeda and Taliban Detainees," memorandum, February 7, 2002, text available on http://www.pegc.us/archive/White_House/bush_memo_20020207_ed.pdf.

11. The air war—the bombing of Afghanistan—began on October 7, 2001. On October 20, 2001, ground forces entered the fray against the Taliban.

12. Suskind, *The One Percent Doctrine,* 79.

13. Jonathan Alter, "Bush's Snoopgate," *Newsweek,* December 19, 2005.

14. Nancy Kassop, "The War Power and Its Limits," *Presidential Studies Quarterly,* no. 3 (September 2003): 509–10.

15. In addition to the president's and vice president's views on this issue, the Department of Justice's Office of Legal Counsel (OLC) and the Pentagon's "working group" developed the legal arguments to support these exceptional views of the powers of the president in the war on terrorism (see chapter 2).

16. Suskind, *The One Percent Doctrine,* 17.

17. "Congress Resolution on Use of Force," *BBC News, World Edition,* October 11, 2002, http://news.bbc.co.uk.

18. "Joint Resolution to Authorize the Use of United States Armed Forces against Iraq," October 2, 2002, text at http://www.whitehouse.gov/news/releases/2002/10/20021002-2.html.

19. Kassop, "The War Power and Its Limits," 513.

20. Suskind, *The One Percent Doctrine,* 157.

21. David Kopel, "Will the War Kill the Bill of Rights?" Cato Institute, October 22,

2001, www.cato.org/pub_display.php?pub_id=3864. The House Judiciary Committee, led by its chairman, F. James Sensenbrenner Jr. (R–WI)—who worked in a bipartisan manner with the Democrats on the committee—marked up the original bill, accepted and rejected amendments to the draft bill, and reported the revised bill out, 36–0. The White House lawyers and the U.S. attorney general wanted a much tougher bill and, at the very last moment, introduced the Bush administration's substitute bill. That was the bill that passed in Congress.

22. *Foreign Intelligence Surveillance Act of 1978,* Public Law 95-511, *U.S. Statutes at Large* 92: 1783, codified as amended at *U.S. Code* 50, secs. 1801–11, 1821–29, 1841–46, 1861–62.

23. See *U.S. Code* 50, sec. 401(a)(3), which defines "counterintelligence" as "information gathered, and activities conducted, to protect against espionage, other intelligence activities, sabotage, or assassinations conducted by or on behalf of foreign governments or elements thereof, foreign organizations, or foreign persons, or international terrorist activities." See http://www.vlex.us/codes/Sec-401a-Definitions/2300-1049,desc_18,docum_19266949).

24. See Howard Ball, *The USA Patriot Act* (Santa Barbara, CA: ABC-CLIO, 2004).

25. Ball, *The USA Patriot Act,* 50–53, passim.

26. Kopel, "Will the War Kill the Bill of Rights?"

27. Fred Barbash, "Justices Reject Appeal over Secret 9/11 Detainees," *Washington Post,* January 12, 2004.

28. David Lindorff and Barbara Olshansky, *The Case for Impeachment: The Legal Argument for Removing President George W. Bush from Office* (New York: St. Martin's Press, 2006), 117.

29. Quoted in ibid., 117ff.

30. Ball, *The USA Patriot Act,* 84–85. In the Passaic, New Jersey, detention center, almost 500 aliens were held from September 11, 2001, until May 30, 2002.

31. David Stout, "Justices Refuse to Review Case on Secrecy and 9/11 Detentions," *New York Times,* January 12, 2004.

32. Both opinions quoted in ibid.

33. Timothy Lynch, "Breaking the Vicious Cycle: Preserving Our Liberties While Fighting Terrorism," CATO Institute, *Policy Analysis* 443, June 26, 2002, 8.

34. Quoted in ibid., 8.

35. Richard Posner, *Llaguno v. Mingey,* 763 Fed. 2d 1560, 1568 (1985).

36. Kopel, "Will the War Kill the Bill of Rights?"

37. Lynch, "Breaking the Vicious Cycle," 12.

38. These military commissions were invalidated by the U.S. Supreme Court in 2006, in the case of *Hamdan v. Rumsfeld.* See chapter 5 for a full discussion of the decision.

39. Lynch, "Breaking the Vicious Cycle," 10.

40. James Risen, *State of War: The Secret History of the CIA and the Bush Administration* (New York: Free Press, 2006), 42.

41. John Dean, "George W. Bush as the New Richard Nixon: Both Wiretapped Ille-

gally, and Impeachably," December 30, 2005, http://writ.news.findlaw.com/dean/20051230.html.

42. Risen, *State of War*, 37, 43.

43. Alter, "Bush's Snoopgate."

44. Quoted in Dan Eggen, "Warrantless Wiretaps Possible in America," *Washington Post*, April 7, 2003.

45. Louis Fisher, letter to author, October 8, 2006.

46. Carol D. Leonnig and Dafna Linzer, "Spy Court Judge Quits in Protest," *Washington Post*, December 21, 2005.

47. Quoted in ibid. A "Potemkin court" is analogous to the classic Potemkin village, which appears elaborate and impressive but in fact lacks substance: "a pretentious, showy or imposing façade intended to mask or divert attention from an embarrassing or shabby fact or condition." *Random House Unabridged Dictionary* (New York: Random House, 1997).

48. Eggen, "Warrantless Wiretaps Possible in America." "Gonzales left open the possibility that President Bush could order warrantless wiretaps on telephone calls occurring solely in the United States—a move that would dramatically expand the reach of a controversial NSA surveillance program."

49. Quoted in ibid.

50. George W. Bush, quoted in Eric Lichtblau, "Gonzales Suggests Legal Basis for Domestic Eavesdropping," *New York Times*, April 6, 2006.

51. Quoted in Eggen, "Warrantless Wiretaps Possible in America."

52. Leslie Cauley, "NSA Has Massive Database of Americans' Phone Calls," *USA Today*, May 11, 2006. As it quickly turned out, the claim made by the paper was largely inaccurate.

53. Barton Gellman and Arshad Mohammed, "Data on Phone Calls Monitored," *Washington Post*, May 12, 2006.

54. Quoted in ibid.

55. The director of the NSA at the time was Air Force General Michael Hayden; he was sworn in as the new director of central intelligence on May 29, 2006.

56. George W. Bush, "Information Sharing, Patriot Act Vital to Homeland Security: Remarks by the President in a Conversation on the USA Patriot Act," April 20, 2004, www.whitehouse.gov/news/releases/2004/04/20040420-2.html.

57. Testimony of Justice Department official Matthew W. Friedrich, reprinted in Walter Pincus, "Silence Angers Judiciary Panel," *Washington Post*, June 7, 2006.

58. Quoted in ibid.

59. U.S. Committee on the Judiciary, statement of the Honorable Patrick Leahy, U.S. senator, Vermont, Ranking Member, Senate Judiciary Committee, hearing on "Examining Department of Justice's Investigation of Journalists Who Publish Classified Information: Lessons from the Jack Anderson Case," June 6, 2006, www.judiciary.senate.gov/member_statement.cfm?id=1928&wit_id=2629.

60. U.S. Senator Arlen Specter to Vice President Richard B. Cheney, June 7, 2006; text available at http://civilliberty.about.com/od/waronterror/a/spectercheney.htm.

61. Ibid.

62. "Specter Warns of 'Confrontation' over NSA Hearings," *CNN*, June 8, 2006, http://www.cnn.com/2006/POLITICS/06/07/nsa/.

63. Phillip W. Cooper, "George W. Bush, Edgar Allan Poe, and the Use and Abuse of Presidential Signing Statements," *Presidential Studies Quarterly* 35, no. 3 (September 2005): 4, text available at http://www.pegc.us/archive/Articles/cooper_35_PSQ_515.pdf.

64. See Charlie Savage, "Bush Challenges Hundreds of Laws," *Boston Globe*, April 30, 2006.

65. Charlie Savage, "Cheney Aide Is Screening Legislation: Adviser Seeks to Protect Bush Power," *Boston Globe*, May 28, 2006.

66. Dahlia Lithwick, "Sign Here," *Slate*, January 30, 2006, www.slate.com/id/2134919/.

67. Savage, "Cheney Aide Is Screening Legislation."

68. Cooper, "George W. Bush, Edgar Allan Poe," 5.

69. George W. Bush, signing statement attached to the *Department of Commerce, Justice, State, Judiciary, and Related Agencies Appropriations Act*, Public Law 107-77, *Weekly Compilation of Presidential Documents* 37 (week ending Friday, November 30, 2001): 1724.

70. Cooper, "George W. Bush, Edgar Allan Poe," 6.

71. George W. Bush, signing statement appended to the *Enhanced Border Security and Visa Entry Reform Act of 2002*, Public Law 107-173, *Weekly Compilation of Presidential Documents* 38 (week ending Friday, May 17, 2002): 822.

72. See Lithwick, "Sign Here."

73. Ibid.

74. Savage, "Cheney Aide Is Screening Legislation."

75. Quoted in Elisabeth Drew, "Power Grab," *New York Review of Books*, June 22, 2006, 12.

76. Editorial, "Veto? Who Needs a Veto?" *New York Times*, May 5, 2006.

77. Kassop, "The War Power and Its Limits," 512.

78. Adam Liptak, "In Terror Cases, Administration Sets Its Own Rules," *New York Times*, November 27, 2005.

79. Ibid.

80. Quoted in ibid.

81. Ibid.

82. Quoted in ibid.

83. See Scott Shane, "Invoking Secrets Privilege Becomes a More Popular Legal Tactic by the U.S.," *New York Times*, June 4, 2006.

84. *United States v. Reynolds*, Vinson, majority opinion, at 6–8, text available at http://supreme.justia.com/us/345/1/case.html.

85. Dana Priest, "Secrecy Privilege Invoked in Fighting Ex-Detainee's Lawsuit," *Washington Post*, May 13, 2006.

86. Sher and Goss both quoted in ibid.

87. Quoted in ibid.

88. *Khalid El-Masri v. George Tenet et al.,* U.S. District Court, Eastern District, Virginia, May 18, 2006, http://www.fas.org/sgp/jud/statesec/elmasri051206.pdf.

89. Priest, "Secrecy Privilege."

90. Quoted in Shane, "Invoking Secrets Privilege."

91. Erwin Chemerinsky, "Enemy Combatants and Separation of Powers," *Journal of National Security Law and Policy* 1 (Fall 2005): 73.

92. Clinton Rossiter, *Constitutional Dictatorship: Crisis Government in the Modern Democracies* (New Brunswick, NJ: Transaction Press, 2002). This is a new edition of a book originally published in 1948, after World War II ended. Rossiter's premise then and now has been a fundamental axiom for some chief executives: The "inescapable truth" is that "no form of government can survive that excludes dictatorship when the life of the nation is at stake." However, Rossiter cannot avoid the Civil War's reality. In that bloody war, where more than 600,000 Americans died, Lincoln repeatedly acknowledged that both Congress and the executive have an equal share in the waging of war—without resorting to dictatorship.

93. Peter Hoekstra to President George W. Bush, May 18, 2006, 4; letter first reported in Eric Lichtblau and Scott Shane, "Ally Warned Bush on Keeping Spying from Congress," *New York Times,* July 9, 2006; text available at http://www.fas.org/irp/congress/2006_cr/hoekstra051806.html.

94. Associate Justice Stephen G. Breyer, *Liberty, Security, and the Courts,* speech given to the Association of the Bar of the City of New York, April 14, 2003, 2, http://www.supremecourtus.gov/publicinfo/speeches/sp_04-15-03.html.

95. Jack M. Balkin, "Who's Afraid of Presidential Signing Statements?" *Balkinization,* January 17, 2006, at http://balkin.blogspot.com/2006/01/whos-afraid-of-presidential-signing.html.

96. Editorial, "A Pattern of Excess," *Washington Post,* May 14, 2006.

97. Grover Norquist, quoted in Drew, "Power Grab," 10.

98. Thomas E. Ricks, *Fiasco: The American Military Adventure in Iraq* (New York: Penguin Press, 2006), 4.

99. Suskind, *The One Percent Doctrine,* 163, 62.

CHAPTER TWO. CAPTURING THE ENEMY

1. Abdur Sayed Rahman was arrested in his village in Pakistan in January 2002 and brought to Afghanistan. Accused of being the Taliban's deputy foreign minister (whose name is Abdur *Zahid* Rahman), he was flown to Guantánamo Bay, where he has since remained in the American military prison, one of countless innocent persons detained by U.S. military authorities in Cuba, Afghanistan, and Iraq. See Editorial, "They Came for the Chicken Farmer," *New York Times,* March 8, 2006.

2. Quoted in Tim Golden, "Administration Officials Split over Stalled Military Tribunals," *New York Times,* October 25, 2004.

3. The Northern Alliance is "an *ad hoc* confederation of anti-Taliban militia and

warlords with whom the United States had formed a loose and strictly expedient partnership in the war in Afghanistan." Erik Saar and Viveca Novak, *Inside the Wire: A Military Intelligence Soldier's Eyewitness Account of Life at Guantanamo* (New York: Penguin Press, 2005), 81–82.

4. See the detailed discussion in chapter 5 of *Hamdan v. Rumsfeld*. In early March 2002, as a critically important action in his run-up to the war with Iraq, the president announced the creation of a radically new national security policy for the nation in the war on terror: preemptive war. In the published policy's part 5, entitled "Prevent Our Enemies from Threatening Us, Our Allies, and Our Friends with Weapons of Mass Destruction," http://www.whitehouse.gov/nsc/nss/2006/sectionV.html, President Bush outlined the new national security–preemptive/preventive war strategy: "It is an enduring American principle that [this duty to protect the American people and American interests] obligates the government to anticipate and counter threats, using all elements of national power, before the threats can do grave damage. The greater the threat, the greater is the risk of inaction—and the more compelling the case for taking *anticipatory action* to defend ourselves, even if uncertainty remains as to the time and place of the enemy's attack. There are few greater threats than a terrorist attack with WMD. To forestall or prevent such hostile acts by our adversaries, *the United States will, if necessary act preemptively in exercising our inherent right of self-defense*" (my emphasis).

5. Kenneth Roth, "The Law of War in the War on Terror," *Foreign Affairs*, January–February 2004, http://www.foreignaffairs.org/20040101facomment83101/kenneth-roth/the-law-of-war-in-the-war-on-terror.html.

6. Saar and Novak, *Inside the Wire*, 82, 110. See also Elisabeth Drew, "Power Grab," *New York Review of Books*, June 22, 2006, 12.

7. See generally Louis Fisher, *Nazi Saboteurs on Trial: A Military Tribunal and American Law* (Lawrence: University Press of Kansas, 2003), 3–16, passim.

8. *Ex Parte Quirin*, 317 U.S. 1 (1942), at 22, text available at http://supreme.justia.com/us/317/1/case.html. See Fisher, *Nazi Saboteurs on Trial*, 43–48, passim, for the reasons the military commission was created. See also Jennifer K. Elsea, "Detention of American Citizens as Enemy Combatants," Congressional Research Service, Library of Congress, report for Congress (Washington, DC: Government Printing Office, March 15, 2004), 8–15, passim. The Articles of War were written and passed by Congress. They were superseded by the Uniform Code of Military Justice (UCMJ—legislation contained in Title 10 of the U.S. Code, Sections 801 through 946), passed by Congress in 1950, taking effect in 1951, and still applicable generations later.

9. Fisher, *Nazi Saboteurs on Trial*, 51.

10. Franklin D. Roosevelt, Proclamation no. 2561, July 2, 1942, *Federal Register* 7: 5101, *Stat*. 56 (1964).

11. *Ex Parte Quirin*, at 24.

12. *Ex Parte Milligan*, 71 U.S. 2 (1866), at 121, text available at http://supreme.justia.com/us/71/2/case.html.

13. *CATO Handbook for Congress: Policy Recommendations for the 108th Congress, "Military Tribunals"* (Washington, DC: CATO Institute, 2005), 127–28.

14. *Ex Parte Milligan,* at 123.

15. See Fisher, *Nazi Saboteurs on Trial,* 49. "Not enough," said President Roosevelt to his attorney general about the punishment the eight might receive in a criminal trial in federal district court.

16. *Ex Parte Quirin,* at 17.

17. See Howard Ball, *Prosecuting War Crimes and Genocide: The Twentieth-Century Experience* (Lawrence: University Press of Kansas, 1999).

18. *Ex Parte Quirin,* at 31.

19. Ibid.

20. In March 2006 the Department of Defense, because of a Freedom of Information Act filing, was forced to release the names and countries of origin of the more than 500 detainees held at Guantánamo Bay Naval Station. The countries the detainees identified as their homes are Afghanistan, Algeria, Australia, Bahrain, Belgium, Canada, China, Denmark, Egypt, Ethiopia, France, Iraq, Iran, Jordan, Kuwait, Libya, Maldives, Mauritania, Morocco, Pakistan, Russia, Saudi Arabia, Spain, Sudan, Sweden, Syria, Tajikistan, Tunisia, Turkey, Uganda, United Kingdom, and Yemen; some detainees answered "unknown." Document published in the *Washington Post,* March 5, 2006, www.washingtonpost.com/. See also Ben Fox, "Pentagon Releases Extensive Gitmo List," http://abcnews.go.com/International/wireStory?id=1863202.

21. The four Geneva Conventions of August 12, 1949, are "I. The Amelioration of the Condition of the Wounded and Sick in Armed Forces in the Field"; "II. The Amelioration of the Condition of the Wounded and Sick and Shipwrecked Members of the Armed Forces at Sea"; "III. Relative to the Treatment of Prisoners of War"; "IV. For the Protection of Civilian Persons in Time of War." The protocols added to the 1949 Geneva Conventions, June 8, 1977, are "Protocol I, Applicable in International Armed Conflicts (including National Liberation Wars)"; "Protocol II, Applicable to Non-International Armed Conflicts."

22. Article 1, Section 6, subpart (a) of U.S. Army Regulation 190-8 states, "In accordance with Article 5, [3rd Geneva Convention], if any doubt arises as to whether a person . . . belongs to any of the categories enumerated in Article 4, [3rd Geneva Convention], such persons shall enjoy the protection of the present Convention until such time as their status has been determined by a competent tribunal." See U.S. Army Regulation 190-8, revised 1997, at http://www.nimj.com/documents/POW_AR_190-8.pdf.

23. Kate Martin and Joseph Onek, "'Enemy Combatants': The Constitution and the Administration's 'War on Terror,'" American Constitution Society White Paper, August 2004, http://www.acslaw.org/pdf/enemycombatants.pdf, 13.

24. Frederic L. Borch, *Judge Advocates in Combat* (Washington, DC: Office of the JAG, 2001), 21. See also Howard S. Levie, *Prisoners of War* (Washington, DC: Naval War College Press, 1978), 57ff.

25. Anthony Lewis, "Introduction," in *The Torture Papers: The Road to Abu Ghraib,* ed. Karen J. Greenberg and Joshua L. Dratel (New York: Cambridge University Press, 2005), xiv.

26. *Conduct of the Persian Gulf War: Final Report to the Congress Pursuant to Title V of the Persian Gulf Conflict Supplemental Authorization and Personnel Benefits Act of 1991* (Washington, DC: Department of Defense, April 1992), appendix L, at 577.

27. Martin and Onek, "'Enemy Combatants,'" 13. However, see *Rasul, Shafiq, et al. v. Bush, President of the United States, et al.* (Case 03-334 [June 28, 2004]; see chapter 4) and the military actions that immediately followed this June 28 U.S. Supreme Court ruling on the question of Article 5 status hearings for foreigners detained by the U.S. military. On July 7, 2004, a few weeks after *Rasul* was announced, the Department of Defense issued an "Order Establishing Combatant Status Review Tribunals," www.defenselink.mil/news/Jul2004/d20040707review.pdf, followed, on July 29, 2004, by "Implementation of Combatant Status Review Tribunal Procedures for Enemy Combatants Detained at Guantanamo Bay Naval Base, Cuba," http://www.defenselink.mil/news/Jul2004/d20040730comb.pdf.

28. Human Rights Watch, "A Policy to Evade International Law," in *The Road to Abu Ghraib,* June 2004, 1, http://hrw.org/reports/2004/usa0604/2.htm.

29. Josh White and Julie Tate, "In Guantanamo Bay Documents, Prisoners Plead for Release," *Washington Post,* March 5, 2006.

30. Human Rights Watch, "A Policy to Evade International Law," 1.

31. Quoted in *In Re Guantanamo Bay Cases, Memorandum Opinion Denying in Part and Granting in Part Respondents' Motion to Dismiss or for Judgment as a Matter of Law,* January 31, 2005, Judge Joyce H. Green, found at http://www.globalsecurity.org/security/library/policy/national/02-299b_31jan2005.pdf, 10. See Judge Green's disagreement with the position of the Bush administration in the matter of the CSRTs in light of the requirement of the Fifth Amendment's due process clause, 38ff. See also Elsea, "Detention of American Citizens as Enemy Combatants," 47.

32. Louis Fisher, *Military Tribunals and Presidential Power: American Revolution to the War on Terror* (Lawrence: University Press of Kansas, 2005), 221.

33. Ibid., 220–21.

34. Congress passed this legislation in 1994 prohibiting torture to fulfill U.S. obligations under the UN *Convention against Torture and Other Cruel, Inhuman, or Degrading Treatment or Punishment,* adopted December 10, 1984.

35. Memorandum for Alberto R. Gonzales, Counsel to the President, from James Bybee, Deputy Attorney General, DOJ, OLC, August 1, 2002, "Re: Standards of Conduct for Interrogation under 18 U.S.C. Sections 2340–2340A," in Greenberg and Dratel, *The Torture Papers,* 200, 203, 204, 206, 207, 213.

36. As of summer 2006, there were at least six separate camps located at Guantánamo Bay Naval Station, Cuba, housing, at their peak, over 750 "enemy combatants." The original Camp Delta had six detention units, levels 1–6. Level 1 was "for the best Gitmo citizens"; Level 2 "was for moderately cooperative detainees"; Level 3 was used for the new arrivals "or [those] who were not cooperating with their interrogators." In

April 2003, a fourth detention unit was set up; it was a medium-security facility, "Camp Delta's version of a college dorm." A fifth unit housed juvenile detainees, and a sixth for detainees was built in 2006. There is also Camp Echo, a permanent 612-unit detention center. Another camp, named Iguana, holds detainees who have not been repatriated to their home countries. Camp X-Ray was the original detention facility. It opened in January 2002 and closed in April 2002, when its detainees were transferred to Camp Delta. See Saar and Novak, *Inside the Wire*, 65, 209. For a critique of Bush administration policies for dealing with the Guantánamo detainees, see Corine Hegland, "Guantanamo's Grip," *National Journal*, February 3, 2006, www.nationaljournal.com/.

37. Memorandum for William J. Haynes, II, DOD, from John Yoo and Robert J. Delahunty, DOJ, January 9, 2002, "Application of Treaties and Laws to al Qaeda and Taliban Detainees," in Greenberg and Dratel, *The Torture Papers*, 38–79.

38. Lewis, "Introduction," xiv.

39. Memorandum for Haynes, from Yoo and Delahunty, "Application of Treaties and Laws to al Qaeda and Taliban Detainees," 48, 50.

40. Ibid., 79.

41. Memorandum for the President, from Alberto Gonzales, Counsel to the President, "Subject: Decision Re: Application of the Geneva Convention on Prisoners of War to the Conflict with al Qaeda and the Taliban," January 25, 2002, in Greenberg and Dratel, *The Torture Papers*, 119.

42. Memorandum, to Counsel to the President, Alberto Gonzales, from Colin L. Powell, "Subject: Draft Decision Memorandum for the President on the Applicability of the Geneva Convention to the Conflict in Afghanistan," January 29, 2002, in Greenberg and Dratel, *The Torture Papers*, 122–25.

43. George W. Bush, "Humane Treatment of al Qaeda and Taliban Detainees," memorandum, February 7, 2002, text available on http://www.pegc.us/archive/White_House/bush_memo_20020207_ed.pdf.

44. Saar and Novak, *Inside the Wire*, 161.

45. Fisher, *Military Tribunals and Presidential Power*.

46. Richard Willing, "Legal Battles of WWII Underpin Bush Strategy," *USA Today*, March 28, 2004.

47. Executive Orders, Military Order of November 13, 2001. 66 *Federal Register*, Number 2, November 16, 2001, "Detention, Treatment, and Trial of Certain Non-Citizens in the War against Terrorism," in Greenberg and Dratel, *The Torture Papers*, 25–28.

48. Ibid., 27.

49. Quotations from the Department of Defense report in Fisher, *Military Tribunals and Presidential Power*, 180–81.

50. Jane Mayer, "The Hidden Power," *New Yorker*, July 3, 2006, 52.

51. Saar and Novak, *Inside the Wire*, 242.

52. Reuters, "Guantanamo Inmates Can Be Held in Perpetuity," June 15, 2006, http://www.truthout.org/cgi-bin/artman/exec/view.cgi/37/11905.

53. One soldier stationed at Guantánamo Bay said of the interrogations, "Between

you and me, the camp is a disaster. Every pissant agency [FBI, DIA, CIA] under the sun has sent someone here to interview the detainees, and they all fight about who gets to talk to the guy first. Then they realize he doesn't know shit." Quoted in Saar and Novak, *Inside the Wire*, 34.

54. Ironically, these enemy belligerents have, with few exceptions, been detained without charges filed against them, for the United States has put forward no evidence of criminal wrongdoing by them.

CHAPTER THREE. TREATMENT OF THE ENEMY

1. James R. Schlesinger, chairman, *Final Report of the Independent Panel to Review DoD Detention Operations* (Arlington, VA: Independent Panel to Review DoD Detention Operations, August 2004) (hereafter referred to as the Schlesinger Report), appendix H, 1.

2. Dick Cheney, September 16, 2001, on *Meet the Press*, quoted in Evan Thomas and Michael Hirsh, "The Debate over Torture," *Newsweek*, November 21, 2005, www. msnbc.msn.com/id/10020629/site/newsweek/.

3. Quoted in Ron Suskind, *The One Percent Doctrine: Deep Inside America's Pursuit of Its Enemies since 9/11* (New York: Simon and Schuster, 2006), 152.

4. Quoted in Seymour M. Hersh, *Chain of Command: The Road from 9/11 to Abu Ghraib* (New York: HarperCollins, 2004), 17. The doctrine of military necessity was defined in the *Instructions for the Government of the Armies of the United States in the Field* (the *Lieber Code of 1863*), April 24, 1863, published as *Army General Orders 100*. Article 14 states that "military necessity, as understood by modern civilized nations, consists in the necessity of those measures which are indispensable for securing the ends of the war, and which are lawful according to the modern law and usages of war." The doctrine "admits of all direct destruction of life or limb of armed enemies, and of other persons whose destruction is incidentally unavoidable" (Article 15), but "military necessity does not admit of cruelty—that is, the infliction of suffering for the sake of suffering or for revenge, nor of maiming or wounding except in fight, nor of torture to extort confessions. It does not admit of the use of poison in any way, nor of the wanton devastation of a district. It admits of deception, but disclaims acts of perfidy; and, in general, military necessity does not include any act of hostility which makes the return to peace unnecessarily difficult" (Article 16). *Lieber Code of 1863*, http://www.civilwarhome.com/liebercode.htm.

5. George W. Bush, 2003 State of the Union address, January 28, 2003, www.white house.gov/news/releases/2003/01/20030128-19.html. From 2002 through June 2005, more than three dozen of these detainees have been killed while being interrogated in the custody of third-party nations. See Tony Judt, "New World Order," *New York Review of Books*, July 14, 2005, 17.

6. See Sidney Blumenthal, "'Abuse'? How About Torture," *Salon.Com*, May 6, 2004, www.salon.com/.

7. Bybee now sits as a federal appeals court judge on the U.S. Court of Appeals for the Ninth Circuit. See Adam Liptak's essay about Bybee, "Author of '02 Memo on Torture: A Gentle Soul for a Harsh Topic," *New York Times,* June 24, 2004.

8. See Memorandum for Alberto R. Gonzales, Counsel to the President, from James Bybee, Deputy Attorney General, DOJ, OLC, August 1, 2002, "Re: Standards of Conduct for Interrogation under 18 U.S.C. Sections 2340–2340A," in Greenberg and Dratel, *The Torture Papers.*

9. Memo, quoted in Hersh, *Chain of Command,* 5. In addition, Bybee noted that Congress did not have the constitutional authority to prohibit the use of torture in order to acquire information from the prisoners.

10. Michael C. Dorf, "The Justice Department's Change of Heart Regarding Torture," *Findlaw Legal News and Commentary,* January 5, 2005, http://writ.news.findlaw.com/dorf/20050105.html.

11. Memo, quoted in Hersh, *Chain of Command,* 5.

12. Michael Byers, *War Law: Understanding International Law and Armed Conflict* (New York: Grove Press, 2005), 133. See appendix 4 for the 1984 Convention against Torture and Other Cruel, Inhuman, or Degrading Treatment or Punishment.

13. Dorf, "The Justice Department's Change of Heart."

14. Martin and Onek, "Enemy Combatants," 13.

15. Tim Golden, "Administration Officials Split over Stalled Military Tribunals," *New York Times,* October 25, 2004.

16. Diane Marie Amann, "Military and Civilian Justice in the United States and the Post–September 11 Military Commissions," in *The Changing Faces of Military Justice and Special Tribunals as They Confront International Law,* a Sixteen-Country Research Project of the Unité Mixte de Recherche de droit comparé, May 30, 2006, 1–2; English final version, submitted August 28, 2006, available at http://testsite.law.ucdavis.edu/faculty/files/Amann_us_fnlreport_engclear_28aug2006_amann.pdf.

17. See UCMJ, subchapter 10, "Punitive Articles," sec. 877.77 to sec. 934.00.

18. *FM 34-52, Intelligence Interrogation* (Washington, DC: Department of the Army, May 8, 1987), found at www.globalsecurity.org/.

19. Ibid., chap. 1, sec. 1, p. 1, found at http://www.globalsecurity.org/intell/library/policy/army/fm/fm34-52/chapter1.htm.

20. Ibid., sec. 3, p. 3.

21. Cited in Stephen Budiansky, "Truth Extraction," *Atlantic Monthly,* June 2005, 32.

22. Ibid., 32.

23. Sherwood F. Moran, quoted in ibid., 32.

24. "In late 2002 the military's Southern Command [Tampa, Florida] had so few interrogators and interpreters that it was forced to employ inexperienced and untrained civilian contractors to perform these jobs at Guantanamo." Ibid., 35.

25. Thomas and Hirsh, "The Debate over Torture," 1. Senator Richard Durbin (D–IL) used the word "gulag," made famous by the Russian writer Aleksandr Solzhenitsyn, much to the chagrin of the president and Secretary of Defense Rumsfeld. Robert Weiner and Emma Dick, "Closing a Prison Won't Put an End to the Torture," *Cleve-*

land Plain Dealer, August 1, 2005, reprinted at www.truthout.org/docs_2005/080105Q. shtml#1.

26. Ibid., 3.

27. Schlesinger Report, 29, 65.

28. Douglas Jehl and Eric Schmitt, "U.S. Military Says 26 Inmate Deaths May Be Homicide," *New York Times,* March 16, 2005.

29. Anthony Lagouranis, "Tortured Logic," *New York Times,* Op-Ed, February 28, 2006.

30. Ibid.

31. See Eric Schmitt, "Army Dog Handler Is Convicted in Detainee Abuse at Abu Ghraib," *New York Times,* March 22, 2006.

32. Schlesinger Report, 68.

33. Douglas Jehl, "U.S. Action Bars Right of Some Captured in Iraq," *New York Times,* October 26, 2004.

34. See Jane Mayer, "The Memo," *New Yorker,* March 6, 2006, www.newyorker.com/ archive/2006/02/27/060227fa_fact. Among those who believed U.S. practices constituted torture were European leaders, the UN High Commissioner for Human Rights, the International Committee of the Red Cross, Amnesty International, and Human Rights Watch—as well as "the Pentagon's own lawyers." See Byers, *War Law,* 129.

35. Ian Wallach, "No Habeas at Guantanamo? The Executive and the Dubious Tale of the DTA," Forum, *Jurist: Legal News and Research,* April 4, 2006, 5–6, http://jurist. law.pitt.edu/forumy/2006/03/no-habeas-at-guantanamo-executive-and.php. The Seton Hall study's research findings were published in 2005 by Mark Denbeaux, Joshua Denbeaux, David Gratz, John Gregorek, Matthew Darby, Shana Edwards, Shane Hartman, Daniel Mann, Megan Sassaman, and Helen Skinner, *Report on Guantanamo Detainees: A Profile of 517 Detainees through Analysis of Department of Defense Data* (South Orange, NJ: Seton Hall University School of Law, April 2005). For a very substantive and less criticized examination of the Guantánamo detainees, see Corine Hegland, "Guantanamo's Grip," *National Journal,* February 3, 2006, www.national journal.com/.

36. Emily Bazelon, "What Is Torture?" *Slate,* June 18, 2006, http://www.slate.com/ id/2143287/.

37. Memo for Secretary of Defense Donald Rumsfeld, from General Counsel, DOD, William J. Haynes, II, November 27, 2002, "Counter-Resistance Techniques," in Greenberg and Dratel, *The Torture Papers,* 237–39.

38. See Alberto Mora, "Memorandum for Inspector General, Department of the Navy, Subject: Statement for the Record. Office of General Counsel Involvement in Interrogation Issues," July 7, 2004, 1, posted at www.newyorker.com/ as "The Mora Memo." Mora was general counsel for the Navy until his recent retirement.

39. See Jane Mayer, "The Memo: How an Internal Effort to Ban the Abuse and Torture of Detainees Was Thwarted," *New Yorker,* March 6, 2006, www.newyorker. com/printables/fact/060227fa_fact.

40. See Mora, "Memorandum for Inspector General, Department of the Navy," July 7, 2004, n45.

41. Ibid., 3, 4, 6, 7, 8, 9, 10–11, 13, 15, 16–17, 18, 19, 20.

42. From Marty Lederman, "The JAG Memos on Military Interrogations and OLC's Legal Analysis," document at www.balkin.blogspot.com/2005/07/jag-memos-on-military-interrogation.html.

43. "Relating to Interrogation of Detainees Held by the U.S. Armed Forces in the War on Terrorism," from ibid.

44. Mayer, "The Memo."

45. See Hegland, "Guantanamo's Grip," for additional stories about the treatment of the detainees by the American military.

46. Kate Zernike, "Newly Released Reports Show Early Concern on Prison Abuse," *New York Times,* January 6, 2005.

47. Schlesinger Report, 82.

48. Zernike, "Newly Released Reports."

49. Andrew Romano, "How Terror Led America to Torture," *Newsweek,* November 21, 2005, www.msnbc.msn.com/id/10020664/site/newsweek/.

50. Tim Golden, "In U.S. Report, Brutal Details of 2 Afghan Inmates' Deaths," *New York Times,* May 20, 2005.

51. Report quoted in ibid. The coroner, Lt. Col. Elizabeth Rouse, told ACIC investigators, "I've seen similar injuries in an individual run over by a bus."

52. Quoted in Zernike, "Newly Released Reports."

53. Quoted in ibid. See also Neil A. Lewis and David Johnston, "New FBI Files Describe Abuse of Iraq Inmates," *New York Times,* December 21, 2004, and Dan Eggen and R. Jeffrey Smith, "FBI Agents Allege Abuse of Detainees at Guantanamo Bay," *Washington Post,* December 21, 2004.

54. *Report of the International Committee of the Red Cross (ICRC) on the Treatment by Coalition Forces of Prisoners of War and Other Protected Persons by the Geneva Conventions in Iraq during Arrest, Internment, and Interrogation,* February 2004, 23, www.newyorktimes.com/. Coalition Forces were the United States, Great Britain, and other allies participating in Operation Iraqi Freedom.

55. See Neil A. Lewis, "Red Cross Finds Detainee Abuse at Guantanamo," *New York Times,* November 30, 2004.

56. Adam Zagorin, "The Abu Ghraib [Medical Care] Scandal You Don't Know," *Time,* February 14, 2005, 36–38. See also Steven H. Miles, "All Too Quiet: Where Were the Doctors and Nurses at Abu Ghraib and Bagram?" *Slate,* June 27, 2006, www.slate.com/id/2144590/.

57. "I took off an ankle and a lower leg. There was no one else, and if it was death or amputation, you just had to do it," said a National Guard physician's assistant, Capt. Kelly Parrson. Quoted in Zagorin, "The Abu Ghraib [Medical Care] Scandal," 37.

58. Mourad Benchellali, "Detainees in Despair," *New York Times,* Op-Ed, June 14, 2006.

59. Josh White, "Writing by Suicidal Detainee Reveals Depths of His Despair," *Washington Post,* March 15, 2006.

60. Erik Saar and Viveca Novak, *Inside the Wire: A Military Intelligence Soldier's Eyewitness Account of Life at Guantanamo* (New York: Penguin Press, 2005), 67.

61. Editorial, "Rebellion against Abuse," *Washington Post,* November 3, 2005.

62. Josh White, "Former Abu Ghraib Guard Calls Top Brass Culpable for Abuse," *Washington Post,* January 23, 2006.

63. Quoted in ibid.

64. See the comprehensive, critical, and very detailed 2005 report by Amnesty International, "Below the Radar: Secret Flights to Torture and 'Disappearance,'" http://web.amnesty.org/library/Index/ENGAMR510512006.

65. See, for example, a recent comprehensive report about these CIA actions: Committee on Legal Affairs and Human Rights of the Parliamentary Assembly of the Council of Europe, "Alleged Secret Detentions and Unlawful Inter-State Transfers Involving Council of Europe Member States," June 7, 2006, rapporteur, Dick Marty, Switzerland, draft report available at http://assembly.coe.int/CommitteeDocs/2006/20060606_Ejdoc162006PartII-FINAL.pdf. See also Dana Priest, "CIA Holds Terror Suspects in Secret Prisons," *Washington Post,* November 2, 2005.

66. James Risen, *State of War: The Secret History of the CIA and the Bush Administration* (New York: Free Press, 2006), 28.

67. Schlesinger Report, 70.

68. Risen, *State of War,* 30–31.

69. Ibid., 29–30.

70. Dana Priest, "A Plan for Indefinite Imprisonment," *Washington Post National Weekly Edition,* January 10–16, 2005, 29.

71. Michael Hirsh, Mark Hosenball, and John Barry, "Aboard Air CIA," *Newsweek,* February 28, 2005, 32–33.

72. Quoted in Editorial, "Director for Torture," *Washington Post,* November 23, 2005.

73. Risen, *State of War,* 32.

74. Quoted in Editorial, "Director for Torture."

75. Hersh, *Chain of Command,* 46. See generally, Jane Mayer, "Outsourcing Torture: The Secret History of America's 'Extraordinary Rendition' Program," *New Yorker,* February 14, 2005.

76. Judt, "New World Order," 17. See also Risen, *State of War,* 33ff.

77. See Amnesty International, "Below the Radar."

78. Hersh, *Chain of Command,* 55.

79. Judt, "New World Order," 17.

80. See, for example, David Johnston and Neil A. Lewis, "Officials Describe Secret CIA Center at Guantanamo Bay," *New York Times,* December 18, 2004.

81. Associated Press, "Report: CIA Has Secret al Qaeda Prison," *Jackson (MS) Clarion-Ledger,* November 2, 2005.

82. Quoted in Dan Bilefsky, "European Inquiry Says C.I.A. Flew 1,000 Flights in Secret," *New York Times*, April 27, 2006.

83. Stephen Grey and Elisabetta Povoledo, "Italy Arrests Two in Kidnapping of Imam in '03," *New York Times*, July 6, 2006. One of the men arrested, Marco Mancini, is the current head of military counterespionage in Italy.

84. Associated Press, "Cleric Seized in Italy Says He Was Tortured," *Arizona Daily Star*, February 23, 2007.

85. See Bob Herbert, "Our Dirty War," *New York Times*, April 20, 2006. Herbert quotes Curt Goering, senior deputy executive director of Amnesty International USA, as saying that rendition "is a kind of netherworld that people disappear into and don't frequently emerge from. It's a world that's outside the reach of law. These individuals might as well be on another planet."

86. Quoted in AP, "No Trial Date for Gitmo Detainees," *CBS News*, September 11, 2003, http://www.cbsnews.com/stories/2003/09/11/attack/main572608.shtml.

87. Byers, *War Law*, 132. See also Hersh, *Chain of Command*.

88. Seymour M. Hersh, "Torture at Abu Ghraib: American Soldiers Brutalized Iraqis. How Far Up Does the Responsibility Go?" *New Yorker*, May 10, 2004; also available at http://www.newyorker.com/archive/2004/05/10/040510fa_fact.

89. Ibid.

90. See Byers, *War Law*. In a 2005 report for the United Nations, Amnesty International listed no fewer than sixty "incarceration and interrogation practices routinely employed at U.S. detention centers, Guantanamo in particular. These include immersion in cold water to simulate drowning, forced shaving of facial and body hair, being urinated upon, sexual taunting, the mocking of religious belief, suspension from shackles, physical exertion to the point of exhaustion (e.g., rock-carrying), and mock execution." Quoted in Judt, "New World Order," 17.

91. See Emily Bazelon, "What Army and Pentagon Investigators Found," in Bazelon, "What Is Torture?" 21–26, quotation at 21–22.

92. George W. Bush, statement on UN International Day in Support of Victims of Torture, *Weekly Compilations of Presidential Documents* 40 (July 5, 2004): 1167–68.

93. At no time did the Bush administration actually "disown" the torture policy, but it had become "too embarrassing." For many, "the spirit [of the 2002 Bybee torture memo is] very much intact." Louis Fisher, letter to author, October 8, 2006.

94. Department of Justice Office of Legal Council, "Legal Standards Applicable under 18 U.S.C. §§ 2340–2340A," December 30, 2004, Memorandum Opinion for the Deputy Attorney General, www.usdoj.gov/olc/18usc23402340a2.htm.

95. Tim Golden and Eric Schmitt, "Detainee Policy Sharply Divides Bush Officials," *New York Times*, November 2, 2005.

96. See Josh White, "Military Lawyers Say Tactics Broke Rules," *Washington Post*, March 16, 2006.

97. Julian Barnes, "Army Manual to Skip Geneva Detainee Rule," *Los Angeles Times*, June 4, 2006.

98. Quoted in ibid.

99. Golden and Schmitt, "Detainee Policy."

100. Unnamed DOD official, quoted in ibid.

101. Ibid.

102. Barnes, "Army Manual."

103. Mark Mazzetti and Kate Zernike, "White House Says Terror Detainees Hold Basic Rights," *New York Times,* July 12, 2006.

104. Ibid. See also Demetri Sevastopulo, "Pentagon to Give Rights to Detainees," *Financial Times,* July 11, 2006, 1, www.ft.com/cms/s/e1de1572-1089-11db-8eec-0000779e 2340,_i_rssPage=6700d4e4-6714-11da-a650-0000779e2340.html.

105. Quoted in T. M. Golden, "U.S. Says It Fears Detainee Abuse in Repatriation," *New York Times,* April 30, 2006.

106. Ibid.

107. On April 19, 2006, under a successful Freedom of Information Act lawsuit, a federal judge ordered the Department of Defense to release the list of enemy detainees.

108. Paul Garwood, "Guantanamo List Stirs Anger," *Burlington (VT) Free Press,* April 21, 2006.

109. Quoted in Golden, "U.S. Says It Fears Detainee Abuse in Repatriation."

110. See Associated Press, "Annan: U.S. Should Shut Guantanamo Prison," February 16, 2006, www.msnbc.msn.com/id/11381321/.

111. Quoted in ibid. The five investigators were representatives of Argentina, Austria, New Zealand, Algeria, and Pakistan.

CHAPTER FOUR. BUSH VERSUS THE U.S.
SUPREME COURT, ROUND ONE, 2003–2004

1. George W. Bush, September 11, 2001. Quoted in Alfred McCoy and Tom Engelhardt, "How Not to Ban Torture in Congress," *Antiwar.Com,* February 9, 2006, www.antiwar.com/engelhardt/?articleid=8517.

2. Robert A. Levy, "Citizen Padilla: Dangerous Precedents," *National Review Online,* June 24, 2002, http://www.cato.org/dailys/07-01-02.html.

3. *Korematsu v. United States,* 323 U.S. 214 (1944); *Youngstown Sheet and Tube Co. v. Sawyer,* 343 U.S. 579 (1952).

4. This judicially created doctrine provides a judge or justices with a tactic to avoid hearing a case on the merits—whether in a trial court or on appeal. If a legal controversy is seen as a "political question," meaning that the controversy must be resolved in the political process, then the judiciary will not decide the matter on the merits.

5. See Howard Ball and Phillip Cooper, *Of Power and Right* (New York: Oxford University Press, 1986).

6. See Jeffrey Toobin, *Too Close to Call: The Thirty Six Day Battle to Decide the 2000 Election* (New York: Random House, 2001).

7. See Joan Biscupic, "President Tests Legal Limits of the War on Terror," *USA Today*, April 19, 2004. The writ of certiorari is an order from an appellate court to a lower court to "produce the record" for examination by the higher court—not of the facts but of the lower court's application of the rule of law. In 1928 Congress gave the Supreme Court total discretion to grant or deny petitions for writs of certiorari. Generally, twenty-nine of thirty certiorari petitions are denied. See Rule 10 of the *Rules of the U.S. Supreme Court,* available at http://www.law.cornell.edu/rules/supct/10.html.

8. Linda Greenhouse, "Justices to Hear Case of Detainees at Guantanamo," *New York Times,* November 11, 2003.

9. McCoy and Engelhardt, "How Not to Ban Torture in Congress," 4.

10. Ibid.

11. "Most said they were humanitarian volunteers who were captured by bounty hunters." Greenhouse, "Justices to Hear Case."

12. *Rasul v. Bush,* Petition for a Writ of Certiorari; text available at http://www.jenner.com/files/tbl_s69NewsDocumentOrder/FileUpload500/108/Rasul_Petition_%20Certiorari.pdf.

13. Ibid., at i–ii, In the *Al Odah v. United States,* Petition for a Writ of Certiorari, four questions were raised by the petitioners' lawyer. Three were essentially the *Rasul* questions; the fourth raised the question of whether government officials can evade judicial examination of their actions "simply by electing to confine their prisoners in an area technically outside U.S. sovereign territory although within its exclusive jurisdiction and control" (at i).

14. *Rasul v. Bush; Al Odah v. United States,* Brief for the Respondents in Opposition, at 15, 19, 26, 5, 10; text at http://www.jenner.com/files/tbl_s69NewsDocumentOrder/FileUpload500/114/BriefForTheRespondents.pdf.

15. For a complete list of the amicus curiae at the pre- and postgrant phases of the litigation before the Court, see Docket for 03-334, Vide 03-343, *Shafiq Rasul, et al., Petitioners v. George W. Bush, President of the United States, et al., Respondents,* docketed September 3, 2003, www.supremecourtus.gov/docket/03-334.htm.

16. See Docket for 03-334.

17. Fred Korematsu was a Japanese American citizen who, during World War II, was sent to one of almost one dozen internment camps for Japanese American citizens and Japanese aliens scattered about the western United States. In 1944, when he was twenty-two years old, he challenged the presidential action in litigation before the U.S. Supreme Court in *Korematsu v. United States* (323 U.S. 214). The Supreme Court, 6–3, upheld the presidential action. After hostilities ended, Korematsu became an attorney, and in these 2004 cases, an amicus curiae brief bearing his name was filed with the Court.

18. See Docket for 03-334.

19. *Rasul v. Bush,* Petitioner's Brief on the Merits, at 9, 29; text available at http://www.jenner.com/files/tbl_s69NewsDocumentOrder/FileUpload500/77/petitioners_brief_on_merits2.pdf. The *Al Odah* brief on the merits made five arguments: "Congress Has Expressly Granted the District Court Jurisdiction"; "Statutory Grants of

Jurisdiction Must Be Construed in Light of Long-Held Canons of Construction"; "There Is No Bar to Jurisdiction . . . *Eisentrager* Does Not Control This Case"; "Denying Judicial Review Is Contrary to the Law of Civilized Nations"; "Judicial Review Neither Threatens National Security Nor Opens the Floodgates to Litigation." *Al Odah*, Brief on the Merits, at 12–42, passim; text available at http://www.jenner.com/files/tbl_s69NewsDocumentOrder/FileUpload500/78/Brief_For_Petitioners.pdf.

20. *Rasul v. Bush*, Petitioners' Brief on the Merits, at 10–11, 15.

21. Ibid., at 29, 30.

22. *Rasul v. Bush; Al Odah v. United States*, Consolidated Brief for the Respondents, at 13, 14, 36; text available at http://www.jenner.com/files/tbl_s69NewsDocumentOrder/FileUpload500/170/respondent_brief.pdf.

23. Ibid., at 16–17.

24. Ibid., at 52ff., 54–55.

25. *Rasul v. Bush*, Reply Brief of Petitioners, at 1–2; text available at http://www.ccr-ny.org/v2/rasul_v_bush/legal/unitedStates/Reply%20Brief%20for%20Petitioners%20Al%20Odah%20v%20USA.pdf.

26. Ibid., at 11–16, passim.

27. Ibid., at 12.

28. *Rasul v. Bush*, Reply Brief for Petitioners, at 17–20, passim., at 20.

29. From the early 1990s to the present, the justices of the Supreme Court have heard fewer and fewer cases on the merits. They heard about seventy cases on the merits during the 2005 term. Also, typically, over 40 percent of the cases are unanimous decisions. In a given term, there may be ten to twenty hard, controversial cases that the justices have agreed to hear and decide. The enemy combatants cases of 2004 and 2006 are among those contentious cases.

30. Greenhouse, "Justices to Hear Case."

31. Linda Greenhouse, "Guantanamo Case about Federal Turf," *New York Times*, November 12, 2003.

32. All from *Rasul v. Bush*, Oral Argument, at 3–4, 8, 19–21, 23, 26, 44, 52, 53–54.

33. *Hamdi v. Rumsfeld*, Case Number 03-6696, October 2003 term.

34. *Rumsfeld v. Padilla*, 542 U.S. 426 (2004), Case Number 03-1027, October 2003 term.

35. Timothy Lynch, "*Hamdi* and Habeas Corpus," at http://www.cato.org/pub_display.php?pub_id=2632.

36. CA-02-348-2, CA-02-382-2 (2002).

37. "*In forma pauperis* is a legal term derived from the Latin phrase *in the form of a pauper*. In the United States, the designation is given by both state and federal courts to someone who is without the funds to pursue the normal costs of a lawsuit or a criminal defense. It is usually granted by a judge without a hearing and it entitles the person to a waiver of normal costs, and sometimes in criminal cases the appointment of counsel. Normal costs such as filing fees are waived but discovery costs like depositions and witness fees are not." "In forma pauperis," *Wikipedia: The Free Encyclopedia*, http://en.wikipedia.org/wiki/In_forma_pauperis.

38. Docket for 03-6696, *Yaser Esam Hamdi; Esam Fouad Hamdi, as Next Friend of Yaser Esam Hamdi, Petitioners, v. Donald Rumsfeld; W. R. Paulette, Commander, Respondents,* Petition for Writ of Certiorari, at i; text available at http://fl1.findlaw.com/ news.findlaw.com/hdocs/docs/hamdi/hamdirums100103pet.pdf.

39. For an excellent book on this subject, see H. W. Perry Jr., *Deciding to Decide: Agenda Setting in the United States Supreme Court* (Cambridge, MA: Harvard University Press, 1991; paperback edition, 2002).

40. *Hamdi v. Rumsfeld,* Petition for Writ of Certiorari, at 13, 19, 30.

41. *Hamdi v. Rumsfeld,* Reply of Respondent in Opposition, at 12–13; text available at http://www.jenner.com/files/tbl_s69NewsDocumentOrder/FileUpload500/154/ 2003-6696.resp.pdf.

42. *Hamdi v. Rumsfeld,* Reply Brief for Petitioners, at 1, 2; text available at http:// www.humanrightsfirst.org/us_law/inthecourts/hamdi_briefs/Hamdi_Reply_Brief.pdf.

43. See Docket for 03-6696.

44. *Hamdi v. Rumsfeld,* Brief for Petitioners, at 50, text available at http://www. abanet.org/publiced/preview/briefs/pdfs_03/6696Pet.pdf.

45. *Padilla v. Rumsfeld,* 352 F. 3rd. 695 (2nd Cir., 2003), Wesley dissent, at 113, 78, 7; text available at http://www.uniset.ca/other/cs5/352F3d695.html.

46. *Rumsfeld v. Padilla,* no. 03-1027, Brief in Opposition to Grant of Certiorari, 19, 16; text available at http://www.jenner.com/files/tbl_s69NewsDocumentOrder/File Upload500/124/PadillaCertOpp.pdf.

47. Docket for 03-1027, *Donald Rumsfeld, Secretary of Defense, Petitioner v. Jose Padilla and Donna R. Newman, as Next Friend of Jose Padilla,* docketed January 20, 2004, at http://www.supremecourtus.gov/docket/03-1027.htm.

48. Benjamin Wittes, "Enemy Americans," *Atlantic Monthly,* July–August 2004, 127–28.

49. See "War and Liberties," *Online NewsHour,* April 28, 2004, http://www.pbs.org/ newshour/bb/law/jan-june04/gb_4-28.html.

50. All from *Hamdi v. Rumsfeld,* Oral Argument, at 3, 24, 21–22, 26–27, 27–28, 35–36, 43, 51, 52–53, 54–56.

51. Justice Ginsburg had in mind a few cases where enemy combatants, including a U.S. citizen, were tried in federal courts: *United States v. Zacarias Moussaoui* (2006); and *United States v. John Philip Walker Lindh* (2002).

52. Dahlia Lithwick, "Cruel Detentions: The Supreme Court Considers Whether the President Can Throw Away the Key," Supreme Court Dispatches, *Slate,* April 28, 2004, www.slate.com/id/2099618/. Zacarias Moussaoui, a French citizen, was arrested in the United States shortly before the attacks of September 11, 2001, and was subsequently charged with participation in their planning. From the beginning, he was brought into the federal criminal justice system, where, in the spring of 2006, he pled guilty to conspiracy and was sentenced to life imprisonment.

53. All from *Rumsfeld v. Padilla,* Oral Argument, at 3, 21, 28–29.

54. *Rasul v. Bush,* Stevens, majority opinion, at 5, 6, 13, 15–16; text available at http:// supct.law.cornell.edu/supct/pdf/03-334P.ZO.

55. *Rasul v. Bush,* Kennedy, concurring opinion, at 3–4; text available at http://supct.law.cornell.edu/supct/pdf/03-334P.ZC.

56. *Rasul v. Bush,* Scalia, dissenting opinion, at 2–3, 19–20; text available at http://supct.law.cornell.edu/supct/pdf/03-334P.ZD.

57. *Hamdi v. Rumsfeld,* O'Connor, plurality opinion, at 8, 9, 17, 24, 26, 29, 30, 33; text available at http://supct.law.cornell.edu/supct/pdf/03-6696P.ZO.

58. *Hamdi v. Rumsfeld,* Souter opinion, at 3, 16; text available at http://supct.law.cornell.edu/supct/pdf/03-6696P.ZX. The Non-Detention Act, *U.S. Code* 18 (1971), sec. 4001(a), literally a one-sentence piece of legislation, states that "no citizen shall be arrested or otherwise detained by the United States except pursuant to an Act of Congress."

59. *Hamdi v. Rumsfeld,* Scalia dissent, at 1–2, 6, 21, 24, 27; text available at http://supct.law.cornell.edu/supct/pdf/03-6696P.ZD.

60. *Hamdi v. Rumsfeld,* Thomas dissent, at 1; text available at http://supct.law.cornell.edu/supct/pdf/03-6696P.ZD1.

61. *Rumsfeld v. Padilla,* Rehnquist for the majority, at 1, 24; text available at http://supct.law.cornell.edu/supct/pdf/03-1027P.ZO.

62. As will be shown in chapter 5, months after the Court's 2004 decision came down, the Bush administration placed Padilla *back* in the criminal justice system, thus ending any further legal questions regarding Padilla's request for habeas.

63. *Rumsfeld v. Padilla,* Kennedy concurrence, at 5; text available at http://supct.law.cornell.edu/supct/pdf/03-1027P.ZC.

64. *Rumsfeld v. Padilla,* Stevens dissent, at 1, 4, 11–12; text available at http://supct.law.cornell.edu/supct/pdf/03-1027P.ZD.

65. Linda Greenhouse, "Justices Affirm Legal Rights of 'Enemy Combatants,'" *New York Times,* June 29, 2004. See also Charles Lane, "Justices Back Detainee Access to U.S. Courts," *Washington Post,* June 29, 2004.

66. Matthew J. Franck, "Harmful Rulings: Enemy Combatants and an Irresponsible Court," *National Review Online,* June 29, 2004, http://www.nationalreview.com/comment/franck200406291303.asp. See also Harvey Silvergate, "Civil Liberties and Enemy Combatants: Why the Supreme Court's Widely Praised Rulings Are Bad for America," *Reasonline,* January 2005, http://www.reason.com/news/show/36440.html.

CHAPTER FIVE. BUSH VERSUS THE U.S. SUPREME COURT, ROUND TWO, 2004–2006

1. Quoted in Deborah Sontag, "Terrorist Suspects Path from Street to Brig," *New York Times,* April 25, 2004.

2. Editorial, "Setting Rules for Detainees," *Washington Post,* January 21, 2005.

3. Ibid.

4. Neil A. Lewis and David E. Sanger, "Administration Changing Review at Guantanamo Bay," *New York Times,* July 1, 2004.

5. Quoted in Neil A. Lewis, "Disagreement over Detainees' Legal Rights Simmers," *New York Times*, November 1, 2004.

6. For example, the following sentence appeared in Olson's argument before the Court in *Rasul*, and although it was rejected by the Court in its June 2004 *Rasul* decision, it appeared again in Department of Justice briefs submitted to the U.S. District Court in the fall of 2004: "The notion that the U.S. Constitution affords due process and other rights to enemy aliens captured abroad and confined outside the sovereign territory of the United States is contrary to law and history." Quoted in Lewis, "Disagreement over Detainees' Legal Rights Simmers."

7. Quoted in ibid.

8. Quoted in Lyle Denniston, "Guantanamo Cases—An Answer Is Due," September 21, 2004, at http://www.goldsteinhowe.com/blog/archive/2004_09_19_SCOTUS blog.cfm

9. Justice O'Connor, for the plurality in *Hamdi*, wrote that hearings under Regulation 190-8 "might be sufficient" to meet due process standards for U.S. citizens like Hamdi. The Department of Defense acted on this dicta to establish the combatant status review tribunals.

10. Department of Defense, "Order Establishing Combatant Status Review Tribunals," July 7, 2004, http://www.defenselink.mil/news/Jul2004/d20040707review.pdf; Department of Defense, "Implementation of Combatant Status Review Tribunal Procedures for Enemy Combatants Detained at Guantanamo Bay Naval Base, Cuba," July 29, 2004, http://www.defenselink.mil/news/Jul2004/d20040730comb.pdf.

11. "Both in common law and in civil law, a rebuttable presumption (in Latin, *praesumptio iuris tantum*) is an assumption that is made that is taken to be true unless someone comes forward to contest it and prove otherwise. Rebuttable presumptions in criminal law are somewhat controversial in that they do effectively reverse the presumption of innocence in some cases." "Rebuttable Presumption," *Wikipedia: The Free Encyclopedia*, http://en.wikipedia.org/wiki/Rebuttable_presumption.

12. Judge Green was appointed to the U.S. District Court, District of Columbia, by President Jimmy Carter (D; 1977–1981).

13. Barbara Olshansky, who participated in the preparation of the three cases heard by the Supreme Court in 2004, said that the government lawyers had stonewalled for seven months after *Rasul*. After Judge Green's ruling, Olshansky said, "The good thing about this ruling is it says, 'Hey, you, in the White House, this law applies to you.'" Quoted in Carol D. Leonnig, "Judge Rules Detainee Tribunals Illegal," *Washington Post*, February 1, 2005.

14. Jonathan Mahler, "Terms of Imprisonment," *New York Times Sunday Book Review*, July 30, 2006, 6. See also Carol D. Leonnig, "Pentagon Tells Detainees about Their Right to Go to Court," *Washington Post*, December 16, 2004.

15. See Joseph Margulies, *Guantanamo and the Abuse of Presidential Power* (New York: Simon and Schuster, 2006).

16. Judge Leon was appointed to the U.S. District Court, District of Columbia, by President George H. W. Bush.

17. Judge Joyce H. Green, quoted in Leonnig, "Judge Rules Detainee Tribunals Illegal."

18. Denniston, "Guantanamo Cases—An Answer Is Due."

19. Department of Justice, press release, September 22, 2004, http://www.usdoj.gov/opa/pr/2004/September/04_opa_640.htm.

20. Dahlia Lithwick, "Nevermind: Hamdi Wasn't So Bad After All," September 23, 2004, http://www.slate.com/id/2107114/. See also Charlie Savage, "Deal Frees U.S. 'Enemy Combatant,'" *Boston Globe,* September 23, 2004; Jerry Markon, "U.S. to Free Hamdi, Send Him Home," *Washington Post,* September 23, 2004.

21. Quoted in Adam Liptak, "For Prisoners, Only Certainty Is Right to a Court Hearing," *New York Times,* June 29, 2004.

22. Associated Press, "Court Won't Review U.S. Citizen's Detention," *Washington Post,* June 14, 2005.

23. *Jose Padilla v. C. T. Hanft, U.S.N. Commander, Consolidated Naval Brig,* U.S. Court of Appeals for the Fourth Circuit, No. 05-6396, September 9, 2005, at 6; text available at http://www.wiggin.com/db30/cgi-bin/pubs/Fourth%20Circuit%20Opinion.pdf.

24. Quoted in Gina Holland, "Terror Suspect Takes Case to High Court," *Washington Post,* October 27, 2005.

25. *United States of America v. Jose Padilla [and Four Co-defendants], Superceding Indictment,* U.S. District Court, Southern District of Florida, Case No. 04-60001-CR-COOKE, November 17, 2005, at 2, 3; text available at http://www.wiggin.com/db30/cgi-bin/pubs/11-17-05%20Indictment.pdf.

26. As cited at "Padilla Transfer of Custody Order [White House]," *Jurist: Legal News and Research,* Gazette Citation, November 22, 2005, http://jurist.law.pitt.edu/gazette/2005/11/padilla-transfer-of-custody-order.php.

27. Quoted in Dan Eggen, "Padilla Is Indicted on Terrorism Charges," *Washington Post,* November 23, 2005.

28. Eggen, "Padilla Is Indicted on Terrorism Charges." "That's an issue the administration did not want to face," said Professor Scott Silliman, of Duke University School of Law. Quoted in David Stout, "U.S. Indicts Padilla after 3 Years in Pentagon Custody," *New York Times,* November 22, 2005. "Analysts," wrote another reporter, "said the decision appeared driven by [an administration] desire to avoid what could be a losing battle before the Supreme Court." Erich Lindblau, "In Legal Shift, U.S. Charges Detainee in Terrorism Case," *New York Times,* November 23, 2005.

29. Editorial, "Three Years Late," *Washington Post,* November 23, 2005.

30. Quoted in Lindblau, "In Legal Shift."

31. Douglas Jehl and Eric Lichtblau, "Shift on Suspect Is Linked to Role of Qaeda Figures," *New York Times,* November 25, 2005.

32. Quoted in Adam Liptak, "Still Searching for a Strategy Four Years after September 11 Attacks," *New York Times,* November 23, 2005.

33. *Jose Padilla v. C. T. Hanft,* Order, December 21, 2005, at 2; text available at http://pacer.ca4.uscourts.gov/opinion.pdf/056396R1.P.pdf.

34. Solicitor General's "Application Respecting the Custody and Transfer of Jose Padilla," as cited at "Padilla Transfer Ruling Appeal [US DOJ]," *Jurist: Legal News and Research,* Gazette Citation, December 29, 2005, http://jurist.law.pitt.edu/gazette/2005/12/padilla-transfer-ruling-appeal-us-doj.php.

35. Quoted in Eric Lichtblau, "Supreme Court Is Asked to Rule on Terror Trial," *New York Times,* December 29, 2005.

36. *Padilla v. Hanft,* 05-533.

37. U.S. Supreme Court, 546 U.S., Order in Pending Case, 05A578, *Hanft, C.T., v. Padilla, Jose,* January 4, 2006, http://www.supremecourtus.gov/orders/courtorders/010406pzr.pdf.

38. *Jose Padilla v. C. T. Hanft,* 547 U.S. ____ (2006), Ginsburg dissenting from the denial of certiorari, at 1; text available at http://www.supremecourtus.gov/opinions/05pdf/05-533Ginsburg.pdf.

39. *Padilla v. Hanft,* Kennedy, with whom the chief justice and Stevens join, concurring in the denial of certiorari, at 3, 3–4; text available at http://www.supremecourtus.gov/opinions/05pdf/05-533Kennedy.pdf.

40. Linda Greenhouse, "Justices Decline Terror Case of a U.S. Citizen," *New York Times,* April 4, 2006.

41. Editorial, "The High Court Punts," *New York Times,* April 4, 2006.

42. See Deborah Sontag, "Defense Calls Padilla Incompetent for Trial," *New York Times,* February 23, 2007. See also Laura Parker, "Psychiatrist: Solitary Confinement Has Made Padilla Unfit for Trial," *USA Today,* February 23, 2007; Jaime Jansen, "Padilla Ruled Competent to Stand Trial," *Jurist: Legal News and Research,* http://jurist.law.pitt.edu/paperchase/2007/02/padilla-ruled-competent-to-stand-trial.php.

43. Charles Lee, "Justices Won't Review Padilla Case," *Washington Post,* April 4, 2006.

44. Alfred McCoy and Tom Engelhardt, "How Not to Ban Torture in Congress," *Antiwar.Com,* February 9, 2006, www.antiwar.com/engelhardt/?articleid=8517.

45. "It was a complete media mirage." Ibid., 7. In this extensively covered media event, Bush said that the McCain amendment makes it "clear to the world that this government does not torture." Quoted in ibid., 7.

46. Ian Wallach, "No Habeas at Guantanamo? The Executive and the Dubious Tale of the DTA," Forum, *Jurist: Legal News and Research,* April 4, 2006, 5–6, http://jurist.law.pitt.edu/forumy/2006/03/no-habeas-at-guantanamo-executive-and.php.

47. Quoted in Charles Lane, "High Court to Hear Case on War Powers," *Washington Post,* November 8, 2005.

48. See Wallach, "No Habeas at Guantanamo?" for the following chronology.

49. Eugene R. Fidell to Senators Specter and Warner, November 14, 2005, quoted in *Congressional Record–Senate,* November 14, 2006, S12728, as quoted at http://www.washingtonwatchdog.org/documents/cr/2005/no/14/cr14no05-46.html. Copies were sent to seven other senators, including Senators Graham, McCain, Bingaman, and Levin.

50. Quoted in Wallach, "No Habeas at Guantanamo?"

51. Lyle Denniston, "*Hamdan* Case Moved Along," September 9, 2005, SCOTUS-BLOG, http://www.scotusblog.com/movabletype/archives/2005/09/hamdan_case_mov.html.

52. Quoted in Dan Eggen and Josh White, "U.S. Seeks to Avoid Detainee Ruling," *Washington Post,* January 13, 2006.

53. Editorial, "The President and the Courts," *New York Times,* March 20, 2006.

54. *United States v. Salim Ahmed Hamdan,* at 2–3; text available at http://news.find law.com/hdocs/docs/tribunals/ushamdan704.html.

55. Neil A. Lewis, "First War-Crimes Case Opens at Guantanamo Base," *New York Times,* August 25, 2004.

56. Judge Robertson was appointed by President Clinton.

57. James Robertson, U.S. District Judge, *Salim Ahmed Hamdan v. Donald Rumsfeld,* U.S. District Court for the District of Columbia, Civil Action, No. 04-1519 (JR), Memorandum Opinion, November 8, 2004, at 1; text available at http://www.global security.org/security/library/policy/national/04-1519_08nov2004.pdf.

58. Ibid., at 9.

59. Ibid., at 13.

60. Neil A. Lewis, "U.S. Judge Halts War-Crime Trial at Guantanamo," *New York Times,* November 9, 2004.

61. Robertson, Memorandum Opinion, at 28ff., 30.

62. Quoted in Carol D. Leonnig and John Mintz, "Judge Says Detainees' Trials Are Unlawful," *Washington Post,* November 9, 2004.

63. Quoted in Marcia Coyle, "Judging the Tribunals," *National Law Journal,* November 22, 2004, 1, 26.

64. *Salim Ahmed Hamdan v. Donald Rumsfeld,* U.S. Court of Appeals for the District of Columbia Circuit, Appeal from the U.S. District Court for the District of Columbia, July 15, 2005. Before Randolph and Roberts, Circuit Judges, and Williams, Senior Circuit Judge; text available at http://www.ll.georgetown.edu/federal/judicial/dc/opinions/04opinions/04-5393a.pdf.

65. Ibid., at 9.

66. Ibid., at 15, 16–20, passim.

67. Ibid., Williams concurring, at 1.

68. Quoted in Neil A. Lewis, "Ruling Lets U.S. Restart Trials at Guantanamo," *New York Times,* July 16, 2005.

69. *Hamdan v. Rumsfeld,* Petition for a Writ of Certiorari, August 8, 2005, at i; text available at http://www.law.georgetown.edu/faculty/nkk/documents/8-7-05_Cert_Petition.nk11.pdf.

70. Ibid., at 8, 5.

71. *Hamdan v. Rumsfeld,* Brief for the Respondents in Opposition, at 1; text available at http://www.law.georgetown.edu/faculty/nkk/documents/HamdanBrief.opp.pdf.

72. An interlocutory order or judgment is "given in an intermediate stage between the commencement and termination" of a legal proceeding. It is "used to provide a

temporary or provisional decision on an issue. Thus, an interlocutory order is not final and is usually not subject to appeal." "Interlocutory," *Wikipedia: The Free Encyclopedia,* http://en.wikipedia.org/wiki/Interlocutory.

73. *Hamdan v. Rumsfeld,* Brief for the Respondents in Opposition, at 10.

74. Emily Bazelon, "Hear Me, Hear Me," *Slate,* October 27, 2005, http://www.slate.com/id/2128917/.

75. All from *Hamdan v. Rumsfeld,* Petitioner's Brief on the Merits, at 5, 6, 8; text available at http://www.hamdanvrumsfeld.com/petbriefhamdanfinal.pdf.

76. All from *Hamdan v. Rumsfeld,* Brief for Respondents, at I, 7, 8; text available at http://www.hamdanvrumsfeld.com/HamdanSGmeritsbrief.pdf.

77. *Youngstown Sheet and Tube Co. v. Sawyer,* 343 U.S., Jackson Concurring Opinion, at 635–37.

78. *Hamdan v. Rumsfeld,* Brief for Respondents, at 9–10.

79. Emily Bazelon, "Invisible Men," *Slate,* March 27, 2006, http://www.slate.com/id/2138750/.

80. *Hamdan v. Rumsfeld,* Reply Brief of the Petitioner, at 5; text available at http://www.hamdanvrumsfeld.com/HAMDANFINAL.march15.reply.pdf.

81. Linda Greenhouse, "Detainee Case Will Pose Delicate Question for Court," *New York Times,* March 27, 2006. *Ex Parte McCardle* dates from the early days of the Civil War Reconstruction. William McCardle, a newspaper publisher and not a member of the military, "published some 'incendiary' articles. He was jailed by a military commander under a law passed by the United States Congress. Mr. McCardle invoked *habeas corpus* in the Circuit Court of the Southern District of Mississippi. The judge sent him back into custody, finding the military actions legal under Congress's law. He appealed to the Supreme Court under a congressional act of 1867 that allowed federal judges to issue writs of *habeas corpus* and hear appeals from circuit courts. After the case was argued but before an opinion was delivered, Congress repealed the statute. . . . The Court, speaking through Chase, validated congressional withdrawal of the Court's jurisdiction. The basis for this repeal was the exceptions clause of Article III Section 2. But Chase pointedly reminded his readers that the 1868 statute repealing jurisdiction 'does not affect the jurisdiction which was previously exercised.'" "*Ex parte McCardle,*" *Wikipedia: The Free Encyclopedia,* http://en.wikipedia.org/wiki/Ex_parte_McCardle.

82. All from *Hamdan v. Rumsfeld,* Oral Argument, at 4–7, passim, 10–12, 14, 17, 19, 21, 22, 25–26, 30.

83. Charles Lane, "Case Tests Power of Judiciary, President," *Washington Post,* March 29, 2006.

84. All from *Hamdan v. Rumsfeld,* Oral Argument, Respondent, at 36, 40, 44–45, 47–48, 56–57, 66, 75, 78.

85. The suspension clause, Article I, Section 9, Clause 2 of the U.S. Constitution, states: "The Privilege of the Writ of Habeas Corpus shall not be suspended, unless when in Cases of Rebellion or Invasion the public Safety may require it."

86. All from *Hamdan v. Rumsfeld,* Oral Argument, Katyal's rebuttal, at 81, 82–83.

87. All from *Hamdan v. Rumsfeld*, Stevens opinion, at 15–16n10, 20, 23–24, 29–30, 30, 31–32, 36, 38, 39–40, 50, 51, 57, 61, 72–73; text available at http://supct.law.cornell.edu/supct/pdf/05-184P.ZO.

88. Article 21 of the UCMJ: "The provisions of this code conferring jurisdiction upon courts-martial shall not be construed as depriving military commissions, provost courts, or other military tribunals of concurrent jurisdiction in respect of offenders or offenses that by statute or by the law of war may be tried by such military commissions, provost courts, or other military tribunals."

89. U.S. Constitution, Article I, Section 8, clause 10.

90. For the relevancy of the Geneva Convention, especially Common Article 3, see *Hamdan v. Rumsfeld*, Majority Opinion, at 64–71, passim.

91. Article 36 of the UCMJ: "(a) The procedure, including modes of proof, in cases before courts-martial, courts of inquiry, military commissions, and other military tribunals may be prescribed by the President by regulations which shall, so far as he considers practicable, apply the principles of law and the rules of evidence generally recognized in the trial of criminal cases in the United States district courts, but which may not be contrary to or inconsistent with this chapter. (b) All rules and regulations made under this article shall be uniform insofar as practicable and shall be reported to Congress."

92. *Hamdan v. Rumsfeld*, Breyer concurring opinion, at 1; text available at http://supct.law.cornell.edu/supct/pdf/05-184P.ZC.

93. *Hamdan v. Rumsfeld*, Kennedy concurring opinion, at 19–20; text available at http://supct.law.cornell.edu/supct/pdf/05-184P.ZC1.

94. *Hamdan v. Rumsfeld*, Scalia dissenting opinion, at 1, 11, 12; text available at http://supct.law.cornell.edu/supct/pdf/05-184P.ZD.

95. *Hamdan v. Rumsfeld*, Thomas dissent, at 1, 29–30, 30, 39, 39–44 passim, 49; text available at http://supct.law.cornell.edu/supct/pdf/05-184P.ZD1.

96. He disagreed with the majority's conclusion "that the commission is unlawful because the President has not explained why it is not practicable to apply the same rules and procedures to Hamdan's [military] commission as would be applied in a trial by court-martial." *Hamdan v. Rumsfeld*, Thomas dissent, at 32.

97. *Hamdan v. Rumsfeld*, Alito dissent, at 2, 3, 4, 7–8, 10; text available at http://supct.law.cornell.edu/supct/pdf/05-184P.ZD2.

98. Aziz Huq, "Hamdan: Not Over Yet," *TomPaine.commonsense*, June 30, 2006, www.tompaine.com/articles/2006/06/30/hamdan_not_over_yet.php.

99. Quoted in Neil A. Lewis, "Detainees May Test Reach of Guantanamo Ruling," *New York Times*, June 30, 2006.

100. Quoted in ibid.

101. Quoted in ibid.

102. Quoted in ibid.

103. William Brannigin, "Supreme Court Rejects Guantanamo War Crimes Trials," *Washington Post*, June 29, 2006.

104. Linda Greenhouse, "Justices, 5:3, Broadly Reject Bush Plan to Try Detainees," *New York Times,* June 30, 2006.

105. Gordon England, "Application of Common Article 3 of the Geneva Conventions to the Treatment of Detainees in the Department of Defense," http://www.washingtonpost.com/wp-srv/nation/nationalsecurity/genevaconvdoc.pdf.

106. "In Retreat," *Economist,* July 15, 2006, 29.

107. Charles P. Pierce, "Best and Brightest 2004: The Iraq Generation. Charles Swift," *Esquire* 142, no. 6 (December 2004), http://www.esquire.com/features/ESQ 1204-DEC_B&BSOCITY_jump_rev_2_5.

108. Quoted in Paul Shukovsky, "Gitmo Win Likely Cost Navy Lawyer His Job," *Seattle Post-Intelligencer,* July 1, 2006.

109. David E. Sanger and Scott Shane, "Court's Ruling Is Likely to Force Negotiations over Presidential Power," *New York Times,* June 30, 2006.

110. Quoted in Kate Zernike, "White House Prods Congress to Curb Detainee Rights," *New York Times,* July 13, 2006.

111. Quoted in ibid.

112. Quoted in R. Jeffrey Smith and Jonathan Weisman, "Policy Rewrite Reveals Rift in Administration," *Washington Post,* July 14, 2006.

113. Quoted in ibid.

114. Joanne Mariner, "It All Depends on What You Mean by Battlefield . . . ," *Findlaw,* July 18, 2006, at http://writ.lp.findlaw.com/mariner/20060718.html.

CHAPTER SIX. BUSH TRUMPS THE U.S. SUPREME COURT: THE 2006 MILITARY COMMISSIONS ACT

1. Joseph Margulies, *Guantanamo and the Abuse of Presidential Power* (New York: Simon and Schuster, 2006), 1.

2. See Harold Myerson, "GOP Conundrum," *Washington Post,* July 6, 2006.

3. Michael R. Gordon and General Bernard E. Trainor, *Cobra II: The Inside Story of the Invasion and Occupation of Iraq* (New York: Pantheon, 2006); Thomas E. Ricks, *Fiasco: The American Military Adventure in Iraq* (New York: Penguin Press, 2006); Ron Suskind, *The One Percent Doctrine: Deep Inside America's Pursuit of Its Enemies since 9/11* (New York: Simon and Schuster, 2006).

4. Jonathan Mahler, "Terms of Imprisonment," *New York Times Sunday Book Section,* July 30, 2006, 6.

5. Jeffrey Rosen, "One Eye on Principle, the Other on the People's Will," *New York Times,* July 4, 2004.

6. International critics criticized Bush's actions, especially after the March 2003 invasion of Iraq. However, as soon as the prison camp at Guantánamo Bay was opened in January 2002, the ICRC was extremely critical of the U.S. treatment of detainees. Until 2005 their criticism was voiced in secret communications to the White House.

The administration ignored these entreaties. Only after 2005 did the ICRC publicly reveal, to the United Nations, the extent of the organization's fears that the Guantánamo detainees were being treated poorly, that they were suffering physical and psychological maladies, and that many were being tortured by U.S. military personnel.

7. Editorial, "The Hamdan Decision," *New York Times,* June 30, 2006.

8. See, in chapter 5, Justice Souter's questions to the attorney general during the *Hamdan* oral argument.

9. Quoted in Kate Zernike, "G.O.P. Senator Resisting Bush over Detainees," *New York Times,* July 18, 2006.

10. Quoted in Peter Baker and Michael Abramowitz, "A Governing Philosophy Rebuffed," *Washington Post,* June 30, 2006.

11. Quoted in ibid.

12. See especially Section 1, subchapter 6, section 950j, "Finality of Proceedings, Findings, and Sentences"; Section 5, "Treaty Obligations Not Establishing Grounds for Certain Claims"; Section 6, "Implementation of Treaty Obligations"; and Section 7, "Habeas Corpus Matters." These sections are found in appendix 6.

13. Quoted in Jonathan Weisman and Michael Abramowitz, "White House Shifts Tack on Tribunals," *Washington Post,* July 20, 2006.

14. The proposed legislation can be found at www.washingtonpost.com/. Sections of the final bill appear in appendix 6 in this book.

15. David S. Cloud and Sheryl Gay Stolberg, "White House Proposes System to Try Detainees," *New York Times,* July 26, 2006.

16. Quoted in ibid.

17. See R. J. Smith, "Top Military Leaders Oppose Plan for Special Courts," *Washington Post,* August 3, 2006.

18. The War Crimes Act of 1996 makes violations of Common Article 3 a war crime. By immunizing those persons who interrogated alleged enemy combatants in violation of the Geneva Conventions, the Bush administration was narrowing the 1996 act, amending it in a very substantive manner.

19. See R. J. Smith, "Military Commissions Act Changes Would Reduce Threat," *Washington Post,* August 9, 2006. See also Jeremy Brecher and Brandon Smith, "Bush Threatens to Kill War Crimes Act of 1996," *Nation,* September 5, 2006, www.thenation.com/.

20. See Josh White, "New Rules of Interrogation Forbid Use of Harsh Techniques," *Washington Post,* September 7, 2006.

21. See Adam Liptak, "Interrogation Methods Rejected by Military Win Bush's Support," *New York Times,* September 8, 2006.

22. See, for example, Frankfurter's opinion for a unanimous (8–0) Court in *Rochin v. California,* 342 U.S. 165 (1952). In overturning Rochin's conviction, Frankfurter wrote of the government's tactics: "This is conduct that shocks the conscience. [The actions of the police to recover evidence from Rochin] is bound to offend even hardened sensibilities. They are methods too close to the rack and the screw to permit of

constitutional differentiation." At 172; text available at http://supreme.justia.com/ us/342/165/case.html.

23. The House Armed Services Committee, however, on the same day, passed the Bush MCA by a vote of 52–8.

24. Letter released by Senator John McCain and published on the *Washington Post*'s Web site, www.washingtonpost.com/.

25. Quoted in Timothy Noah, "Powell Trumps Bush," *Slate*, September 14, 2006, http://www.slate.com/id/2149744/.

26. See Rick Klein, "Bush Raps McCain's Detainee Proposals," *Boston Globe*, September 16, 2006.

27. Quoted in Jim Rutenberg and Sheryl Gay Stolberg, "Bush Says GOP Rebels Are Putting Nation at Risk," *New York Times*, September 16, 2006.

28. See Editorial, "A Bad Bargain," *New York Times*, September 22, 2006.

29. Senator Patrick Leahy, speech found in www.tompaine.com/print/. http://www.tompaine.com/articles/2006/09/26/showdown_over_habeas.php.

30. Quoted in John W. Dean, "The Controversy over Curtailing Habeas Corpus Rights: Why It Is a Bad Day for the Constitution Whenever Attorney General Alberto Gonzales Testifies," January 26, 2007, http://writ.lp.findlaw.com/dean/20070126.html.

31. Quoted in R. J. Smith and Charles Babington, "Detainee Bill in Final Stages," *Washington Post*, September 27, 2006.

32. The section numbers referred to in the following notes are taken from the version of the MCA of 2006 as voted on in the Senate. After a conference session, a final version of the MCA (S. 3930 and H.R. 6166) was passed on to the president for his signature. Appendix 6 contains excerpts from the MCA.

33. See Section 4, subchapter 6, section 950e, "Providing Material Support for Terrorism."

34. See Section 5, subchapter 7, section 950j(b), "Finality of Proceedings, Findings, and Sentences"; Section 6, "Habeas Corpus Matters."

35. Section 4, "Military Commissions," section 948b. "Military Commissions Generally," "Inapplicability of Certain Provisions," (1) "The following provisions shall not apply to trial by military commission, Section 810 [UCMJ] relating to speedy trial, . . . Sections 831 (a) (b), and (d), relating to compulsory self-incrimination."

36. See Section 4, "Military Commissions," section 948c(f), "Geneva Conventions Not Establishing Source of Rights"; Section 7, "Treaty Obligations Not Establishing Grounds for Certain Claims."

37. See Section 4, "Military Commissions," section 948r, "Statements Obtained before enactment of DTA of 2005," "coerced statements may be admitted only if the military judge finds that (1) the totality of the circumstances renders it reliable and possessing sufficient probative value."

38. See Section 8, "Implementation of Treaty Obligations," (a)(3) "Interpretation by the President."

39. See Section 8(d) "Common Article 3 Violations," (G) "Rape."

40. Scott Shane and Adam Liptak, "Detainee Bill Shifts Power to President," *New York Times,* September 30, 2006.

41. Ibid.

42. Andrew Cohen, "The Ball Is Now in the Supremes' Court," Bench Conference, *Washington Post,* September 29, 2006, http://blog.washingtonpost.com/benchconfer ence/2006/09/.

43. Ibid.

EPILOGUE: THE 2006 MIDTERM ELECTIONS AND A RETURN TO THE U.S. SUPREME COURT

1. Editorial, "The Verdict on Rumsfeld," *Boston Globe,* November 9, 2006, http://www.boston.com/news/nation/washington/articles/2006/11/09/the_verdict_on _rumsfeld/.

2. Richard A. Posner, *Not a Suicide Pact: The Constitution in a Time of National Emergency* (New York: Oxford University Press, 2006), 149.

3. Robert Dreyfuss, "The Iraq Mandate," *TomPaine.commonsense,* November 8, 2006, http://www.tompaine.com/articles/2006/11/08/the_iraq_mandate.php.

4. Peter Baker and Jim VanderHei, "A Voter Rebuke for Bush, the War, and the Right," *Washington Post,* November 8, 2006.

5. Greenberg Quinlin Rosner Research, "Campaign for America's Future," November 7–8, 2006, http://www.tompaine.com/.

6. In the same poll, voters overall were very negative toward the job congresspersons were doing: 29 percent approved; 67 percent disapproved. Ibid.

7. See Phillip Carter, "A Catalog of Failure: Rumsfeld's Biggest Blunders and How They've Harmed America," *Slate,* November 8, 2006, http://www.slate.com/id/2153319/.

8. See, for example, John Heilprin, "Bush Faces GOP Ire over Rumsfeld Timing," Associated Press, November 12, 2006, http://abcnews.go.com/Politics/wireStory?id= 2647858&CMP=OTC-RSSFeeds0312.

9. Ibid.

10. See Katherine Shrader and Ann Sanner, "Gates' Views Have Differed from Bush," *Washington Post,* November 10, 2006.

11. *Ali Kahlah Al-Marri v. S. L. Wright, USN Commander, Consolidated Naval Brig,* No 06-7427, U.S. CA 4, November 13, 2006.

12. Ibid., 2–3.

13. Associated Press, "U.S. Defends Legal Limits for Detainees," *Washington Post,* November 14, 2006. See also www.brennancenter.org for more information on the *Al-Marri v. Wright* litigation.

14. Ibid. In mid-December 2006, U.S. District Court Judge James Robertson ruled that the MCA could bar detainees held at Guantánamo from seeking redress in federal court but could not bar the more than 12 million legal immigrants living in America

from doing so. See David G. Savage, "Federal Judge Issues Split Decision on New MCA," *Seattle Times,* December 14, 2006.

15. Quoted in Roxana Tiron, "Senate Democrats Plan Overhaul of Military Tribunals Bill," *Hill,* November 17, 2006, 1, http://thehill.com/leading-the-news/senate-dems-plan-overhaul-of-military-tribunals-bill-2006-11-16.html. Dodd's proposal is entitled "The Effective Terrorists Prosecution Act of 2006."

16. Jennifer Van Bergen, "Damage Control," *TomPaine.commonsense,* October 27, 2006, http://www.tompaine.com/articles/2006/10/27/damage_control.php.

17. Quoted in Associated Press, "Leahy Seeks Documents on Detention," *Washington Post,* November 18, 2006.

18. Leahy and Specter clearly spelled out the bill's aims: It "strikes the new limitations on habeas corpus created in the Military Commissions Act of 2006, Public Law 109-366, 2006 Stat. 3930.

"The MCA added two new habeas provisions—

"(1) A new paragraph in the federal habeas statute, 28 U.S.C. Sec. 2241(e), that would bar any alien detained by the United States as an enemy combatant from filing a writ of habeas corpus. The new paragraph [applied] to all pending cases 'without exception' thereby barring all pending habeas corpus applications pending on behalf of Guantanamo Bay detainees.

"(2) An entirely new habeas corpus limitation that barred any habeas review of military commission procedures. Had this bill been passed before the *Hamdan v. Rumsfeld* case was decided, the Supreme Court would not have had jurisdiction to review and reject the military commission procedures that were at issue. This new habeas limitation was added to federal law as 10 U.S.C. Sec. 950j(b).

"The Habeas Corpus Restoration Act would strike these two provisions from the law in their entirety, thereby restoring the right of aliens detained within U.S. territorial jurisdiction (including at Gitmo) to challenge their detention via file writs of habeas corpus.

"Because the Military Commissions Act already completely repealed and superseded the habeas limitations created by the Graham Amendment to the Detainee Treatment Act of 2005, the bill would restore the state of play before the DTA.

"Actual effect—The MCA would deprive federal courts of jurisdiction to hear the 196 habeas corpus applications currently pending on behalf of the detainees at Guantanamo Bay, Cuba. This bill would restore jurisdiction and allow those cases to be decided on their merits. It would also allow habeas corpus challenges to military commission procedures." Arlen Specter, for himself and Patrick Leahy, Senate, 109th Cong., 2nd sess., *Congressional Record* 152 (December 5, 2006), S11197. http://frwebgate.access.gpo.gov/cgi-bin/getpage.cgi?dbname=2006_record&page=S11197&position=all.

19. Congressional Record for December 5, 2006, at http://www.fas.org/irp/congress/2006_cr/s4081.html.

20. Jeffrey Rosen, "The Subpoena Wars: House Arrest," *New Republic,* November 20, 2006, https://ssl.tnr.com/p/docsub.mhtml?i=20061120&s=rosen112006.

21. Editorial, "Reform on Detentions," *Washington Post,* November 19, 2006.

22. Quoted in Associated Press, "Leahy Seeks Documents on Detention."

23. Quoted in Savage, "Federal Judge Issues Split Decision."

24. Quoted in Laurie Kellman, "Warrantless Wiretaps Unlikely to Be OK'd," *New York Times,* November 11, 2006.

25. Quoted in Tiron, "Senate Democrats Plan Overhaul."

26. Stanley Brand, "Let the Investigations Begin," *New York Times,* November 12, 2006.

27. Posner, *Not a Suicide Pact,* 156. He also observed, "Terrorist suspects should have a constitutional right to demand, by applying to a court for habeas corpus, that a judicial officer determine whether their detention has a legal basis—the right, in short, to due process of law." 12.

28. Ibid., 39.

29. Rosen, "The Subpoena Wars."

30. See ibid. for such a possible scenario for constitutional crisis.

31. Jonathan Hafetz, "Government Seeks to Strip Immigrants of Habeas Corpus," Brennan Center for Justice, November 14, 2006, http://www.brennancenter.org/press_detail.asp?key=100&subkey=38766. See also Dan Eggen, "Justice Department's Brief on Detention Policy Draws Fire," *Washington Post,* November 15, 2006.

32. Josh White, "Guantanamo Detainees Lose Appeal," *Washington Post,* February 21, 2007. See also Stephen Labaton, "Court Endorses Law's Curb on Detainees," *New York Times,* February 21, 2007.

33. Vice President Cheney, quoted in Dreyfuss, "The Iraq Mandate."

34. Quoted in White, "Guantanamo Detainees Lose Appeal."

35. In a 243–141 vote in September 1987, the House of Representatives approved the redress legislation. The U.S. Senate overwhelmingly passed a similar measure in April 1988, and on August 10, 1988, President Reagan signed the bill authorizing redress payments for Japanese Americans.

36. Bob Herbert, "The Definition of Tyranny," *New York Times,* July 7, 2006. "Slapstick justice is a process," Herbert wrote, "worthy of a Marx Brothers routine":

"You have been accused of being a terrorist."

"Where is the evidence?"

"We can't show it to you."

"That's ridiculous!"

"So is this court. We find you guilty. Take him away."

Index

Abu Ghraib prison, 62, 70–71, 85
  atrocities in, 176
  photos of torture at, 171
  torture at, 71ff.
  torture scandal at, 71–73, 79–81
ACLU (American Civil Liberties Union),
    81, 83
"Actionable suspicion" doctrine, 35–36
Addington, David, 24–26, 52, 68, 83
  response of, to Hamdan, 172
Administrative Review Boards (ARB), 131
Air CIA, 76–77. See also CIA, rendition
    practice of
Al Odah v. U.S., 85, 90–95, 194
Al Qaeda, 2, 7, 19–20, 27, 45, 49, 57, 62–63,
    75, 89, 105, 172
Al-Dossari, Juna, 73–74
Alito, Samuel, 126
  dissent of, in Hamdan, 168–169
  participation of, in Hamdan, 150
Al-Marri, Ali Saleh Kahlah, 27–29
Alter, Jonathan, 9, 19, 34
Ambuhl, Megan, 73–74
America, vulnerability of, 196
American Civil Liberties Union (ACLU),
    81, 83
Amnesty International, 53–54
Amsterdam, Anthony G., 128
Arar, Maher, 31
Army Criminal Investigation Command
    (ACIC), 70–74
Ashcroft, John, 1, 13, 14, 54
Authorization for Use of Military Force
    (AUMF), 2, 10–13, 20, 51, 53, 90, 191
  as blank check for president, 2
  constitutionality of, 133–134
  text of, 199–200

Bagram prison, 62–63, 70–72
Bartlett, Dan, 182
Bazelon, Emily, 154–155
BBC News, 12
Benchellali, Mourad, 72–73
Bingaman, Jeff, 142, 143
Bin Laden, Osama, 37, 53, 63
Black sites, 74–75. See also CIA
Bolton, Joshua, 182
Boumediene v. Bush, 194
  dissent from denial of certiorari in,
    195
Bradbury, Stephen, 179
Brand, Stanley, 192
Breyer, Stephen G., 33
  concurring opinion of, in Hamdan,
    166
Bright Light, 75. See also CIA
Brown v. Board of Education of Topeka,
    Kansas, 128
Bush administration, 2, 9, 31, 77, 87
  antiterrorism policies of, 27–29
  blind trust of public in, 12
  definition of war on terror of, 9–10,
    32–35, 42–44
  divisions in, after Hamdan, 173–174
  military orders and, 16–17
  no debates regarding torture, 64–65
  noncompliance with U.S. Supreme
    Court opinions, 126–133
  plans of, for Iraq invasion, 7
  rebuke of, by Supreme Court in
    Hamdan, 170
  role of Dick Cheney in, 9
  torture debate after Abu Ghraib,
    82–83
  "trumps" Supreme Court, 175–186

Bush administration, *continued*
  undermining of due process by, 16–19
  view of enemy combatants by, 8, 38–39
  view of Geneva Conventions of, 49–51
Bush, George W., 1, 3, 4, 6, 8, 16, 24, 45, 56,
    65, 84, 125, 171, 172–173, 191, 193,
    196–197
  assertion of unilateral executive power
    by, 175–176
  CIA torture practices and, 74–76
  comparison of, to George III, 172
  condemnation of torture by, 81
  critics of, 10ff., 26–28
  defense of MCA by, 182
  defense of warrantless wiretap
    programs by, 18–22
  and enemy combatant concept, 37
  on judicial review in wartime, 88
  and MCA, 182, 184–185
  military order of, 37, 126
  powers of, as commander in chief, 2, 11
  preemptive war doctrine announced
    by, 37
  radical view of war on terror, 175
  rebuke of, by Supreme Court in
    Hamdan, 177
  Republican anger at, after 2006
    elections, 188–189
  response of, to *Hamdan,* 171–172
  response of, to McCain amendment,
    139–140
  signing statements of, 24–27, 33–34
  statement of regarding treatment of
    detainees, 71
  "thumped" in 2006 election, 187
  unilateral executive doctrine defended
    by, 193
  veto record of, 26–27
  view of DTA, 141–142
  view of, as "coronated" president, 177
Bybee, Jay S., 47
Bybee torture memo, 56–58, 65, 69

Cambone, Stephen A., 83
Card, Andrew, 8
CBS *60 Minutes,* and Abu Ghraib
    scandal, 79–80
*Center for National Security Studies v.
    U.S. DOJ,* 2003, 15–16
Central Intelligence Agency. *See* CIA
Cheney, Dick, 1, 3, 7, 8, 22–24, 26, 32, 66,
    83, 125, 171, 172, 193
  lobbying by, in Congress for MCA, 182
  majordomo in Bush administration,
    9–10
  manipulation of Judiciary Committee
    by, 23–24
  on McCain amendment to DTA, 139
  position of, on actionable suspicion,
    35ff.
  powers of, 24–26
  on presidency, 175
  review by, of military orders, 52–54
  on 2006 election, 194
Church, Albert, 66–69
Church, Frank, 18–19
CIA (Central Intelligence Agency), 8,
    13–14, 54, 61, 63
  counterresistance techniques of,
    65–67, 71–73
  high-value detainees held by, 71ff.
  immunity for, in MCA, 182
  interrogation techniques of, 76–77
  rendition practice of, 77–82
  role of, in torture of detainees, 74–77
CIA Counterterrorism Center (CTC),
    74–76
CIA Special Access Program (SAP), 77–78
Civil liberties, threats to, in war on
    terror, 34
Clement, Paul, 109, 112, 144, 176
  argument of, in *Padilla II,* 136–137
  Hamdan oral argument of, 157–160
Clinton, Bill, 24
Cohen, Andrew, 185–186

Combat Status Review Tribunals, 46–48
Convention Against Torture, 1984, 56–57
  text of, 215–220
Conyers, John, 190–191
Cooke, Marcia, 138–139
Corallo, Mark, 147
Counterintelligence, definition of,
  236n23
Coyle, Marcia, 108

Dean, John, 19
Defense Authorization Bill (2006), 140,
  142–144. *See also* DTA; McCain,
  John
Defense Intelligence Agency (DIA),
  13–14, 73–74
Delahunty, Robert J., 48, 49
Department of Defense. *See* U.S.
  Department of Defense
Department of Justice. *See* DOJ
Department of State, 59. *See also* Powell,
  Colin
Detainees
  abuse of, 70–74
  citizenship of, 241n20
  constitutional questions raised in
    2004 petitions, 91–93
  despair of, 72–74
  habeas petitions of, 141
  history of, 34ff.
  innocence of many, 54
  interrogation of, 54ff.
  lawyers for, frustrated by tactics of
    Bush, 128–129
  medical treatment for, 72–73
  status of, 88–89
  treatment by U.S. forces, 60–61
  treatment of, after September 11, 54
  and 2004 petitions, 91–93
Detainee Treatment Act. *See* DTA
DIA (Defense Intelligence Agency),
  13–14, 73–74

Dinh, Viet, 13–14
DOD. *See* U.S. Department of Defense
Dodd, Chris, 193, 195
DOJ (Department of Justice), 15–16, 59.
  briefs to dismiss habeas petitions of
    detainees, 189–190
  criminal indictment of Padilla by,
    134–135
  See also Gonzales, Alberto; Office of
    Legal Counsel
Douglas, William O., 87
DTA (Detainee Treatment Act; 2005), 2,
  7, 139ff., 176
  challenged in *Hamdan*, 152ff.
  and jurisdiction of federal courts, 126
  text of, 221–228
Due process, 58
Dunham, Frank W., 100, 108
Durbin, Richard, 143, 193

Economist, 172
Election of 2006, 185–186
Ellis, T. S., III, 30–31
El-Masri, Khalid, 30
Enemy combatants, 7–8, 27–29, 38–44,
  46–50, 56–58, 233n2
England, Gordon, 83–84, 171, 177
  Geneva Convention memo of,
    171–172
Enhanced Border Security and Visa
    Entry Reform Act (2002), 25–26
Ex Parte McCardle (1868), 155, 259n81
Ex Parte Milligan (1866), 39–40
Ex Parte Quirin (1942), 38–42, 47, 87, 146

"Failed state," 49. *See also* Taliban
FBI (Federal Bureau of Investigation),
  13–15, 59, 70, 73–74
Federalist Papers, 3–4
Fein, Bruce, 177–178
Fidell, Eugene, 135, 142–143
  DTA concerns of, 142–143

Floyd, Henry F., 28
Foreign Intelligence Surveillance Act
    (1978), 13–15, 18–19, 20–21
Foreign Intelligence Surveillance Court,
    18–20, 21
Franck, Matthew J., 123
Freiman, Jonathan, 133
Friedrich, Matthew H., 22
Frist, Bill, 182

Gates, Robert M., 189
Geneva Accord on Prisoners of War,
    Third Convention (1929), 41
Geneva Convention (1949), 7–8, 43–46,
    48, 53–54, 56–57, 58, 60, 83, 84,
    87–88, 170–172
    rejection of, in MCA, 180
    text of, 205–214
Gingrich, Newt, 188
Ginsburg, Ruth Bader, 176
Golden, Tim, 85
Gonzales, Alberto R., 1, 8, 38, 49, 56–57,
    59, 64–65, 134, 178, 190–191
    on enemy combatants, 7–8
    on *Padilla*, 27–29
    threat to investigate reporters by,
    20–21
Goodman, Bill, 170
Gordon, Jeffrey, 85
Goss, Porter J., 76
Graham, Lindsey, 154, 177, 178
    amendment of, to DTA, 142–143
    DTA manipulation by, 140–144
    opposition of, to MCA, 178, 180–183
Green, Joyce H., 129–131
Greenberg Quinlin Rosner Research Poll,
    187–188
Greenhouse, Linda, 123, 138
Guantánamo Bay Naval Station, Cuba
    (GTMO), 2, 7, 48, 62, 66
    detainee camps at, 242–243n36
    detainees, 84–85

Habeas corpus, 1–2, 17, 39, 58–59, 176
    as central ingredient of constitutional
    rights, 192–193
    defense of by Center for
    Constitutional Rights, 142
    legislative avoidance of protection of,
    129–131
    prohibition on use of, in MCA,
    183–184
Habeas Corpus Restoration Act (2007),
    191. *See also* Leahy, Patrick; Specter,
    Arlen
Habeas Corpus Statute, 90–91
Hadley, Stephen J., 182
Hague Conventions (1899, 1907), 41
Hamdan, Salim Ahmed, 53
Hamdan v. Rumsfeld, 2, 8, 53, 83–84,
    144–145, 176–178, 233–234nn 3, 4
    amici briefs in, 154–155
    background of, 145–170
    briefs filed in, 148–152
    certiorari granted in, 126ff.
    government merits brief in, 152–153
    government reply brief, 149–150
    grant of certiorari in, 150–151
    MCA as a response to, 185
    oral arguments in, 155–160
    petitioner merits brief in, 150–152
    questions presented in, by petitioners,
    148–149
    rebuke of Bush policy in, 178
    relevance of Geneva Conventions
    raised in, 154
    Supreme Court opinions in, 162–170
Hamdi, Yaser Esam, 99–100
    release of, conditions for, 131–132
Hamdi v. Rumsfeld, 85, 125, 130
    background, 99–105
    government brief filed in, 105–106
    government brief in opposition,
    102–103
    oral argument in, 108–112

petition for certiorari, 100–103
plaintiff brief on the merits, 104–105
questions by Supreme Court in,
    103–104
Supreme Court opinion in, 117–121
Hamilton, Alexander, 4, 176
Haynes, William J., 48, 49, 65
Hersh, Seymour, 79
Hicks, David, 150
"High value" detainees, 63, 71. *See also*
    CIA
Hill, James T., 65–66
Hoekstra, Peter, 33
Human Rights Watch, 53
Hussein, Saddam, 12, 63
alleged possession of WMD by, 37

ICRC (International Committee of the
    Red Cross), 56, 58, 71–72
MCA concerns of, 180
reports on detainees, 71, 85
Immigration and Naturalization Service
    (INS), 14–16
In forma pauperis, definition of, 252n37
Interlocutory judgment, definition of,
    258–259n72
International Committee of the Red
    Cross. *See* ICRC
International laws of war, 43
Interrogation Rules of Conduct (IROC),
    66–69, 82–83
Iraq Resolution, 2002, 2, 10–13
IROC (Interrogation Rules of Conduct),
    66–69, 82–83

Jackson, Robert H., concurring opinion
    in steel seizure case, 153–154
JAG (Judge Advocate General), 59–60,
    66, 90
opposition to MCA by, 178ff.
Japanese American internment in World
    War II, 196

Jay, John, 4
Johnson v. Eisentrager, 88, 91–94
Johnson, Lyndon B., 13, 87
Judge Advocate General. *See* JAG

Katyal, Neal K., 148, 150–152, 170
    Hamdan oral argument of, 155–157,
    161
Kennedy, Anthony, 88
concurrence of, in *Padilla II*, 138
concurring opinion of, in *Hamdan*,
    166–167
concurring opinion of, in *Rasul*,
    115–116
concurring opinion of, in *Rumsfeld*,
    122
Kmiec, Douglas W., 128
Koh, Harold, 170
Kollar-Kotelly, Colleen, 91–92, 150
Kopel, Dave, 17
Korean War, 44
Korematsu, Fred, 251n17
Korematsu v. U.S., 87
Kyl, Jon, 144, 154

Lagourarnis, Anthony, 62
Landler, Mark, 6–7
Lawful combatants, 43–45
Leahy, Patrick, 22, 26–27, 193, 195
introduction by, of MCA overturn
    bill, 190ff.
opposition of, to MCA, 183
Leahy-Specter proposed MCA Overturn
    Bill, 265n18
Lederman, Martin, 181
Leon, Richard J., 130
Levin, Carl, 142, 143, 191–192, 193
Levin, Daniel, 58
Lieber Code (1863), 41
Lincoln, Abraham, 32
Liptak, Adam, 28
Lithwick, Dahlia, 132

Madison, James, 4
Martin, Kate, 14
Martinez, Jennifer, 113
MCA. *See* Military Commissions Act
McCain, John
    anti-torture amendment of, 26,
        139–140
    opposition of, to MCA, 178, 180–183
McClellan, Scott, 107
McNeill, Daniel, 80–81
Meyers, Richard, 8
Military Commissions Act (MCA; 2006)
        2, 178ff., 195
    Bush draft of, given to Congress, 180
    draft of, leaked to press, 179
    excerpts from, 229–232
    final version of, 184
    politics of, 178–185
    Warner-McCain-Graham substitute,
        181–182
"Military necessity" doctrine, 244n4
Miller, Geoffrey, 62, 63, 80–81
Mora, Alberto J., 66–69
Moran, Sherwood F., 61
Muslims, 14–16

National Law Journal, 108
National Security Agency (NSA), 10,
        18–20, 21–23
    warrantless wiretap program of,
        192ff.
Navy Criminal Investigation Command
        (NCIC), 66–69, 73–74
New Yorker, 79
New York Times, 19, 27, 70, 77–78, 85, 123,
        144, 178
Newman, Donna, 106, 134, 136
Newsweek, 76
Nixon, Richard M., 13
Norquist, Grover, 34–35
Northern Alliance, 38
NSA. *See* National Security Agency

O'Connor, Sandra Day, 88
    majority opinion of, in *Hamdi,*
        117–118
    participation of, in *Hamdan,* 150
    retirement of, 126
Office of Legal Counsel (OLC), 65, 81–83,
        179
Olson, Theodore B., 92, 95, 102
    arguments in 2004 detainee cases,
        92–93
"One percent" doctrine. *See* "Actionable
    suspicion" doctrine
Operation Desert Storm, 45
Operation Enduring Freedom, 62–63, 66,
        71

Padilla, Jose, 27–28, 31–32, 105–106,
        133–138
    competency of to stand trial, 139
    federal criminal trial of, 138–139
Padilla and Donna Newman v. Rumsfeld,
        32, 106
Padilla v. Hanft (Padilla II), 32, 123,
        135–139
Pakistan, 38
Pike, Otis, 18–20
Political question doctrine, 87, 250n4
Posner, Richard, 17, 192–193
Powell, Colin, 8, 49–50, 64
    opposition of, to MCA, 181–182
Presidential Military Order 1 (2001), text
    of, 201–204
Presidential signing statements, 24–27
Presidential war powers, 1
"Preventive detention" concept, 54. *See
    also* CIA; Detainees
Public opinion polling, 187–188

Randolph, Raymond, 148
Rasul v. Bush, 46, 85, 127–128, 130–131
    arguments in, 93–99
    background, 90–95

decision of Supreme Court in, 114ff.
petitioner reply brief in, 94–95
Reagan, Ronald, 24, 30
Rebuttable presumption, 129, 255n11
Rehnquist, William H., 88
death of, 126
majority opinion of, in *Rumsfeld*,
121–122
Rice, Condoleezza, 7, 8, 191
Ricks, Thomas, 35
Risen, James, 19
Rives, Jack L., 69
Roberts, John
appointment as Chief Justice, 126
recusal of, in *Hamdan*, 150
Robertson, James, 53
Hamdan order of, 146–147
Roehrkasse, Brian, 191–192
Rogers, Judith W., 194
Roosevelt, Franklin D., 32, 39–40, 50
Roth, Kenneth, 37
Rumsfeld, Donald, 1, 3, 7, 8, 45, 56, 62, 65,
66, 77–78, 80–81, 83, 102, 106, 125, 175
resignation of, 188
response of, to *Hamdan*, 172
and rules for interrogation, 51–52
Rumsfeld v. Padilla, 85
background, 105–110
certiorari petition granted, 108
oral arguments in, 112–114
Supreme Court opinion in, 121–124

Saar, Erik, 50
Salt Pit, 75. *See also* CIA
Sanchez, Ricardo, 80–81
Scalia, Antonin, 88, 127
dissenting opinion of, in *Hamdan*, 167
dissenting opinion of, in *Hamdi*,
120–121
dissenting opinion of, in *Rasul*, 116–117
view of government of, in *Hamdi*, 176
Schiff, Adam, 20

Schlesinger Report, 62
Scolinos, Tasia, 21
Seton Hall University Study, 63–64
Sher, R. Joseph, 30
Skelton, Ike, 191
Smith, Michael J., 62
Snow, Tony, 172
rebuke of Colin Powell by, 182
Souter, David H., opinion of in *Hamdi*,
119–120
Specter, Arlen, 22–24, 142, 188, 191
Specter-Leahy-Smith substitute
amendment (MCA), 183
State secrets privilege, 28–31
Steel seizure case. *See Youngstown Sheet
and Tube Co. v. Sawyer*
Stevens, John Paul, 127–128
dissenting opinion of, in *Rumsfeld*,
122–123
majority opinion of, in *Hamdan*,
162–166
opinion of, in *Padilla II*, 138
majority opinion of, in *Rasul*, 114–115
"Stress and duress" interrogation
technique, 63. *See also* CIA
Suspension clause. *See* Habeas corpus;
under U.S. Congress
Swift, Charles, 146ff., 150–152
Taft, William H., IV, 64

Taliban, 7, 34, 37, 45, 49, 65, 88
Tatel, David A., 16
Tenet, George, 8
Thomas, Clarence, 88
dissenting opinion of, in *Hamdan*,
167–168
dissenting opinion of, in *Hamdi*, 121
on unitary executive, 168, 175
Torture
U.S. definition of, 57
use of, 61ff. *See also* Bush
administration; CIA; "Torture Lite"

"Torture Lite," 61ff., 69–73, 180–181. *See also* Rumsfeld, Donald

Truman, Harry S., 18

UCMJ (Uniform Code of Military Justice), 41, 48, 60, 74

U.S.A. Patriot Act (2001), 13–15, 26

U.S. Army Field Manual, 34–52, 60–61

U.S. Articles of War, 60

U.S. Congress, 3, 90
  power of to suspend habeas corpus, 91
  Democratic control of, 187
  suspension of habeas corpus only by, 2

U.S. Constitution, 10–11, 16–18
  suspension clause, 2
  coexistence of, with national security, 196

U.S. Court of Appeals, D.C. circuit, 16, 190
  overturn of *Hamdan* district court opinion, 147–149

U.S. Court of Appeals for the Fourth Circuit
  decision of, in *Boumediene,* 194
  Padilla II appeal in, 135–136

U.S. Department of Defense, 59
  noncompliance with *Hamdi,* 129–130

U.S. detention policy after September 11, 54–56

U.S. federal courts, 15–16, 31–33
  limits of, in wartime, 2

U.S. immigrant community, 15ff.

U.S. interrogators, 58–59. *See also* CIA; FBI

U.S. Supreme Court, 3, 5, 15–16, 37, 85, 197
  and *Boumediene* case, 195
  compliance with orders of, 126–127
  docket of, 252n29
  grant of certiorari in 2004 detainee cases, 89–91
  and *Hamdi* case, 88
  jurisprudence of, in 2003, 88ff.

and *Odeh* case, 88
and *Padilla* cases, 88, 136–138
and petitions from detainees, 88
power of, 176–177
procrastination by in 2007, 195–196
and *Rasul* case, 88
rationale for hearing cases, 125
rules of, for granting certiorari, 101–102
vote of four in, 102

U.S. v. O'Brien, 87

U.S. v. Reynolds, 28–31

Uniform Code of Military Justice (UCMJ), 41, 48, 60, 74

"Unitary Executive" doctrine, 25–26. *See also under* Bush, George W.; Cheney, Dick; Thomas, Clarence

United Nations, 53

United Nations Human Rights Commission, 85

Universal Declaration of Human Rights (1948), 57–58

Unlawful combatants, 43–45. *See also* Geneva Convention

USA Today, 21

Vietnam War, 44–46, 87

Vinson, Fred M., 29

War against terror, 6, 9–10

War crimes, 51–53

War Crimes Act (1996), 38, 48–49

War Crimes Act, MCA amendments to, 180

Warner, John W., 142, 173
  opposition of, to MCA, 178, 180–183

Washington Post, 11, 63, 77–78, 135, 179, 185–186

Waxman, Matthew C., 83

Weapons of mass destruction (WMD), 12, 37, 38ff.

Wesley, Richard, 107

Wiggins, J. Michael, 54

Wilson, Woodrow, 32
Wizner, Ben, 30–31
WMD (weapons of mass destruction), 12, 37, 38ff.
Wolfowitz, Paul, 46

Yoo, John C., 47, 48–49, 179–180
Youngstown Sheet and Tube Co. v. Sawyer, 87, 153, 234n5

Zapf, Patricia A., 138–139